Women in the Third World

Women
in the
Third World

A Historical Bibliography

Pamela R. Byrne
Suzanne R. Ontiveros
Editors

ABC-CLIO

Santa Barbara, California
Oxford, England

Library of Congress Cataloging-in-Publication Data

Byrne, Pamela R.
  Women in the Third World.

  (ABC-Clio research guides ; 15)
  Bibliography: p.
  Includes index.
  1. Women—Developing countries—History—Bibliography.
2. Feminism—Developing countries—History—Bibliography.
3. Women—Developing countries—History—Abstracts.
4. Feminism—Developing countries—History—Abstracts.
I. Ontiveros, Suzanne R.   II. ABC-Clio Information
Services.   III. Title.   IV. Series.
Z7964.D44B96   1985 [HQ1870.8]   016.3054'09172'4   85-19968
ISBN 0-87436-459-0

*This book is Smyth sewn and printed on acid-free paper to
meet library standards.*

ABC-Clio, Inc.
2040 Alameda Padre Serra, Box 4397
Santa Barbara, California 93140-4397

Clio Press Ltd.
55 St. Thomas Street
Oxford, OX1 1JG, England

Manufactured in the United States of America.

ABC-CLIO RESEARCH GUIDES

The ABC-CLIO Research Guides are a new generation of annotated bibliographies that provide comprehensive control of the recent journal literature on high-interest topics in history and the related social sciences. These publications are compiled by editor/historians and other subject specialists who examine article entries in ABC-CLIO's vast history data base and select abstracts of all citations that relate to the particular topic of study.

Each entry selected from this data base—the largest history data base in the world—has been reviewed to ensure consistency in treatment and completeness of coverage. The subject profile index (ABC-SPIndex) accompanying each volume has been evaluated and revised in terms of the specific subject presented to allow precise and rapid access to the entries.

The titles in this series are prepared to save researchers, students, and librarians the considerable time and expense usually associated with accessing materials manually or through online searching. ABC-CLIO's Research Guides offer unmatched access to significant scholarly articles on the topics of most current interest to historians and social scientists.

ABC-CLIO RESEARCH GUIDES

Pamela R. Byrne, Executive Editor
Suzanne R. Ontiveros, Managing Editor

1. **World War II from an American Perspective** *(1982)*;
ISBN 0-87436-035-8

2. **The Jewish Experience in America** *(1982)*;
ISBN 0-87436-034-X

3. **Nuclear America** *(1983)*;
ISBN 0-87436-360-8

4. **The Great Depression** *(1983)*;
ISBN 0-87436-361-6

5. **Corporate America** *(1983)*;
ISBN 0-87436-362-4

6. **Crime and Punishment in America** *(1983)*;
ISBN 0-87436-363-2

7. **The Democratic and Republican Parties** *(1983)*;
ISBN 0-87436-364-0

8. **The American Electorate** *(1983)*;
ISBN 0-87436-372-1

9. **The Weimar Republic** *(1984)*;
ISBN 0-87436-378-0

10. **The Third Reich, 1933-1939** *(1984)*; ISBN 0-87436-379-9

11. **The Third Reich at War** *(1984)*;
ISBN 0-87436-393-4

12. **American Family History** *(1984)*; ISBN 0-87436-380-2

13. **The Sino-Soviet Conflict** *(1985)*;
ISBN 0-87436-382-9

14. **The United States in East Asia** *(1985)*; ISBN 0-87436-452-3

15. **Women in the Third World** *(1986)*; ISBN 0-87436-459-0

RELATED TITLES PUBLISHED BY ABC-CLIO

CONTENTS

LIST OF ABBREVIATIONS

A.	Author-prepared Abstract	*Illus.*	Illustrated, Illustration
Acad.	Academy, Academie, Academia	*Inst.*	Institute, Institut-.
Agric.	Agriculture, Agricultural	*Int.*	International, Internacional,
AIA	Abstracts in Anthropology		Internationaal, Internationaux,
Akad.	Akademie		Internazionale
Am.	America, American	*J.*	Journal, Journal-prepared Abstract
Ann.	Annals, Annales, Annual, Annali	*Lib.*	Library, Libraries
Anthrop.	Anthropology, Anthropological	*Mag.*	Magazine
Arch.	Archives	*Mus.*	Museum, Musee, Museo
Archaeol.	Archaeology, Archaeological	*Nac.*	Nacional
Art.	Article	*Natl.*	National, Nationale
Assoc.	Association, Associate	*Naz.*	Nazionale
Biblio.	Bibliography, Bibliographical	*Phil.*	Philosophy, Philosophical
Biog.	Biography, Biographical	*Photo.*	Photograph
Bol.	Boletim, Boletin	*Pol.*	Politics, Political, Politique, Politico
Bull.	Bulletin	*Pr.*	Press
c.	century (in index)	*Pres.*	President
ca.	circa	*Pro.*	Proceedings
Can.	Canada, Canadian, Canadien	*Publ.*	Publishing, Publication
Cent.	Century	*Q.*	Quarterly
Coll.	College	*Rev.*	Review, Revue, Revista, Revised
Com.	Committee	*Riv.*	Rivista
Comm.	Commission	*Res.*	Research
Comp.	Compiler	*RSA*	Romanian Scientific Abstracts
DAI	Dissertation Abstracts	*S.*	Staff-prepared Abstract
	International	*Sci.*	Science, Scientific
Dept.	Department	*Secy.*	Secretary
Dir.	Director, Direktor	*Soc.*	Society, Societe, Sociedad,
Econ.	Economy, Econom-.		Societa
Ed.	Editor, Edition	*Sociol.*	Sociology, Sociological
Educ.	Education, Educational	*Tr.*	Transactions
Geneal.	Genealogy, Genealogical,	*Transl.*	Translator, Translation
	Genealogique	*U.*	University, Universi-.
Grad.	Graduate	*US*	United States
Hist.	History, Hist-.	*Vol.*	Volume
IHE	Indice Historico Espanol	*Y.*	Yearbook

INTRODUCTION

Throughout the world, women are pursuing major goals for social, economic, and political parity. Despite some significant progress as educational and economic opportunities expanded and as traditional family roles have taken new shapes, in Western and non-Western nations alike, there have also been a number of serious setbacks. The setbacks have perhaps most critically affected women in the Third World.

Ten years have elapsed since the United Nations proclaimed International Women's Year, and a recent worldwide conference in Nairobi marked the end of the Women's Decade, 1975-1985. During those ten short years, many of the advances of the women's movement, particularly in Third World countries, have been stalled or overturned. In May of 1985, for example, the Egyptian Supreme Court struck down the "personal status" amendments of 1979. These laws, supported and extolled by liberals worldwide, made Egypt a pioneer in the Arab world's women's movement, but Muslim fundamentalists there, as in Iran, opposed liberalizing legislation as inconsistent with Islamic religious tradition.

In those Third World countries where there is official endorsement of equal or increased opportunity for women, there yet remains a gap between *de jure* equality and *de facto* inequality. For much of the Third World's female populations, little has changed, indeed. Perhaps the greatest and most encouraging achievement of the Women's Decade is simply the growing international recognition of women's issues *as* issues of global political consequence.

Since the 1970's, scholarship in women's studies, international in scope, has developed a firm theoretical foundation and has produced a wide-ranging body of periodical literature. During that time there has been an equally explosive interest in the social, economic, and political developments in the Third World. These two foci are brought together here in a single bibliographic sourcebook that summarizes the journal scholarship in history on the subject.

Women in the Third World contains 600 abstracts and citations of journal articles drawn from ABC-CLIO's vast history database, which covers over 2,000 periodicals published in some 90 countries. In creating this bibliography, editors reviewed thousands of article abstracts published between 1970 and 1985. They selected only those articles relevant to women in countries traditionally considered Third World. Entries are arranged alphabetically by author within geographic chapters. Chapter 1 includes overviews treating more than one developing nation or entries that are not nation-specific. Chapters 2-6 cover Africa, Asia, the Middle East (including Egypt and the Ottoman Empire), the Pacific Region, and Latin America and the West Indies, respectively. Differences in the size of chapters do not represent editorial predisposition; rather, they reflect the relative volume of journal coverage during 1970-1985. Consequently, this bibliography says as much about what has not been written or published as it does about what has appeared in the journal literature of history.

Additional access to the abstracts and citations in *Women in the Third World* is provided through ABC-SPIndex (Subject Profile Index), a highly specific subject index. Key subject terms are linked with the historical dates to form a complete profile of the article. Each set of index terms is rotated alphabetically so that the complete profile appears under each of the subject terms. Thus, the accuracy and specificity of subject access is enhanced as compared to conventional, hierarchical indexes. Care has been taken to eliminate inconsistencies that might have appeared in the subject index as a result of merging many years of database material. The explanatory note at the beginning of the subject index provides further information for using ABC-SPIndex.

This volume represents the collaboration of a skilled and diverse group. Electronic Publishing Group Managing Editor Suzanne R. Ontiveros oversaw all major editorial work on the abstracts and indexes. Assistant Editors Susan K. Kinnell and Terry H. Elkiss were responsible for reviewing the subject index. The Data Processing Services Department, under the supervision of Ken Baser, Director, and Deborah Looker, Production Supervisor, ably manipulated the database to fit the editorial specifications of this bibliography. David R. Blanke, Applications Programmer, provided critical support in assuring high-quality photocomposition. Terri Wright MacRae, Graphics Production Staff Supervisor, and Tanya Cullen were responsible for essential paste-up corrections and book design.

Sincere appreciation is extended to the worldwide community of scholars who wrote the abstracts and citations that comprise this volume. Their efforts mark an early contribution to the growing scholarly interest in the effects of the women's movement in countries where centuries-old patriarchal attitudes prevail.

1

GENERAL

1. Badran, Margot Farranto. MIDDLE EAST AND NORTH AFRICA: WOMEN. *Trends in Hist. 1979 1(1): 123-129.* Review essay of periodical literature published from 1973 to 1979, on the traditional and changing or modern worlds of Middle Eastern and North African women, primarily in the 19th and 20th centuries.

2. Bhattacharyya, Amit K. ROLE OF RURAL-URBAN INCOME IN-EQUALITY IN FERTILITY REDUCTIONS: CASES OF TURKEY, TAI-WAN, AND MOROCCO. *Econ. Development and Cultural Change 1977 26(1): 117-138.* Examines the role of rural-urban income inequality in fertility reductions in Turkey, Taiwan, and Morocco. Compares the three countries, discussing several methodological considerations: literacy and education; rural-urban differences in ideal number of children and mean live births; knowledge and practice of birth control; and rural-urban differences in exposure to mass communication and mass media. Ranks the effectiveness of family-planning programs in the following order—Taiwan, Turkey, and Morocco. The author demonstrates that higher educational levels of these rural populations correlated with fertility reduction. Based on government surveys, 1963-67, and published works; 19 tables, 12 notes. J. W. Thacker, Jr.

3. Blitz, Rudolph C. AN INTERNATIONAL COMPARISON OF WOM-EN'S PARTICIPATION IN THE PROFESSIONS. *J. of Developing Areas 1975 9(4): 499-510.* Analyzes the role of women in the professions and the labor market in 49 countries in various stages of economic development. Historically the percentage of women in the professions has increased as per capita income has increased. Using equally weighted indicators of per capita energy consumption and percentage of male labor force in nonagricultural pursuits, it was discovered that female labor force participation increases with advancing economic development. In the early stages of development where conservative values predominate, women were employed primarily in the lower skill strata. Based on 1950-67 censuses of 49 nations; 3 tables, 24 notes. O. W. Eads, Jr.

4. Carr, Shirley. WOMEN'S YEAR—UNION ROLE. *Can. Labour 1975 20(2): 2-6, 34.* Discusses worldwide sex discrimination and the role played by labor unions to eliminate it.

5. Copley, Anthony. THE DEBATE ON WIDOW REMARRIAGE AND POLYGAMY: ASPECTS OF MORAL CHANGE IN NINTEENTH-CENTURY BENGAL AND YORUBALAND. *J. of Imperial and Commonwealth Hist. [Great Britain] 1979 7(2): 128-148.* The attempt by the Victorians to impose their moral codes through the empire in the quest for political power caused existing codes to be questioned and changed. Different effects were felt by the various social classes and cosmopolitan areas. Here widow remarriage in Hindu India is contrasted with polygamy in West Africa. Based on materials at the India Office Library and Church Missionary Society records, London, and secondary sources; 92 notes.   M. C. Rosenfield

6. Croll, Elizabeth J. WOMEN IN RURAL PRODUCTION AND RE-PRODUCTION IN THE SOVIET UNION, CHINA, CUBA, AND TAN-ZANIA: SOCIALIST DEVELOPMENT EXPERIENCES. *Signs 1981 7(2): 361-374.* Collectivization as a tenet of socialist economic development should free women economically by removing patriarchal authority patterns. While women have been recruited into agriculture, they are paid less, maintaining a strong sexual division of labor. Although they were promised state aid in reducing domestic tasks, women instead have fallen under the "double burden" of domestic work and employment. The women's revolution appears to have been lost within the socialist revolution to the detriment of women. 11 notes.
                                                                    S. P. Conner

7. Croll, Elizabeth J. WOMEN IN RURAL PRODUCTION AND RE-PRODUCTION IN THE SOVIET UNION, CHINA, CUBA, AND TAN-ZANIA: CASE STUDIES. *Signs 1981 7(2): 375-399.* More than half of the workers on Soviet farms are women, yet Communist Party membership is only 23% women. Policy decisions including the birth rate are determined predomi-nantly by men. In China, where 90% of the able-bodied women are employed, agrarian tasks are ranked on the basis of strength, skill, and experience. Women fall behind in wages and in access to power. In Cuba, laws have been enacted to force domestic sharing, and in Tanzania laws encouraging "villagi-zation" attempt unsuccessfully to bring economic equality to women. Either the policies are not being carried out to assist women or the ideology is inherently incorrect. Based on newspaper accounts and secondary sources; 119 notes.   S. P. Conner

8. Cuca, Roberto. FAMILY PLANNING PROGRAMS AND FERTILI-TY DECLINE. *J. of Social and Pol. Studies 1980 5(4): 183-190.* Based on a 1978-79 World Bank study of 63 developing nations to determine the conditions that may have brought about the decline in fertility in the developing world during the last two decades, including a survey of the implementation of family planning and programs with specific demographic objectives.

9. Ende, Werner. EHE AUF ZEIT *(MUT'A)* IN DER INNERISLAMIS-CHEN DISKUSSION DER GEGENWART [Temporary marriage *(mut'a)* in recent intra-Islamic discussion]. *Welt des Islams [Netherlands] 1980 20(1-2): 1-43.* Although *mut'a* marriage is permissible among Twelver Shi'ites and its legality has been supported by the major mujtahids (Shi'ite ulama jurisconsult)

of the 20th century, its merit has been a matter of discussion among Shi'ite scholars until the 1979 revolution. In practice it is not common and is limited to women of the lower classes. Attacks on *mut'a* form a significant part of the anti-Shi'a polemics of Sunnite fundamentalists, but some modern Sunnite scholars have argued that *mut'a* is permissible under certain circumstances. Based on Arabic and Western published sources; corrigenda, addendum, 194 notes.   W. J. Wilson

10. Iglitzin, Lynne B. THE PATRIARCHAL HERITAGE. Iglitzin, Lynne B. and Ross, Ruth, ed. *Women in the World* (Santa Barbara, Ca.: Clio Books, 1976): pp. 7-24. Although some advances have been made since the recent revival of feminism, Western and non-Western nations are still characterized as patriarchal. Four sources of patriarchalism—biological, anthropological, religious, and economic ideas and events—contributed to the pervasively male-dominated societies that are the norm today. A model of five attitudes toward women, applied to the contemporary United States, demonstrates that patriarchal attitudes are still prevalent. Primary and secondary sources; 29 notes.
                                                                J. Holzinger

11. Iglitzin, Lynne B. et al. WOMEN AROUND THE WORLD. *Center Mag. 1974 7(3): 44-80.*

12. Jacobs, Sue-Ellen. WOMEN IN DEVELOPMENT. *Am. Anthrop. 1982 84(2): 366-371.* Reviews *Women and Technological Change in Developing Countries,* edited by Roslyn Dauber and Melinda L. Cain (1981), Elizabeth Moen, Elise Boulding, Jane Lillydahl, and Risa Palm's *Women and the Social Costs of Economic Development: Two Colorado Case Studies* (1981), and Barbara Rogers's *The Domestication of Women: Discrimination in Developing Societies* (1981).

13. Jaquette, Jane S. WOMEN AND MODERNIZATION THEORY: A DECADE OF FEMINIST CRITICISM. *World Pol. 1982 34(2): 267-284.* The literature on women's roles in economic and political development, and on the impact of development policies on women, illuminates both the process of modernization and the nature of male-female relations. Three main kinds of approaches—liberal modernization theory and its feminist critiques, socialist approaches and their feminist critiques, and an eclectic "female sphere" position that emphasizes the need to replace male-dominated theory and practice with female experience and values—are discussed. Each approach has a distinct view of the causes, consequences, and significance of women's inferior status during modernization, and each proposes different strategies of change. The clarification of theoretical differences suggests new opportunities for productive research with implications for public policy.   J

14. Lindsay, Beverly. PERSPECTIVES OF THIRD WORLD WOMEN: AN INTRODUCTION. Lindsay, Beverly, ed. *Comparative Perspectives of Third World Women: The Impact of Race, Sex, and Class* (New York: Praeger, 1980): 1-22. Introduction to a collection of essays on Third World women. Defines "Third World" and discusses the impact of dependency,

colonialism, and development on the Third World and specifically on women's social, educational, and economic status.

15. Lindsay, Beverly. THIRD WORLD WOMEN AND SOCIAL REALITY: A CONCLUSION. Lindsay, Beverly, ed. *Comparative Perspectives of Third World Women: The Impact of Race, Sex, and Class* (New York: Praeger, 1980): 297-310. Examines how race, sex, and class affect all women of color, relating these concepts to "colonialism, neocolonialism, internal colonialism, internal neocolonialism, dependency, and development" and to articles in this collection.

16. Lutfi, Huda. AL-SAKHAWI'S *KITAB AL-NISA* AS A SOURCE FOR THE SOCIAL AND ECONOMIC HISTORY OF MUSLIM WOMEN DURING THE FIFTEENTH CENTURY A.D. *Muslim World 1981 71(2): 104-124.* Although some information on the life of Moslem women can be obtained from extant documents, a major untapped source has been biographical dictionaries, and this study is based on such a source by al-Sakhawi. The study outlines the limitations of this literary genre and details the range of women covered before dealing with specific aspects of women's position in the family, their economic position, and women and education based on the 1,075 biographees covered in this work. Such a study has limitations but can provide valuable insights into the social life of women among the Moslems. Based on Arabic secondary sources; 117 ref.   F. A. Clements

17. Martin, Anita Shilton. WOMEN AND IMPERIALISM. *Can. Dimension 1975 10(8): 19-25.* Socialist women in Canada systematically analyze how women have been affected by the operation of capitalism on a world scale, from the late 19th century to the present.

18. Menken, Jane; Trussell, James; and Watkins, Susan. THE NUTRITION FERTILITY LINK: AN EVALUATION OF THE EVIDENCE. *J. of Interdisciplinary Hist. 1981 11(3): 425-441.* Examines the physiological link between nutrition and fertility in women who are chronically malnourished. Historians are often eager to accept the view that low birth rates throughout history can be tied to times of famine. Studies show that there is in fact little variation from the normal among malnourished women in contemporary societies. There are many more complex reasons for low fertility rates. 29 notes.   A. Drysdale

19. Montes, Segundo. LA LIBERACIÓN FEMININA [Women's liberation]. *Estudios Centro Americanos [El Salvador] 1975 30(316-317): 115-128.* Discusses the international status of the women's movement in 1975, International Women's Year, discussing Old and New Testament conceptions of women and comparing them with women's social reality in the world today.

20. Musallam, Basim F. WHY ISLAM PERMITTED BIRTH CONTROL. *Arab Studies Q. 1981 3(2): 181-197.* Discusses the current attitude in Islamic jurisprudence toward contraception, traces the development of Islamic thought on the subject from Al-Ghazali (1058-1111), and compares the Judaeo-Christian difficulties in dealing with it.

21. Mutti, Antonio. LA SOCIOLOGIA DELLA MODERNIZZAZIONE [The sociology of modernization]. *Quaderni di Sociologia [Italy] 1970 19(3/4): 338-375.* Reviews the main approaches of the last twenty years to the study of the modernization process, with special reference to the American sociological literature on developing countries. This study deals particularly with some fundamental and ideological problems, emphasizing both the efforts of the analysts to overcome the limits of the excessively specialist approaches to the study of modernization and the persistence of important faults in the proposed models. The basic limitations of the American sociological literature on the Third World, emerging from this study, are the persistence of the ethnocentric attitude, i.e. the tendency to interpret the experience of modernizing countries in terms of Western experience, the abstraction and rigidity of the models, and their inability to analyze adequately the conflicts and strains that the process of social change inevitably brings forth and enhances. The special importance of the contribution of J. P. Nettl is emphasized, in so far as it inspires a critical revision of the sociology of modernization. The critical contribution of some other authors opposed to the prevalent trend of the studies on modernization in American culture is also emphasized; these authors have justly approached the problems of the Third World in the context of the international stratification system. J

22. Perinbam, B. Marie. PARROT OR PHOENIX? FRANTZ FANON'S VIEW OF THE WEST INDIAN AND ALGERIAN WOMAN. *J. of Ethnic Studies 1973 1(2): 45-55.* Analyzes Frantz Fanon's comparisons between two types of colonial women; the West Indian woman who attempted to copy white society, and the Algerian woman who rejected colonial society and clung to her cultural roots. Based on Fanon's works; 36 notes. T. W. Smith

23. Reanda, Laura. HUMAN RIGHTS AND WOMEN'S RIGHTS: THE UNITED NATIONS APPROACH. *Human Rights Q. 1981 3(2): 11-31.* Though fundamental international instruments of the UN have established the principle of equality of men and women in international law, the interpretation and implementation of these instruments by the competent organs has fallen short of protecting the rights of women.

24. Robert, Annette. THE EFFECTS OF THE INTERNATIONAL DIVISION OF LABOUR ON FEMALE WORKERS IN THE TEXTILE AND CLOTHING INDUSTRIES. *Development and Change [Great Britain] 1983 14(1): 19-37.* Discusses the new international division of labor, the deteriorating employment situation for women in industrialized countries, and the specific working conditions for women in developing countries.

25. Safa, Helen Icken. RUNAWAY SHOPS AND FEMALE EMPLOYMENT: THE SEARCH FOR CHEAP LABOR. *Signs 1981 7(2): 418-435.* Third World countries are turning more toward "export processing" to achieve economic stability. Following the 19th-century American pattern, women in Southeast Asia, Mexico, and Jamaica are being recruited and forced to enter a market "already determined as inferior." Native rural labor augmented by immigrant labor, provides the source of a large-scale female industrial proletariat. The dangers of "export processing" are the further exploitation of women

and government action to keep women from organizing. Based on US Government statistics and secondary sources; 60 notes.   S. P. Conner

26. Schultz, T. Paul. FERTILITY AND CHILD MORTALITY OVER THE LIFE CYCLE: AGGREGATE AND ADDITIONAL EVIDENCE. *Am. Econ. Rev. 1978 68(2): 208-215.* Based on samples from rural and urban households in India and Latin America, statistically significant relationships exist between cumulative child mortality and cumulative fertility. Compensating reductive responses to child mortality have occurred in low income countries where child survival has markedly improved. Why? This article calls for further research and study concerning economic determinants in this complex human and cultural situation. Tables, ref.   D. K. Pickens

27. Semyonov, Moshe. THE SOCIAL CONTEXT OF WOMEN'S LABOR FORCE PARTICIPATION: A COMPARATIVE ANALYSIS. *Am. J. of Sociol. 1980 86(3): 534-550.* Analyzes data from 61 societies on the participation of women in the labor force.

28. Sipila, Helvi. CHANGING ROLES OF WOMEN IN THE DEVELOPING REGIONS OF THE WORLD. *J. of Int. Affairs 1976-77 30(2): 183-190.* The status of women in the developing nations, as evidenced by their role in national politics and in international bodies, has considerably improved but much needs to be done. The World Plan of Action adopted at the 1975 International Women's Year Conference states the goals which need to be realized.   V. Samaraweera

29. Üçok, Bahriye. ISLAMDEVELETLERINDE BAZI NAIBELER [Some female regents in Moslem states]. *Belleten [Turkey] 1967 31(122): 169-190.* Discusses examples of female regents from various medieval and modern Islamic states, with particular reference to the Khanate of Kazan.

30. White, Elizabeth H. PURDAH. *Frontiers 1977 2(1): 31-42.* Because purdah, the Moslem practice of secluding women from contact with men, is essential to the maintenance of the family under Islam, the restrictions of early marriage and limited education and recreation will change only when outside influence is effective in destroying the image of women as sensual objects.

31. Youssef, Nadia H. EDUCATION AND FEMALE MODERNISM IN THE MUSLIM WORLD. *J. of Int. Affairs 1967-77 30(2): 191-209.* Given adequate incentives a tremendous female potential exists in the Moslem world which could be channeled into development efforts. Available data supports incentives in the form of intensified education of Moslem women at the secondary and higher education levels. 6 tables, 23 notes.   V. Samaraweera

32. Youssef, Nadia H. WOMEN AND AGRICULTURAL PRODUCTION IN MUSLIM SOCIETIES. *Studies in Comparative Int. Development 1977 12(1): 41-58.* Examines conceptual problems in labor force comparisons and analyzes 1) the characteristics of the female agricultural work force; 2) contrasting patterns of female employment in agriculture; and 3) undercounting. Women in Islamic society do not have a historical tradition in farming,

nor do they bring to the economic process any particular skill or talent. Under plough cultivation a woman's work value diminishes as does her social status. The obvious, though by no means easily implemented, objective is to devise a policy of employment expansion which can provide stimulus to raising the level of rural economic output and enhancing the prestige and status of women. Based on UN demographic data; note, 6 refs. S. A. Farmerie

33. Youssef, Nadia H. WOMEN IN THE MUSLIM WORLD. Iglitzin, Lynne B. and Ross, Ruth, ed. *Women in the World* (Santa Barbara, Calif.: Clio Books, 1976): 375-389. The first evidence of female modernism in Moslem society is due not to a feminist movement, but to economic and political transition. *Shari'a* law promotes patriarchy and polygamy, denying sexual equality within the home. Moslem women are absent from the work force and 87% are illiterate. Cultural norms deny contact with the opposite sex, even for those few who are educated and employed in the professions. Since 1960, some countries have initiated change, liberalizing laws regarding marriage, enfranchisement, and elementary education. Future economic modernization is apt to have further effect, but change in this tradition-entrenched society will be gradual. Secondary sources; 16 notes. N. Barron

34. —. WOMEN, JOBS AND DEVELOPMENT. *Afro-Asian Econ. Rev. [Egypt] 1973 15(164-165): 11-15.* Discusses the economic factors involved in the employment of women in developing nations, 1960-73. There will be greater interest in female employment because of a change in "the strategy and objectives of economic development with more emphasis on the human and personal side." R. T. Brown

2

WOMEN IN AFRICA

35. Abraham, Arthur. WOMEN CHIEFS IN SIERRA LEONE: A HISTORICAL REAPPRAISAL. *Odu: a J. of West African Studies [Nigeria] 1974 (10): 30-44.* After the proclamation of the protectorate in 1896, the colonial government in Sierra Leone popularized the practice of women holding the office of Paramount Chief. But until this practice became legitimized, women chiefs were a source of much local instability. In precolonial times women had no historical right to claim the office. Based on Colonial Office records, documents in the archives of Sierra Leone, and secondary sources; 60 notes.   M. M. McCarthy

36. Adams, Lois. WOMEN IN ZAIRE: DISPARATE STATUS AND ROLES. Lindsay, Beverly, ed. *Comparative Perspectives of Third World Women: The Impact of Race, Sex, and Class* (New York: Praeger, 1980): 55-77. Discusses the conflict between the status of women in Zaire based on the Zairian constitution and its legal code, and their traditional role which results in their dependence on men, tracing women's status in marriage and the family, their opportunities for education, and their position in the labor force and in public life since colonial times, focusing on the 1960's and 1970's. Since historical conditions have changed, women's status and role will change in the future also.

37. Afonja, Simi. CHANGING MODES OF PRODUCTION AND THE SEXUAL DIVISION OF LABOR AMONG THE YORUBA. *Signs 1981 7(2): 299-313.* Modernization theory cannot explain the cause and effect of female subordination in cultures like the Yoruba, where the economy is characterized by a low level of specialization. A multidimensional approach proves that there is some continuity between traditional and modern Africa. Not until the 19th century did long-distance trade patterns change the scale and unit of trade, thereby changing the woman's role. While women engaged actively in trade, their sphere was only the small retail shop. The value structure continued to place the woman's function as biological and social reproduction. Based on interviews and research financed by the Ford Foundation; 33 notes.   S. P. Conner

38. Armagnac, Catherine and Retel-Laurentin, Anne. RELATIONS BETWEEN FERTILITY, BIRTH INTERVALS, FOETAL MORTALITY AND MATERNAL HEALTH IN UPPER VOLTA. *Population Studies [Great Britain] 1981 35(2): 217-234.*

39. Berger, Iris. REBELS OR STATUS-SEEKERS? WOMEN AS SPIRIT MEDIUMS IN EAST AFRICA. Hafkin, Nancy J. and Bay, Edna G., ed. *Women in Africa: Studies in Social and Economic Change* (Stanford U. Pr., 1976): 157-181. In the interlacustrine and Nyamwezi regions of precolonial East Africa, where women were subordinate and enjoyed limited participation in religious activity, women played a prominent role in spirit-possession cults and ceremonies. Where ordinary rules of society were suspended, they could express hostility and protect themselves from excess demands without threatening the idea of female inferiority. Women could share in the status and prerogatives of men. As priestesses and mediums, some gained long-term high status while a few rose to national prominence. Interviews and secondary sources; 25 notes.   S. Tomlinson-Brown

40. Bernus, S. STRATÉGIE MATRIMONIALE ET CONSERVATION DU POUVOIR DANS L'AIR ET CHEZ LES IULLEMMEDEN [Matrimonial policy and the retention of power in Aïr and among the Yullemmeden]. *Rev. de l'Occident Musulman et de la Méditerranée [France] 1976 (21): 101-104.* Examines how the various strata within the society of the Yullemmeden Tuareg of the Aïr region have guaranteed their privileges through endogamous marriage since the 19th century. The Yullemmeden have preserved endogamy virtually intact until recently, but political conflict has forced other groups to relax this policy in order to survive and preserve their autonomy. Note, biblio.   R. O. Khan

41. Boals, Kay. THE POLITICS OF CULTURAL LIBERATION: MALE-FEMALE RELATIONS IN ALGERIA. Carroll, Berenice A., ed. *Liberating Women's Hist.* (Chicago: U. of Illinois Pr., 1976): 194-211. Establishes a framework for the systematic comparative analysis of the process of cultural liberation. There are six process-oriented types of consciousness which reflect the dialectic between dominant and oppressed groups on the external (economic, military, technological) and psychic (emotional, cultural) levels. These include traditional, traditionalist, assimilationist, reformist, revolutionary, and transforming consciousnesses, each of which is examined in terms of male-female and colonizer-colonized relationships in Algeria. In the areas of political rights, employment opportunity, and equal primary education, traditionalist attitudes toward male-female relations in Algeria have been bypassed under the pressure of commitment to development goals. In the more private realms, traditionalist consciousness has combined with Marxist ideology to stifle liberation in male-female relations. Primary and secondary sources; 36 notes.

42. Boals, Kay and Stiehm, Judith. THE WOMEN OF LIBERATED ALGERIA. *Center Mag. 1974 7(3): 74-76.*

43. Brain, James L. LESS THAN SECOND-CLASS: WOMEN IN RURAL SETTLEMENT SCHEMES IN TANZANIA. Hafkin, Nancy J. and Bay, Edna G., ed. *Women in Africa: Studies in Social and Economic Change* (Stanford, Ca.: Stanford U. Pr., 1976): 265-282. In Ujamaa settlements of Tanzania, established in the 1960's, settlers' wives were denied the rights exercised in traditional society where they had participated in the choice of a political leader and had rights to land and offspring in cases of divorce. In the

settlement, however, all proceeds of labor went to their husbands. Since it was assumed that man and wife should function as two equal working units, women had to work eight hours in the fields as well as perform domestic and childrearing duties. Moreover, no provisions were made for them in the event of their husbands' deaths. Fieldwork and secondary sources; note.

S. Tomlinson-Brown

44.   Brooks, George E. ARTISTS' DEPICTIONS OF SENEGALESE SIG-NARES: INSIGHTS CONCERNING FRENCH RACIST AND SEXIST ATTITUDES IN THE NINETEENTH CENTURY. *Genève-Afrique [Switzerland] 1980 18(1): 75-89.* Signares, African women who headed the households of resident Frenchmen in Senegal, underwent a significant loss of status in the 19th century. A study of five artistic depictions of these women chronicles their stereotypes from the authoritative head of a large household to the sensuous and corrupting mistress of a colonial. 13 notes, biblio.

B. S. Fetter

45.   Brown, Barbara B. THE IMPACT OF MALE LABOUR MIGRATION ON WOMEN IN BOTSWANA. *African Affairs [Great Britain] 1983 82(328): 367-388.* Since the end of the last century, Batswana have gone to work in the mines, factories, kitchens, and farms of white South Africa. Since the independence of Botswana in 1966, however, the Botswana economy has undergone major changes that have affected the size and direction of labor migration. Currently, rural Botswana is a labor reserve for both South Africa and urban areas in Botswana, and 23% of the national population of the country are now migrant wage earners. This has had a serious effect on marriage patterns, nativity, and family dynamics, and the decline in the position of women in Tswana society has resulted in a feminization of poverty. Based on field research and primary and secondary sources; 3 tables, 68 notes.

L. J. Klass

46.   Brydon, Lynne. WOMEN AT WORK: SOME CHANGES IN FAMILY STRUCTURE IN AMEDZOFE-AVATIME, GHANA. *Africa [Great Britain] 1979 49(2): 97-111.* Examines developments in family, child rearing, and residential group structure in the village of Amedzofe-Avatime and outlines the economic and social factors that have resulted in the practice of fostering. Discusses various models that have been proposed to account for women's migration in West Africa in the 20th century and notes similarities between Avatime and West Indian fostering patterns. The Avatime practice indicates the versatility of the formal kin group in adapting to meet new externally imposed socioeconomic conditions. Based mainly on author's field research; 21 notes, biblio., appendix.

P. J. Taylorson

47.   Bujra, Janet M. WOMEN ENTREPRENEURS OF EARLY NAIRO-BI. *Can. J. of African Studies 1975 9(2): 213-234.* Focuses on the independent role played by women in the society of early Nairobi, Kenya. Through prostitution and beer brewing many women accumulated savings which they invested in houses. In order to have someone to bury them, that is, some "relatives," these women converted to Islam. Another practice to which these women resorted was "woman to woman" marriages. These landholding women

became an important part of the African middle class urban economy, not susceptible to male control. Based on government documents, interviews, and secondary works; 43 notes.   E. R. Campbell

48. Burton, John W. INDEPENDENCE AND THE STATUS OF NILOT-IC WOMEN. *Africa Today 1981 28(2): 54-60.* Points out that the traditional parallel power role of Nuer women was ignored by colonial and Arab institutions which has relegated Nuer women to an inferior status. Some changes are occurring. Based on secondary sources; 21 notes.

                                                              G. O. Gagnon

49. Burton, John W. NILOTIC WOMEN: A DIACHRONIC PERSPEC-TIVE. *J. of Modern African Studies [Great Britain] 1982 20(3): 467-491.* Women among the Nilotic-speaking pastoral societies of the Upper Nile in the Southern Sudan were long the subject of inaccurate stereotyping as backward and degraded primitives by European observers. Professional anthropologists since the mid-1900's have altered this image of Nilotic women. E. E. Evans-Pritchard pioneered a "new" view, which linked women, the rivers, and the generation of life. Recent field research among the Atuot has confirmed this view and stressed the important role of Nilotic women in social and economic affairs. Based on field research and published primary sources; 94 notes.

                                                              L. W. Truschel

50. Callaway, Barbara J. WOMEN IN GHANA. Iglitzin, Lynne B. and Ross, Ruth, ed. *Women in the World* (Santa Barbara, Calif.: Clio Books, 1976): 189-201. "In Ghana, the superimposition of Western values under the colonial aegis disrupted the whole fabric of traditional societies." Before the British colonization of southern Ghana, women were an important and independent group in the matrilinear society. The division of labor was equal, with no hierarchical constructs imposed on tasks. Outside of certain responsibilities, such as feeding their children, women were free to earn profits from their labor or trade and to run their households; they were also entitled to inherit property. After the British conquest, Ghanaian men were recruited to work the colonial network, and only boys were sent to colonial schools. Thus, the division of labor was upset; women were isolated from the job market and were forced to depend on the men's earnings. The Convention People's Party (1952-66) formed an auxiliary party to involve women in the political process, the National Council of Ghana Women (NCGW). Ideologically and economically controlled by the CPP, the NCGW did not succeed in restoring many lost rights to women. It concentrated on maintaining traditional marriage laws that would hold men responsible for children they fathered. Primary and secondary sources; 19 notes.   J. Holzinger

51. Campbell, Penelope. PRESBYTERIAN WEST AFRICAN MISSIONS: WOMEN AS CONVERTS AND AGENTS OF SOCIAL CHANGE. *J. of Presbyterian Hist. 1978 56(2): 121-132.* In spite of the secular (colonial administration) and religious (Catholic) forces working against them, Presbyterian women missionaries were able to accomplish a considerable work among female African converts who became the backbone and sustaining power in the indigenous mission churches. Less vulnerable to societal ways, women were

able to grow in the Christian faith. Their groups served both religious needs and social and economic hopes. The author also chronicles missionary educational work in late 19th-century West Africa. Based largely on Board of Foreign Missions Correspondence and Report Files, African Letters, in the Presbyterian Historical Society, Philadelphia; 38 notes.   H. M. Parker, Jr.

52.   Cassell, Kay Ann. AN INTERNATIONAL WOMAN—ASSIGNMENT: MOROCCO. *Wilson Lib. Bull. 1973 47(10): 848-851.* Suggests goals for library education and administration in developing nations.

53.   Chauncey, George, Jr. THE LOCUS OF REPRODUCTION: WOMEN'S LABOUR IN THE ZAMBIAN COPPERBELT, 1927-1953. *J. of Southern African Studies [Great Britain] 1981 7(2): 135-164.* Great Britain's colonial administration and the local Native Authorities in Northern Rhodesia opposed the migration of African women from rural tribal areas to the industrial copperbelt region, the government fearing proletarianization of rural society and the tribal elders resenting their loss of authority and labor. The mining companies, however, took positive steps to encourage this migration, since women on the copperbelt made substantial economic and social contributions by providing food, housekeeping, and other supportive services for the miners. Based on official Zambian colonial and company documents and reports and on interviews; 111 notes.   L. W. Truschel

54.   Cheater, Angela. WOMEN AND THEIR PARTICIPATION IN COMMERCIAL AGRICULTURAL PRODUCTION: THE CASE OF MEDIUM-SCALE FREEHOLD IN ZIMBABWE. *Development and Change [Netherlands] 1981 12(3): 349-377.* Examines female participation in production oriented to the national market on medium-scale freehold farms in Zimbabwe and analyzes Zimbabwe's present state of economic evolution from a Marxist perspective.

55.   Ciancanelli, Penelope. EXCHANGE, REPRODUCTION AND SEX SUBORDINATION AMONG THE KIKUYU OF EAST AFRICA. *Rev. of Radical Pol. Econ. 1980 12(2): 25-36.* Polygynous household as the unit production, social regulaton of fertility through group regulation of household formation, and specific goods traded all determine the position of women. Women's status in precapitalist society cannot be deciphered, their social status fell when men only gained control of the ivory trade. Outside trade affected the status of women, in this case adversely. 4 notes, 20 ref.   D. R. Stevenson

56.   Clark, Carolyn M. LAND AND FOOD, WOMEN AND POWER, IN NINETEENTH CENTURY KIKUYU. *Africa [Great Britain] 1980 50(4): 357-370.* In the 19th century Kikuyu women performed most horticultural and food processing activities, while men were responsible for the livestock and for controlling local or regional councils. Wealth among the Kikuyu was measured in livestock, land, and people, and could be increased by bridewealth, by children who would work the land, and by the produce of the land. In turn, wealth could be translated into political advantage. As wives and mothers, the women were responsible for the allocation of harvests stored in their granaries, and therefore had a say in their distribution. Women also contributed to the

size of the herds by trading vegetable produce for livestock which could not be disposed of without their agreement; thus they contributed to the political economy. Based on fieldwork, 1971-72; 6 notes.   R. L. Collison

57. Cliffe, Lionel. LABOUR MIGRATION AND PEASANT DIFFEREN-
TIATION: ZAMBIAN EXPERIENCES. *J. of Peasant Studies [Great Britain]*
1978 5(3): 326-346. Peasants in Zambia, as elsewhere in Southern Africa, were
drawn into the world economy as labour migrants, and even now, when urban
employment is more permanent, the rural areas are given over more to the
reproduction of labour than to the production of commodities. The resulting
general impoverishment has not, however, precluded significant differentiation
among the various regional peasantries. Moreover, in these peasantries, where
many men are absent, changes in property rights related to kinship and the
division of labour between sexes take place. Differentiation and the special
position of women have to be taken into account in assessing the political
potential in societies whose complexity gives special meaning to the "worker-
peasant alliance."   J

58. Clignet, Remi. SOCIAL CHANGE AND SEXUAL DIFFERENTIA-
TION IN THE CAMEROUN AND THE IVORY COAST. *Signs: J. of*
Women in Culture and Soc. 1977 3(1): 244-260. A comparison of the rates of
social change and sexual differentiation in Cameroon and Ivory Coast, societies
which have contrasting histories and ethnic structures. Examines the interrela-
tion of changes in women's status as affected by complexity of social structures
and by past and present cultural models and stereotypes. 9 tables, 25 notes.
                                                              L. M. Maloney

59. Clignet, Remi. L'INFLUENCE DU CONCEPT DE COHORTE SUR
LA DEMOGRAPHIE DES PAYS EN VOIE DE DEVELOPPEMENT: LE
CAS DU CAMEROUN DE L'OUEST [The influence of the concept of
cohort on the demography of developing countries: the case of western
Cameroon]. *Population [France] 1983 38(4-5): 707-732.* Provides a reconstruction of the fertility rates among women of the Duala and Widekum groups
from the 1965 census records; reproductive behavior varies between different
communities and ethnic groups because their historical development and social
organization has differed.

60. Crapuchet, Simonne. FEMMES AGNI EN MILIEU URBAIN [Anyi
women in an urban environment]. *Cahiers d'Études Africaines [France] 1971*
11(2): 298-307. A 10-year follow-up study of a group of village women from
the Ivory Coast who had migrated to the capital of Abidjan. Describes the new
opportunities for mothers freed from the social restraints of the village,
particularly the domination of older female relatives, and shows that educated
mothers who migrated to the city were better able to improve the position of
their children than uneducated mothers. Based on personal interviews; 4 notes.
                                                              B. S. Fetter

61. Crummey, Donald. FAMILY AND PROPERTY AMONGST THE
AMHARA NOBILITY. *J. of African Hist. [Great Britain] 1983 24(2):*
207-220. By tracing the affairs of one Abyssinian noble family from the mid-

18th to mid-19th centuries, the Amhara of Ethiopia are shown to have had a distinct kinship pattern. The Amhara form an ambilineal society in which lineage is traced through the maternal and paternal lines. Similar to European nobility, Amhara nobility formed something comparatively close to transgenerational families, which based their structure and lineage on land holdings. There existed a strong interrelationship between property and public office. The nobles used wills and marriage settlements such as *alaquenat* to consolidate the family and property holdings under one family member. Based on wills in the British Library and manuscripts in the Cambridge University library; 2 descent charts, 49 notes.   J. M. Gilbert

62. Crummey, Donald. WOMEN AND LANDED PROPERTY IN GONDARINE ETHIOPIA. *Int. J. of African Hist. Studies 1981 14(3): 444-465.* A statistical analysis of document collections of 6,500 land records from the Ethiopian province of Gondar. These show that noble women did hold, inherit, and engage in land transactions, although at a much lower rate than men. Based on Ethiopian documents in the British Museum and at Cambridge University; 15 tables, 30 notes.   R. T. Brown

63. Decraene, Philippe. ESQUISSE D'UNE NOUVELLE POLITIQUE ÉTRANGÈRE GABONAISE [Outline of a new Gabonese foreign policy]. *Rev. Française d'Études Pol. Africaines [France] 1973 (90): 58-66.* Discusses the efforts of President Albert Bernard Bongo following his 25 February 1972 election in strengthening international ties, including the opening of new relations, normalization of US-Gabon ties, the establishment of diplomatic relations with Egypt and Algeria, and a policy of general rapprochement with neighboring countries.

64. Denzer, LaRay. CONSTANCE A. CUMMINGS-JOHN OF SIERRA LEONE: HER EARLY POLITICAL CAREER. *Tarikh [Nigeria] 1981 7(1): 20-32.* Traces the early life and political career of Constance Agatha Cummings-John (née Horton), founder of the Sierra Leone Women's Movement, from her birth in 1918 in Freetown, Sierra Leone to the 1950's, focusing on her involvement in anticolonial and independence movements in West Africa and on her dealings with other African leaders, including I. T. A. Wallace-Johnson (1894-1965) and H. C. Bankole Bright (1883-1958).

65. Devis, T. L. F. FERTILITY DIFFERENTIALS AMONG THE TRIBAL GROUPS OF SIERRA LEONE. *Population Studies [Great Britain] 1973 27(3): 501-514.* Estimates of fertility levels have already been made for the administrative districts of Sierra Leone. These made use of conventional techniques and were based on age data from the 1963 Census. As such methods assume the hypothetical situation where a population is closed to migration, an attempt was made to approximate it more closely by using the larger tribal groups of the country. Distinct differences were found between the two largest groups, the Mende and Temne, and in general tribes inhabiting the south and east displayed lower levels than those in the north. Other sources provided some confirmation of these results. In view of the lack of information reasons for such differentials can only be guessed at, but it seems likely that the pattern of development in Sierra Leone is a major contributing factor. Cultural

influences and religion probably affect the issue also, but the extent of this cannot be assessed. J

66. Dobert, Margarita and Shields, Nwanganga. AFRICA'S WOMEN: SE-CURITY IN TRADITION, CHALLENGE IN CHANGE. *Africa Report 1972 17(7): 14-20.*

67. Dolghin, Florentina. O REGINĂ AFRICANĂ ÎMPOTRIVA COLO-NIALISMULUI [An African queen against colonialism]. *Magazin Istoric [Rumania] 1978 12(6): 58-61.* A biography of Zinga (1582-1663) Queen of Ndongo (Angola), emphasizing her successful opposition to Portuguese colonial expansion.

68. Egboh, Edmund O. POLYGAMY IN IBOLAND. *Civilisations [Belgium] 1972 22(3): 431-444.* Polygamy was universally accepted in pre-Christian Iboland in southeastern Nigeria in order to provide wealth, property and power, and the development of a labor force, and to overcome rivals or enemies. With the introduction of Christianity polygamy has declined. Today most reasons for which polygamy was instituted have disappeared, however, it is doubtful if it will completely disappear in Iboland. Table, 44 notes.
H. L. Calkin

69. Ejiogu, Aloy M. SEX DIFFERENCES IN THE LEADER BEHAV-IOUR OF NIGERIAN COLLEGE PRINCIPALS. *J. of Educ. Administration and Hist. [Great Britain] 1982 14(1): 55-61.* Considers barriers placed to keep women from prestigious positions in organizations, in particular a number of incidents in Nigeria involving the appointment of female principals in secondary schools, and the downgrading of their capabilities, 1977-82.

70. Ekechi, Felix K. AFRICAN POLYGAMY AND WESTERN CHRIS-TIAN ETHNOCENTRISM. *J. of African Studies 1976 3(3): 329-350.* Examines the attitude of church and colonial government officials toward polygamy and their attempts to replace the African with the Western marriage system. Efforts of 19th- and 20th-century Christian missionaries to impose monogamy was an attempt to destroy the West African social and economic structure and to Europeanize the Africans. Though less so today, polygamy has met the economic needs of the community while conferring social status on its practitioners and continues as a revered African social institution.
E. P. Stickney/S

71. Etienne, Mona. WOMEN AND MEN, CLOTH AND COLONIZA-TION: THE TRANSFORMATION OF PRODUCTION-DISTRIBUTION RELATIONS AMONG THE BAULE (IVORY COAST). Etienne, Mona and Leacock, Eleanor, ed. *Women and Colonization: Anthropological Perspectives* (New York: Praeger, J. F. Bergin Publ., 1980): 214-238. Before colonization of east central Ivory Coast in 1893, the Baule maintained a sexual division of labor in their production activities. Women cultivated yams and cotton and controlled their distribution. Men owned the land and spun and wove cotton. Colonization altered this interdependent relationship and provided new opportunities for cloth production. The appearance of imported European cloth and

thread and the establishment of the R. Gonfreville textile factory in Bouaké, 1923, diminished women's economic independence. The development of cotton, cocoa, and coffee into cash crops for export under colonial administration further increased male domination of agriculture. Photo, 24 notes, ref.

72. Etienne, Mona. WOMEN AND MEN, CLOTH AND COLONIZA-TION: THE TRANSFORMATION OF PRODUCTION-DISTRIBUTION RELATIONS AMONG THE BAULE (IVORY COAST). *Cahiers d'Études Africaines [France] 1977 17(1): 41-64.* Baule men and women were interdependent in their production relationships before colonization in the early 20th century. As a result of colonial demands and the industrialization of the textile-making process, women lost control of the production of cotton cloth and became alienated from the production process, although cloth remained an item of high prestige. Based on field research and secondary literature; 36 notes.   B. S. Fetter

73. Farrag, Amina. SOCIAL CONTROL AMONGST THE MZABITE WOMEN OF BENI-ISGUEN. *Middle Eastern Studies [Great Britain] 1971 7(3): 317-327.* A study of the effectiveness of the sanctions practiced in Beni-Isguen, one of the seven towns of Mzab, in connection with the control of the women of the community, in a period of the loosening of social restraints. Not all norms are sanctioned equally, some depending on the social status of the deviant. Examines the function and operation of the Azzabat, the female institution through which social, moral, and religious control is exercised over the women. Sex offenses are handled with great strictness, but going to a doctor, educating girls, and traveling get varied treatment depending on circumstances. This increased flexibility is preventing complete breakdown of authority in a time of great economic and social change. Note.   R. V. Ritter

74. Fieloux, Michele. "FEMMES INVISIBLES" ET "FEMMES MUETTES": À PROPOS DES ÉVÉNEMENTS IBO DE 1929 ["Invisible women" and "silent women": the Ibo incidents of 1929]. *Cahiers d'Études Africaines [France] 1977 17(1): 189-194.* A bibliographical essay demonstrating that male scholars have failed to understand the feminine role in the Aba riots of 1929 in Nigeria. Three female anthropologists have demonstrated that what has been called the Aba riots might better be called the women's war. Based on the secondary literature; 15 notes.   B. S. Fetter

75. Fleming, C. J. W. THE CONSTITUTION OF THE INDIGENOUS FAMILY. *NADA [Rhodesia] 1973 10(5): 56-65.* Provides succinct descriptions of the three traditional extended family systems of Central Africa: the matripotestal, collateral patripotestal, and primogenitary patripotestal. Discusses marriage, succession, and property-holding within these family systems. These family forms continue to exert great influence despite the inevitable modern tendency toward legal, social, and economic independence of individuals. Based on published Rhodesian court cases and secondary works; 4 diagrams, 36 notes, biblio.   L. W. Truschel

76. Fleming, C. J. W. THE NATURE OF AFRICAN CUSTOMARY LAW IN CENTRAL AFRICA. *NADA [Rhodesia] 1972 10(4): 93-102.* A

concise and comprehensive overview of customary law among the Bantu-speaking peoples of Central Africa. Stresses the legal roles of matripotestal and patripotestal family units. Cites recognized authorities on the legal systems of Central African peoples. Based on published Rhodesian court cases and secondary works; biblio. L. W. Truschel

77. Gadant, Monique. LES FEMMES, LA FAMILLE ET LA NATION-ALITÉ ALGÉRIENNE [Women, family, and Algerian nationality]. *Mediterranean Peoples [France] 1981 (15): 25-56.* Discusses the position of women in Algerian society since independence in 1962. Women's status remains tied to religious values, which consign them to the private sphere of the family. The authorities appeal to Islamic tenets and family solidarity in order to halt Algerian progress toward democracy.

78. Gaitskell, Deborah. INTRODUCTION. *J. of Southern African Studies [Great Britain] 1983 10(1): 1-16.* Introduces the articles of a special thematic issue, "Women in Southern Africa," which surveys the history of scholarship on women in Southern African studies. This scholarship began in the 1930's and has included anthropological examinations of the role of women in precolonial African societies, studies of female African welfare in modern South Africa from the perspective of liberal South African circles, Marxist studies of women's involvement in class and national liberation struggles, and a very recent feminist trend. Based on secondary works; 52 notes. L. W. Truschel

79. Goody, Jack and Buckley, Joan. INHERITANCE AND WOMEN'S LABOUR IN AFRICA. *Africa [Great Britain] 1973 43(2): 108-121.* Examines the contribution of women to cultivation in pastoral as well as purely farming economies, tracing the correlates throughout Africa of the dominant part played by women in hoe cultivation; although women are excluded from ownership of the means of production there is social recognition of the key role they play.

80. Gould, T. F. A NEW CLASS OF PROFESSIONAL ZAIRIAN WOMEN. *African Rev. [Tanzania] 1977 7(3-4): 92-105.* The efforts of Mobutu's government to encourage the education and employment of Zaire's women are adversely affected by class and ethnic considerations, as well as historical factors.

81. Guyer, Jane I. FEMALE FARMING AND THE EVOLUTION OF FOOD PRODUCTION PATTERNS AMONGST THE BETI OF SOUTH-CENTRAL CAMEROON. *Africa [Great Britain] 1980 50(4): 341-356.* In worked by women with hoes. *Esep* crops included plaintain, taro, melon seeds, and sugarcane. *Afub owondo* produced groundnuts, maize, and cassava. Lab 1920's upset the existing system, but the spread of cocoa cultivation helped to retain the men and was responsible for a monetarized system. Women are now largely responsible for producing food, the men for cocoa production, which has limited the ground available for *esep.* Urban demand for food gives women the chance to make a regular cash income. Based on field research in Cameroon, 1975-77; table, map, 8 notes. R. L. Collison

82. Guyer, Jane I. FOOD, COCOA, AND THE DIVISION OF LABOUR BY SEX IN TWO WEST AFRICAN SOCIETIES. *Comparative Studies in Soc. and Hist. [Great Britain] 1980 22(3): 355-373.* Examines the development of the division of labor by sex among the Yoruba of western Nigeria and the Beti of south central Cameroon as cocoa was introduced as a cash crop.

83. Guyer, Jane I. HOUSEHOLD AND COMMUNITY IN AFRICAN STUDIES. *African Studies Rev. 1981 24(2-3): 87-137.* A review of the literature on the changing concepts of African household, family, and community prepared for the American Council of Learned Societies and the Social Science Research Council. 15 notes, biblio.   R. T. Brown

84. Handwerker, W. Pen. CHANGING HOUSEHOLD ORGANIZATION IN THE ORIGINS OF MARKET PLACES IN LIBERIA. *Econ. Development and Cultural Change 1974 22(2): 229-248.* Examines the effect of government-sponsored market places on Liberian society (1950-70). Originally a government response to the dislocation caused by industrial innovation, the market places have also enabled women to assume more of the responsibility for household subsistence by market selling. Based primarily on a sample of 783 Liberian market sellers; illus., 9 tables, 13 notes.   J. W. Thacker, Jr.

85. Hay, Margaret Jean. LUO WOMEN AND ECONOMIC CHANGE DURING THE COLONIAL PERIOD. Hafkin, Nancy J. and Bay, Edna G., ed. *Women in Africa: Studies in Social and Economic Change* (Stanford U. Pr., 1976): 87-109. Innovations in agriculture and trade by Luo women from Kowe, Kenya, had resulted in increased production and capital investment since the 1890's. With deteriorating conditions in the 1930's, however, their experimentations were crucial to the maintenance of the same level of food production. Because of declining soil fertility, the withdrawal of male labor for wage employment, and increased colonial taxation through the 1940's, women reduced their concentration on agriculture, reinvesting it in trade. Education and long-term employment replaced agriculture and land ownership as the sources of economic security and social status. Based on interviews and secondary sources; 26 notes.   S. Tomlinson-Brown

86. Hay, Margaret Jean. WOMEN'S STATUS, FEMINIST CONSCIOUSNESS, AND STUDIES ABOUT AFRICAN WOMEN. *Int. J. of African Hist. Studies 1980 13(4): 699-713.* Reviews Margaret Strobel's *Muslim Women in Mombasa, 1890-1975* (1979), Deborah Pellow's *Women in Accra: Options for Autonomy* (1977), Martin King Whyte's *The Status of Women in Preindustrial Societies* (1978), and Lois Beck and Nikki Keddie's *Women in the Muslim World* (1978). 20 notes.   R. T. Brown

87. Heggoy, Alf Andrew. ALGERIAN WOMEN AND THE RIGHT TO VOTE: SOME COLONIAL ANOMALIES. *Muslim World 1974 64(3): 228-235.* Describes the plight of Algerian women during the French colonial period and during the first few years of independence. Although their husbands were granted the franchise in 1919, women were not allowed to vote until 1958. The French colonials had sought to maintain the existing religious limitations on women. The Algerian women were nonpersons not only

politically, but legally and socially as well. It was not until the French reforms of the 1950's that women gained some rights. These gains were continued after Algeria became independent in 1962, because the nationalists, for a variety of reasons, accepted woman suffrage. Secondary French works; 9 notes.

P. J. Mattar

88. Heggoy, Alf Andrew. CULTURAL DISRESPECT: EUROPEAN AND ALGERIAN VIEWS ON WOMEN IN COLONIAL AND INDEPENDENT ALGERIA. *Muslim World 1972 62(4): 323-335.* A study of attitudes of Algerians and Frenchmen toward women in Algeria. The French misinterpreted such customs as the veil and the dowry, since they lacked an understanding of Algerian customs relating to women. To the European such practices were degrading. Algerian men could not accept the freedom allowed Western women, such as walking the streets unescorted. At the same time some attempted to have sexual relations with French women in order to gain revenge over their "masters." Because of such attitudes, mixed marriages and assimilation were minimal. Based on French and English primary and secondary sources; chart, 41 notes.

P. S. J. Mattar

89. Heggoy, Alf Andrew. THE EVOLUTION OF ALGERIAN WOMEN. *African Studies Rev. 1974 17(2): 449-456.* A research note on the small change in the role of women in Algerian society from the colonial era to the present. Biblio.

R. T. Brown

90. Hill, Sylvia. LESSONS FROM THE MOZAMBICAN WOMEN'S STRUGGLE. *TransAfrica Forum 1983 2(1): 77-90.* Examines the theoretical basis for the women's liberation movement in Mozambique.

91. Hilton, Anne. FAMILY AND KINSHIP AMONG THE KONGO SOUTH OF THE ZAIRE RIVER FROM THE SIXTEENTH TO THE NINETEENTH CENTURIES. *J. of African Hist. [Great Britain] 1983 24(2): 189-206.* From their early origins to the 19th century, Kongo kinship relations were ruled by the ideology of the *kanda,* a matrilineal descent group which based its power on land. With the onslaught of the slave trade, Kongo economics and politics began to change and in the late 15th century, the *kanda* developed a ruling elite, or Mwissikongo, which based its power and membership on patrilateral ties. At the end of the 17th century, new trade patterns and routes caused the Kongo kingdom to decline and led to a consolidation of the power of the Mwissikongo. As the Kongo's power diminished in the 19th century the divisions between free and slave dissolved, and all sought identification through the descent system of the *kanda* and the lineage of Mbanza Kongo. Primary sources; 67 notes.

J. M. Gilbert

92. Hirschmann, David and Vaughan, Megan. FOOD PRODUCTION AND INCOME GENERATION IN A MATRILINEAL SOCIETY: RURAL WOMEN IN ZOMBA, MALAWI. *J. of Southern African Studies [Great Britain] 1983 10(1): 86-99.* The traditional matrilineal inheritance patterns in the Zomba district of Malawi has given rural women a secure position of land tenure rights over the small plots they farm with hoe technology. In recent times, men throughout Malawi have left their home rural

areas as migrant laborers to earn cash incomes elsewhere. Interviews with Zomba women cultivators reveal that increasing needs to purchase commodities ranging from fertilizers to Malawi Congress Party membership cards and the growing shortage of arable land is eroding their traditional security in land, creating an ever greater dependence on other income from their local efforts and their husbands' work in more distant areas. These tendencies are serving to subordinate the women to their male relations. Based on interviews and published Malawian official reports; 2 tables, 20 notes.   L. W. Truschel

93.   Johnson, Cheryl P. GRASSROOTS ORGANIZING: WOMEN IN ANTI-COLONIAL ACTIVITY IN SOUTHWESTERN NIGERIA. *African Studies Rev. 1982 25(2-3): 137-157.* Short histories of the Lagos Market Women's Association, the Nigerian Women's Party and the Abeokuta Women's Union. Based on interviews and participants' papers; 4 notes, biblio.
R. T. Brown

94.   Johnson, Cheryl P. MADAM ALIMOTU PELEWURA AND THE LAGOS MARKET WOMEN. *Tarikh [Nigeria] 1981 7(1): 1-10.* Traces the life of Alimotu Pelewura from 1900 to her death in 1951. Describes her role as a market leader for women in Lagos, Nigeria and discusses her influence along with Herbert Macaulay (died 1946), the father of Nigerian nationalism, on the formation of nationalist political parties, including the Nigerian National Democratic Party and the Nigerian Union of Young Democrats, during the 1920's and 1930's in Nigeria.

95.   Kalu, Wilhemina J. MODERN GA FAMILY LIFE PATTERNS: A LOOK AT CHANGING MARRIAGE STRUCTURE IN AFRICA. *J. of Black Studies 1981 11(3): 349-352.* The traditional residence pattern of Ga families in Ghana was patrilocal. Modernization has led to new residence patterns—matrilocal kin (most common), patrilocal nuclear (usually well-educated professionals), matrilocal (the newest form, where the woman is financially dominant), and matrilocal- patrilocal (an unstable form found among some new marriage partners). Biblio.   R. G. Sherer

96.   Kenny, Michael G. THE RELATION OF ORAL HISTORY TO SO-CIAL STRUCTURE IN SOUTH NYANZA, KENYA. *Africa [Great Britain] 1977 47(3): 276-288.* Discusses the lineage organization, as revealed by oral history and genealogy, of sections of the Basuba peoples from the islands and southern mainland of the Gulf of Kavirondo and compares it to that of the Kenyan Luo. Points to possible explanations of the dynastic struggles in the kingdom of Buganda, and of the history of the Luo. Presents extracts from Basuba folklore which clearly illustrate the close connection between tradition and present-day attitudes, and show that some aspects of genealogy function as charters for and explanations of de facto political and economic relationships. Based on fieldwork; 2 maps, 13 notes, bibliography.   R. L. Collison

97.   Kinsman, Margaret. BEASTS OF BURDEN: THE SUBORDINATION OF SOUTHERN TSWANA WOMEN, CA. 1800-1840. *J. of Southern African Studies [Great Britain] 1983 10(1): 39-54.* During precolonial times, southern Tswana women, living in the region between the Orange and Molopo

rivers, were clearly subordinated within their society. Labor among the Tswana was determined by sex, with chiefs, elders, and headmen controlling the arable plots on which women farmed. Children were thoroughly socialized on the basis of normalized gender behavior and labor. Married women were subordinated to their husbands, and all women were rendered politically powerless. Men could beat daughters and wives and desert their spouses with relative impunity. Contemporary accounts indicate that these precolonial Tswana women viewed themselves as beasts of burden within their society. Based on missionary papers, archival records, and published diaries and first hand accounts; 72 notes. L. W. Truschel

98. Kitching, Gavin. PROTO-INDUSTRIALIZATION AND DEMOGRAPHIC CHANGE: A THESIS AND SOME POSSIBLE AFRICAN IMPLICATIONS. *J. of African Hist.* [Great Britain] 1983 24(2): 221-240. Recent studies by the British historians Peter Laslett on family reconstitution and David Levine on protoindustrialization in England offer theoretical guidelines for interpreting family change in Africa. The respective studies explore the correlation between the lowering of the marriage age and the increased fertility of women, as well as the effect of protoindustrialization on population growth. These studies suggest research possibilities on the transition from polygyny to monogamy and increased fertility in Africa. 55 notes. J. M. Gilbert

99. Kruks, Sonia. MOZAMBIQUE: SOME REFLECTIONS ON THE STRUGGLE FOR WOMEN'S EMANCIPATION. *Frontiers: A J. of Women Studies* 1983 7(2): 32-41. Women in Mozambique made considerable gains after independence. For the first time they were incorporated in political processes, had equal legal rights and responsibilities with men, and gained increased access to education. Oppressive practices such as child marriage and initiation rites declined, and women were encouraged to choose their own marriage partners. In the cooperative sector, a cash income and the experience of collective work were opened to them.

100. Ladipo, Patricia. DEVELOPING WOMEN'S COOPERATIVES: AN EXPERIMENT IN RURAL NIGERIA. *J. of Development Studies* [Great Britain] 1981 17(3): 123-136. Focuses on two groups of Yoruba women that organized cooperatives, one following government regulations, and another more successful group that formed its own regulations.

101. Ladner, Joyce. TANZANIAN WOMEN AND NATION BUILDING. *Black Scholar* 1971 3(4): 22-28. Discusses the role of women in the political, social, and economic development of Tanzania since 1961. Traditionally, women were considered inferior, exploited for their labor, subjugated by the Islamic religion, and oppressed by sexual inequality. Since 1961, when Tanzania became an independent nation, deliberate efforts have been made to combat traditional sexual discrimination. The United Women of Tanzania formed to become a political force. Women's economic importance is recognized, particularly in agriculture on the farms and in the *ujaama* villages. Women also actively participate in the National Service where they acquire military, civil service, and social service skills necessary for nation-building.

Despite persistent resistance to and prejudices against women's new roles, women's activities and opportunities are institutionalized parts of Tanzania's national development.   A. E. Wiederrecht

102.   Ladner, Joyce A. RACISM AND TRADITION: BLACK WOMAN-HOOD IN HISTORICAL PERSPECTIVE. Carroll, Berenice A., ed. *Liberating Women's Hist.* (Chicago: U. of Illinois Pr., 1976): pp. 179-193. Past historiography has generally compared the black family to middle-class whites, a method which emphasizes the weaknesses of the blacks and overlooks their positive features. To begin to comprehend the position of black women in today's society, an analysis must be undertaken of family life in pre-colonial African cultures and the structural effects of slavery and modern oppression of blacks. In this way a true assessment of the strengths of the black personality can be made. 39 notes.   B. Sussman

103.   Lamba, Isaac C. AFRICAN WOMEN'S EDUCATION IN MALAWI, 1875-1952. *J. of Educ. Administration and Hist. [Great Britain] 1982 14(1): 46-54.* Surveys the development of women's education in Malawi, 1875-1952, in particular the assistance of European missionaries and the change in status that came with education.

104.   Lewis, Shelby. AFRICAN WOMEN AND NATIONAL DEVELOPMENT. Lindsay, Beverly, ed. *Comparative Perspectives of Third World Women: The Impact of Race, Sex, and Class* (New York: Praeger, 1980): 31-54. Rejects various existing views about the concept of African development and women's place in it, focusing on women's role in society, their contributions to development, why women have been excluded from development programs, and the commitment of African states to change the economic, social, and political situation to improve women's status.

105.   Lindsay, Beverly. ISSUES CONFRONTING PROFESSIONAL AFRICAN WOMEN: ILLUSTRATIONS FROM KENYA. Lindsay, Beverly, ed. *Comparative Perspectives of Third World Women: The Impact of Race, Sex, and Class* (New York: Praeger, 1980): 78-95. Describes the professional woman in a Kenyan context as one who has completed postsecondary formal education and is employed, focusing on factors such as domestic roles, social conditions, and educational and career conditions which affect women's participation in the paid labor force, and examines some policy implications for the future.

106.   MacGaffey, Wyatt. LINEAGE STRUCTURE, MARRIAGE AND THE FAMILY AMONGST THE CENTRAL BANTU. *J. of African Hist. [Great Britain] 1983 24(2): 173-187.* Until the 1960's, there existed a degree of cultural and social homogeneity among the Central Bantu people. A social structure identified as the "lineage mode of production" influenced this uniformity. Within this structure, lineage, house, and clan-section existed as corporate groups that served an economic function. Based on fictive or real kinship, this patrilineal structure included both free and slave. The Atlantic slave trade resulted in the coastal societies' becoming more complex and

stratified. Eventually, this division also influenced the central regions, segmenting a once bilateral structure. 55 notes.   J. M. Gilbert

107. Mandala, Elias. PEASANT COTTON AGRICULTURE, GENDER, AND INTER-GENERATIONAL RELATIONSHIPS: THE LOWER TCHIRI (SHIRE) VALLEY OF MALAWI, 1906-1940. *African Studies Rev. 1982 25(2-3): 26-44.* The development of cotton as a cash crop allowed African male elders to tighten their economic and social grip over the labor of youth and women. The collapse of cotton production in the 1930's reversed the trend. Based on fieldwork and government archives; 2 tables, 11 notes, biblio.
                                                                                                              R. T. Brown

108. Mandeville, Elizabeth. POVERTY, WORK AND THE FINANCING OF SINGLE WOMEN IN KAMPALA. *Africa [Great Britain] 1979 49(1): 42-52.* Examines the financial position of all-female households in a poor area of Kampala, Uganda in the 1960's to indicate the relative standards of living of households of various composition and to decide whether the practice of soliciting money from lovers is better viewed as a preferred alternative to employment or as an essential supplementing of inadequate incomes. Based on author's field research; 6 tables, 3 notes, biblio.   P. J. Taylorson

109. Mann, Kristin. THE DANGERS OF DEPENDENCE: CHRISTIAN MARRIAGE AMONG ELITE WOMEN IN LAGOS COLONY, 1880-1915. *J. of African Hist. [Great Britain] 1983 24(1): 37-56.* By the 1880's an educated Christian subculture existed in Lagos, centered upon the churches, schools, and Government House, headed by an elite of educated Christian men and women. Christian marriage, supported by the Marriage Ordinance, 1884, conflicted sharply with the Yoruba marriage system, though consent and a modified form of Yoruba bridewealth contrived to be regarded as vital preliminaries to Christian marriages. Ordinance marriage failed to guarantee women's status, and, at the beginning of the 20th century, elite women began to probe the problems posed by Christian marriage, discovering that it could leave them dependent, vulnerable, and unhappy. Based on field work and published sources; 117 notes.   R. Collison

110. Mann, Kristin. MARRIAGE CHOICES AMONG THE EDUCATED AFRICAN ELITE IN LAGOS COLONY, 1880-1915. *Int. J. of African Hist. Studies 1981 14(2): 201-228.* A survey of marriage practices among 200 Yoruba professionals. The decision to practice either traditional or western marriage was based on ideological or pragmatic reasons. Toward the end of the period there was a growth of traditional marriage in conjunction with a rise in colonial authority. Based on family data and personal papers; 2 tables, 121 notes.   R. T. Brown

111. Marks, Shula and Rathbone, Richard. THE HISTORY OF THE FAMILY IN AFRICA: INTRODUCTION. *J. of African Hist. [Great Britain] 1983 24(2): 145-161.* Concerned that the history of the family was being neglected in Africa, the School of Oriental and African Studies, in conjunction with the British Social Science Research Council held a conference in September 1981 to present papers on the subject. In researching this topic, the

lack of documentation and a workable definition of "family" renders the use of standard methodology useless. Faced with this dilemma, researchers have begun to consider the concepts of house, household, and homestead, which may lead to the classification of family by the functions and roles it performs. Historians are now examining the interaction of the family as an autarkic unit within the state, kinship authority in the family, and the nature of outside influences such as Christianity, capitalism, and colonialism on familial relations. 76 notes.   J. M. Gilbert

112. Marks, Shula. RUTH FIRST: A TRIBUTE. *J. of Southern African Studies [Great Britain] 1983 10(1): 123-128.* From her student days in Johannesburg in the 1940's to her assassination in 1982, Ruth First was a prominent South African Marxist radical and writer. Following her arrests and detentions in South Africa in the 1950's and 1960's, First went into exile and worked to topple the South African state from abroad and to build socialism in Mozambique under FRELIMO. Her many works included books on her imprisonment in South Africa, South-West Africa, Libya, ruling elites in independent Africa, and the life of Olive Schreiner. Based on Ruth First's writings; 16 notes.   L. W. Truschel

113. Marshall, Susan E. and Stokes, Randall G. TRADITION AND THE VEIL: FEMALE STATUS IN TUNISIA AND ALGERIA. *J. of Modern African Studies [Great Britain] 1981 19(4): 625-646.* National policy on the status of women in society has diverged since independence in Algeria and Tunisia. While the law and national leadership under Bourguiba in Tunisia have pioneered among Arab countries in the emancipation of women from traditional Islamic constraints, the political elite of the ruling FLN in Algeria has, despite its radical rhetoric, actually reintroduced such traditional practices as polygyny marriage by familial arrangement, and the husband's right to repudiate his spouse. Tunisia under Bourguiba has pursued Westernization, even to the point of openly challenging Islamic law and reputed statements of Mohammed on the status of women. The Algerians, suffering from a protracted crisis of political instability, elite fragmentation, and local ethnic revitalization, have retreated to a position of reaffirming Islamic tradition on the status of women. 2 tables, 42 notes.   L. W. Truschel

114. Matsepe, Ivy. UNDERDEVELOPMENT AND AFRICAN WOMEN. *J. of Southern African Affairs 1977 2(2): 135-143.* Studies the role of southern African women in economic, political and ideological terms. The integration of Africa into the capitalist system has produced underdevelopment, with women the main victims. Women initiated political resistance in the face of racist policies, but they hold no important posts in liberation organizations. The dominant ideology in this patriarchal, traditional society with the internalized socialization of women reinforces feelings of inferiority and subordination. 3 tables, 27 notes.   J. Tull

115. Matthews, T. I. THE TONGA AND THE ANTHROPOLOGIST. *Rhodesian Hist. [Zimbabwe] 1978 9: 115-122.* Reviews Aquina Weinrich's *The Tonga People of the Southern Shore of Lake Kariba* (1977) and discusses the methodological and interest differences between history and anthropology.

116. Mazrui, Ali A. PHALLIC SYMBOLS IN POLITICS AND WAR: AN AFRICAN PERSPECTIVE. *J. of African Studies 1974 1(1): 40-69.* A discussion of objects which represent both male sexual virility and military or political power. The bull, cock, sword, and spear are widespead examples, both in Africa and elsewhere. War dances often are sexual dances as well; military and sexual conquest are seen as one and the same. Christianity proved to be counter-phallic, as was Gandhianism. Both have played a large role in the politics of Africa, but both declined rapidly when military weaknesses were replaced by strength and virile male images could viably replace symbols of feminine weakness. 32 notes, 2 appendixes. V. L. Human

117. Mbilinyi, Marjorie J. EDUCATION, STRATIFICATION AND SEX-ISM IN TANZANIA: POLICY IMPLICATIONS. *African R. [Tanzania] 1973 3(2): 327-340.* Analyzes the factors used by families to determine school enrollment of their children. Indices included sex, standard of living, education of head of household, children per household, and the community. Parents generally educate their children anticipating an eventual economic "return." Argues that urban and rural education be the same to bridge the gap between rural peasantry and urban dwellers. Outlines proposed changes in the educational system. Fig., 39 notes. H. G. Soff

118. Meer, Fatima. WOMEN AND THE FAMILY IN THE INDIAN ENCLAVE IN SOUTH AFRICA. *Feminist Studies 1972 1(2): 33-47.* The need to protect a minority culture from its surrounding culture is a compelling excuse for the oppression of women, as seen in the case of Indian women in South Africa. In the 1920's the unusual relationship between men and women and the abnormal structure of the family among immigrant indentured Indians gave way to traditional conservatism. The woman became the guardian of Indian culture and the family the bastion of Indian life against the alien milieu. The men, however, became sophisticated and urbane from their contact with the wider world, thus creating a status and cultural gap between husband and wife. The new Indian woman in South Africa does not seek liberation; she seeks to overcome the limitations of her traditional role and to realize her womanhood, not reject it. J. D. Falk

119. Mikell, Gwendolyn. AFRICAN WOMEN WITHIN NATIONS IN CRISIS. *TransAfrica Forum 1983 2(1): 31-34.* Considers Liberia and Ghana, two nations which experienced economic and political crises affecting women's roles.

120. Miller, Joseph C. NZINGA OF MATAMBE IN A NEW PERSPEC-TIVE. *J. of African Hist. [Great Britain] 1975 16(2): 201-216.* A reassessment of Queen Nzinga who from 1622 to 1663 was involved in murder, the slave trade, and other violence. She sought aid from the Portuguese, Dutch, and Africans, but was never fully recognized by her own people due to her sex and eventual conversion to Catholicism. 2 maps, 24 notes. H. G. Soff

121. Mullings, Leith. WOMEN AND ECONOMIC CHANGE IN AFRI-CA. Hafkin, Nancy J. and Bay, Edna G., ed. *Women in Africa: Studies in Social and Economic Change* (Stanford, Ca.: Stanford U. Pr., 1976): 239-264.

Precolonial African villages were characterized by sexual equality and equal access to the means of production. However, the acceleration of class stratification under colonialism resulted in the deterioration of the position of women relative to men, as evidenced in Labadi, a Ga town in Ghana. The introduction of large-scale production for exchange, and the transfer of production resources into private property, disrupted the reciprocal division of labor. Women have found themselves in a money economy where the products of their labor are considered inferior and they are denied access to resources. On the other hand, in Mozambique and Guinea-Bissau, where postcolonial societies are committed to the eradication of class stratification, the liberation of women has been declared a major step in the social revolution. Field work and secondary sources; 26 notes.   S. Tomlinson-Brown

122. Murray, Jocelyn. THE CHURCH MISSIONARY SOCIETY AND THE "FEMALE CIRCUMCISION" ISSUE IN KENYA, 1929-1932. *J. of Religion in Africa [Netherlands] 1976 8(2): 92-104.* The Church Missionary Society opposed clitoridectomy as a ritual of entry into adulthood. Their activity peaked in Kenya during 1929-30 when the various missions disagreed over the religious justification of such an operation. Based on oral interviews, it was determined that as late as 1972 60% of the girls in one area had undergone circumcision. 38 notes.   H. G. Soff

123. Nzotta, Briggs C. THE LITERATURE ON LIBRARIANS' CA-REERS AND MOBILITY IN THE USA, UK AND NIGERIA. *Int. Lib. Rev. [Great Britain] 1983 15(4): 317-334.* A survey of the 20th-century sociological literature on career and mobility studies in librarianship, comparing that of the United States with the United Kingdom and Nigeria and assessing different methodologies.

124. Obichere, Boniface I. WOMEN AND SLAVERY IN THE KING-DOM OF DAHOMEY. *Rev. Française d'Hist. d'Outre-mer [France] 1978 65(1): 5-20.* In precolonial Dahomey women participated equally in all aspects of life. The country was always at war and slaves were needed—whether by capture, birth, or sale—to maintain population levels. Women both owned and traded slaves of either sex. The amazons (agodogie) were an elite female force of the Dahomey army who also had female slaves as helpers. Movement from slavery to freedom and vice versa was not uncommon, since slavery was considered an economic circumstance and not a mark of natural inferiority. The Transatlantic slave trade extended rather than created the procurement of slaves by war as a feature of Dahomey society. Based on records in the National Archive of Dahomey; 33 notes.   D. G. Law

125. O'Connell, Patricia A. BANDI ORAL NARRATIVES. *Liberian Studies J. 1976-77 7(2): 87-98.* Analyzes Bandi oral narratives from around Bolahun, northwestern Liberia recorded from the Wawoma clan. Old and honored men narrate history, while everyone tells folktales. Tales of legendary leaders, wars, or town histories do not emphasize performance; but folktales include performance interaction and audience song refrains. Common folktale themes include: the jealous co-wife who takes revenge on her rival's children; the foolish, jealous husband; the deadly disguised suitor; people who refuse

good advice; and dilemma tales. Based on field interviews; 15 notes.

W. D. Piersen

126. Okeyo, Achola Pala. DAUGHTERS OF THE LAKES AND RIVERS: COLONIZATION AND THE LAND RIGHTS OF LUO WOMEN. Etienne,- Mona and Leacock, Eleanor, ed. *Women and Colonization: Anthropological Perspectives* (New York: Praeger, J. F. Bergin Publ., 1980): 186-213. Examines the interrelationship between land tenure and social organization in the Luo community in West Kenya. Historically women played a key role in the rural economy in terms of food production and reproduction. British attempts in the early 20th century to create a colonial socioeconomic structure through land tenure reforms changed corporate, lineage-based land tenure systems to individualized ones which altered the interdependent roles of men and women and created disputes within the descent group. Photo, 7 notes, ref.

127. Okonjo, Kamene. THE DUAL-SEX POLITICAL SYSTEM IN OP-ERATION: IGBO WOMEN AND COMMUNITY POLITICS IN MID-WESTERN NIGERIA. Hafkin, Nancy J. and Bay, Edna G., ed. *Women in Africa: Studies in Social and Economic Change* (Stanford U. Pr., 1976): 45-58. Igbo society on the western side of the Niger in Nigeria can be characterized as a dual-sex political system wherein each sex managed its own affairs and women's interests were represented on all levels. The *omu* was in charge of the female sector of the community, overseeing the community market, the institution of title-taking, and women's rituals, while the *otu omuada* acted as a political pressure group for women's interests. With British colonialism in the 1910's, women's political and religious functions were usurped by Christianity and the colonial government. Although there has been a resurgence of women's social position and traditional roles since 1960, women do not function in national political, status-bearing roles. Based on fieldwork and secondary sources.

S. Tomlinson-Brown

128. Okonkwo, Rina. ADELAIDE CASELY HAYFORD: CULTURAL NATIONALIST AND FEMINIST. *Phylon 1981 42(1): 41-51.* Adelaide Casely Hayford (1868-1960) was a prominent cultural nationalist and feminist on the Gold Coast of West Africa. She organized a technical training school for girls, headed the Ladies' Division of the Universal Negro Improvement Association, and traveled and spoke to refute the stereotype of African barbarism. She combined feminism and cultural nationalism to improve the lives of African women.

A. G. Belles

129. Okorafor, A. E. COMMUNICATION AND POPULATION CHANGE IN AFRICA. *J. of Black Studies 1982 13(1): 73-85.* Africa's rising birth rate and declining mortality rate make its population growth rate the world's highest. Population growth aided economic development in the major industrial countries during the past four centuries, but it now retards development in Africa. One, though not the major, means of controlling African population growth is effective communication about the means and importance of birth control and the interaction of population limits and economic growth or development. Table, biblio.

R. G. Sherer

130. Oliver, Roland. MARGERY PERHAM. *African Affairs [Great Britain] 1982 81(324): 409-412.* Stresses Margery Perham's early experiences in Africa, her belief in the enduring nature of the British Empire, and her disillusionment during World War II, when she perceived that the age of empire had ended. After the war she helped train African leaders and establish an educational system for Africa.   V. L. Human

131. Opoku, K. T. LE MARIAGE AFRICAIN ET SES TRANSFORMA-TIONS [African marriage and changes in marriage rules]. *Genève-Afrique [Switzerland] 1972 11(1): 3-37.* Discusses African marriage laws, including attempts by the colonial government of Great Britain and France to reform them and suggests that they have also been modified by other factors, such as religious conversion and the introduction of European law codes.

132. Oppong, Christine. ATTITUDES TO FAMILY SIZE AMONG UN-MARRIED JUNIOR CIVIL SERVANTS IN ACCRA. *J. of Asian and African Studies [Netherlands] 1974 9(1/2): 76 -82.* A test of variables concerning attitudes toward family size in Ghana. 4 tables, 3 notes, biblio.
                                                          R. T. Brown

133. Oppong, Christine. FROM LOVE TO INSTITUTION: INDICA-TIONS OF CHANGE IN AKAN MARRIAGE. *J. of Family Hist. 1980 5(2): 197-209.* In the marriages of traditional Akan society in Ghana, love rather than social or economic roles bound the couple. Modernization has given marriage more social and economic duties and diminished the role of love. Biblio.   T. W. Smith/S

134. Oyemade, Adefunkẹ. THE CARE OF MOTHERLESS BABIES: A CENTURY OF VOLUNTARY WORK IN NIGERIA. *J. of the Hist. Soc. of Nigeria 1974 7(2): 369-371.* Research note on the evolution of care for orphans in Nigeria. The author describes the types of care and changes in the precolonial, colonial, and independence eras. Based on the author's medical thesis at the University of Glasgow; biblio.   J. A. Casada

135. Peters, Pauline. GENDER, DEVELOPMENTAL CYCLES AND HIS-TORICAL PROCESS: A CRITIQUE OF RECENT RESEARCH ON WOM-EN IN BOTSWANA. *J. of Southern African Studies [Great Britain] 1983 10(1): 100-122.* Most recent research on the status of women in Botswana has centered on females as household heads and consequences of male labor migration out of the rural areas. The concepts of patriarchy and matrifocality have been poorly handled, and there has been an inaccurate equating of the socioeconomic situation in Botswana with that pertaining to Lesotho. Most errors by researchers, however, stem from their failures to carefully examine the often intricate relationships found within and between households in Botswana. Based on field research, unpublished papers, the Botswana National Migration Study, and secondary sources; table, 64 notes.   L. W. Truschel

136. Phiri, Kings M. SOME CHANGES IN THE MATRILINEAL FAMI-LY SYSTEM AMONG THE CHEWA OF MALAWI SINCE THE NINE-TEENTH CENTURY. *J. of African Hist. [Great Britain] 1983 24(2):*

257-274. The matrilineal family is the primary lineage structure among the Chewa of Malawi and was built around the concept of "mother right." This was the right of the wife to reside with her kinsmen and for her brother to act as her guardian. Her husband lived within the kingroup as an outsider. With the coming of the slave trade, the matrilineal structure incorporated the concept of slavery and the practice of adding to the kingroup through the marriage of female slaves occurred frequently. In the 19th century, the matrilineal structure changed through the influence of invading patrilineal groups, missionary work, colonialism, and capitalism. All circumstances combined to produce small nuclear families in opposition to the old matrilineal, uxorilocal system. Based on oral history; map, 73 notes.   J. M. Gilbert

137.   Roberts, Simon. KGATLA LAW AND SOCIAL CHANGE. *Botswana-Notes and Records [Botswana] 1970 2: 56-61.* Examines changes in the laws of succession to property amongst the Kgatla tribe of Botswana since 1875.

138.   Robertson, Claire. THE DEATH OF MAKOLA AND OTHER TRAGEDIES. *Can. J. of African Studies [Canada] 1983 17(3): 469-495.* The market of Makola in Accra was razed by government order on 18 August 1979. The government has encouraged the persecution of Ghana's women market traders because of its need to have a scapegoat for its own poor economic policies, which have created food shortages. There was considerable public support for the destruction of the markets and the goverment's view of the women traders, who are seen as wealthy and powerful figures by the public. The separation between the female-dominated food distribution system and the male-dominated government has exaggerated male-female distrust, and in reality the women have little means of fighting back. Weighs the advantages and liabilities of the market system and concludes that a market system of small-scale entrepreneurs should be encouraged by positive government regulation. Graph, 30 notes, biblio.   L. Moore

139.   Robertson,   Claire. GA   WOMEN   AND   SOCIOECONOMIC CHANGE IN ACCRA, GHANA. Hafkin, Nancy J. and Bay, Edna G., ed. *Women in Africa: Studies in Social and Economic Change* (Stanford, Ca.: Stanford U. Pr., 1976): 111-133. The Ga women of Ussher Town in Accra, Ghana, had been highly successful as traders of fish, vegetables, and small luxury items since the late 19th century. By the 1960's, they exercised greater economic independence from their husbands and were less cooperative in sharing information with them about their business dealings. However, women have not been able to make a success of their independence, and their position in relation to men has worsened as men have begun to earn salaries. Trading conditions have deteriorated due to the growth of monopolies in the fish and cloth trade. Because husbands are less willing to fulfill their support obligations, women have been saddled with the added financial burden of their children's education. Interviews and secondary sources; 2 tables, 16 notes.
                                          S. Tomlinson-Brown

140.   Sabean, David Warren. THE HISTORY OF THE FAMILY IN AFRICA AND EUROPE: SOME COMPARATIVE PERSPECTIVES. *J. of African Hist. [Great Britain] 1983 24(2): 163-171.* In comparing and evaluating

the history of the family in Europe and Africa, there are problems concerning the concept of "family." During certain periods in Europe, as in many African societies, no single word was synonymous with the English term "family." Recently, researchers have defined family by the functions and roles it performed. As a result, they have begun to identify concepts of house, household, and homestead, as being more specific. These concepts are directly related to a consideration of how sources of authority have perceived the family as a unit of production, consumption, and reproduction. Further refinement in the analysis of societies including the correlation of reproduction to production and the reevaluation of kinship relationships must occur before comparison and analysis can be more precise. 48 notes.   J. M. Gilbert

141. Saha, S. C. ROLES AND STATUSES OF WOMEN IN A TRADI-TIONAL AFRICAN SETTING: A STUDY OF WOMEN IN LIBERIA. *Africa Q. [India] 1982 22(1): 25-33.* An analysis of the subordinate status of adult and married women in Liberian tribal areas, which is in sharp contrast to the high social and political position attained by Americo-Liberian women.

142. Salvaing, Bernard. LA FEMME DAHOMEENNE VUE PAR LES MISSIONNAIRES: ARROGANCE CULTURELLE, OU ANTIFEMIN-ISME CLERICAL? [The Dahomeyan woman viewed by missionaries: cultural arrogance, or clerical antifeminism?]. *Cahiers d'Etudes Africaines [France] 1981 21(4): 507-521.* Analyzes the view of the missionaries in Africa, on the Dahomeyan woman, as degraded and corrupted, comparable to the country priests' appraisal of French peasant women; this opinion derived not from racial prejudice but from a clerical hostility to women, prevalent in the Catholic Church since the 14th century.

143. Sarr, Dominique. JURISPRUDENCE DES TRIBUNAUX INDI-GÈNES DU SÉNÉGAL (LES CAUSES DE RUPTURE DU LIEN MATRI-MONIAL DE 1872 À 1946) [The jurisprudence of the native courts of Senegal: the causes of rupture of matrimonial bonds, 1872-1946]. *Ann. Africaines [Senegal] 1975: 143-178.* Surveys the reasons for divorce in Senegal as argued in the native courts between 1872 and 1946; these include cases in both traditional and Moslem law. In general, four types of divorce action are surveyed: adultery, desertion, ill-treatment, and requests for annulment (due to nonconsent, impotence, nonpayment of brideprice, etc.). Summarizes 75 cases, divided by category, listing the court hearing the matter, date, citation, and presenting the facts, the native law or custom invoked, and the decision of the court. 5 notes.   R. Garfield

144. Saul, Mahir. BEER, SORGHUM AND WOMEN: PRODUCTION FOR THE MARKET IN RURAL UPPER VOLTA. *Africa [Great Britain] 1981 51(3): 746-764.* The beer industry in Upper Volta is a major factor in the economy of the villages. The Manga region exports over 1,800 tons of sorghum as malt each season, thus generating an income of about 116,000,000 francs. Sorghum production is in the hands of the men, but beer production is almost entirely the province of the women. European-style bottled beer is increasingly competitive, particularly as a status symbol. Beer consumption is adversely

affected by the rapid growth of Islam, which sees sorghum beer as a symbol of primitive culture. Based on fieldwork; map, 14 notes, biblio.   R. L. Collison

145. Schuster, Ilsa. CONSTRAINTS AND OPPORTUNITIES IN POLITICAL PARTICIPATION: THE CASE OF ZAMBIAN WOMEN. *Gevève-Afrique [Switzerland] 1983 21(2): 7-37.* Although some Zambian women played important political roles before colonial conquest, opportunities for political participation diminished substantially under British rule because women lacked access to education, jobs, and political office. Women again assumed leadership roles in the drive for independence in the late 1950's and early 1960's, but after independence women came to conclude that party political interests have not represented their own concerns. Based on field work and secondary sources; 2 photos, 37 notes, biblio.   B. Fetter

146. Schuster, Ilsa. PERSPECTIVES IN DEVELOPMENT: THE PROBLEM OF NURSES AND NURSING IN ZAMBIA. *J. of Development Studies [Great Britain] 1981 17(3): 77-97.* Traditional Zambian society does not associate the healing process with young women; therefore, young Zambian nurses must act within the area of conflict created by their western medical training and traditional attitudes.

147. Shuteriqi, Mediha and Najdeni, Nexhmije. ASPEKTE MBI PJESE-MARRJEM E GRUAS SHQIPTARE NE LUFTEN NATIONALCIMTARE [Aspects of Albanian women's participation in the national liberation war]. *Studime Hist. [Albania] 1974 28(1): 163-184.* A selection of 30 documents containing the instructions of enemy authorities concerning the resistance of Albanian women, 1942-44.

148. Shvetsova, S. I. PROBLEMI SOTSIAL'NOGO OSVOBOZHDENIIA ZHENSHCHIN V TROPICHESKOI AFRIKE [The problems of social emancipation of women in tropical Africa]. *Narody Azii i Afriki [USSR] 1979 (1): 91-99.* Analyzes measures taken for the social liberation of women in Ethiopia, Congo, Guinea, Tanzania, and Angola. The All-African Organization of Women, founded in 1962, discusses the right to vote, activity in local and national governments, women in education, and medical services for women. Today in almost all states of tropical Africa, there are organs dealing with the position of women in society, either in the form of sections of ruling parties or as national women's organizations. Tables, biblio.   S. R. Gudgin

149. Sosne, Elinor. OF BIASES AND QUEENS: THE SHI PAST THROUGH AN ANDROGYNOUS LOOKING GLASS. *Hist. in Africa 1979 6: 225-252.* Analysis of data from the Shi kingdom of Ngweshe in eastern Zaire requires correction both for Western androcentrism and for African androcentrism. Although only men participate openly in politics, the backstage activities of women are an essential, often decisive, and always unmentioned part of the process. Based on published accounts and oral interviews; 3 tables, 61 notes.   R. Grove

150. Steady, Filomina Chioma. PROTESTANT WOMEN'S ASSOCIATIONS IN FREETOWN, SIERRA LEONE. Hafkin, Nancy J. and Bay,

Edna G., ed. *Women in Africa: Studies in Social and Economic Change* (Stanford, Ca.: Stanford U. Pr., 1976): 213-237. The Protestant religious organizations of Freetown Creole women have fostered Christian values and have provided financial support to the church, 1960's-70's. At the same time, they have promoted a conservative ideology that has prevented the emancipation of women. By providing an outlet for the development of female religious leadership, the organizations have helped maintain the male-dominated clergy. The organizations support a system of morality based on marriage in which men are granted the double sexual standard. Their opposition to divorce is a form of economic protection for the women, who depend on their husbands as breadwinners. The organizations are a form of manipulation to encourage women to conform to society's standards and do not recognize women's needs or potential. Field research and secondary sources; table, 19 notes.

S. Tomlinson-Brown

151. Steel, William F. FEMALE AND SMALL-SCALE EMPLOYMENT UNDER MODERNIZATION IN GHANA. *Econ. Development and Cultural Change 1981 30(1): 153-165.* Examines the effect of large-scale industrialization on female and small-scale employment in Ghana. Ghana's industrial policies, sectoral absorption of increased female labor supply, and the role of female employment in small-scale manufacturing are discussed in detail. Concludes that "Ghana's industrialization policies favoring large-scale, capital-intensive production clearly worked to the disadvantage of small-scale female employment." 5 tables, 19 notes.

J. W. Thacker, Jr.

152. Stiehm, Judith. ALGERIAN WOMEN: HONOR, SURVIVAL, AND ISLAMIC SOCIALISM. Iglitzin, Lynne B. and Ross, Ruth, ed. *Women in the World* (Santa Barbara, Ca.: Clio Books, 1976): 229-241. Although Algerian women were granted equal rights with men in the constitution of 1963, the Arabic custom of secluding women from public life still prevails. Male honor has long been "closely linked to female purity." In order to insure women's fidelity, men traditionally segregated them from the rest of society. Although the 19th-century French colonialists tried to discourage female exclusion, polygamy, and the wearing of the veil, Algerians held fast to the old ways. Women participated in the fight for independence against the French, but after the emergency of war passed, women fell back into their submissive role. Moreover, after the constitution of 1963 was overthrown in a military takeover by Houari Boumedienne in 1965, women lost the small political power they had accumulated. Today, educational opportunities are greater for women than ever before and the female literacy rate has risen to 15%, but women are not trained for technical jobs with the result that "less than 3% of the labor force is female." Secondary sources; 10 notes.

J. Holzinger

153. Strobel, Margaret. AFRICAN WOMEN'S HISTORY. *Hist. Teacher 1982 15(4): 509-522.* Historians of women in Africa confront several special problems not faced by other women's history practitioners. The nonexistence of a wide range of sources and documentary evidence is the most severe restriction. The author explains how she has tried to deal with these problems in a course on African women's history. A brief description of the course includes discussions of women and the slave trade, the impact of colonialism

on women, women in national liberation movements, and women in postcolonial African society. Review essay of secondary sources; 32 notes.

L. K. Blaser

154.   Strobel, Margaret. FROM *LELEMAMA* TO LOBBYING: WOMEN'S ASSOCIATIONS IN MOMBASA, KENYA. Hafkin, Nancy J. and Bay, Edna G., ed. *Women in Africa: Studies in Social and Economic Change* (Stanford, Ca.: Stanford U. Pr., 1976): 183-211. In the 1930's-50's, Mombasa saw the rise of self-help, community-oriented Moslem women's organizations whose goals were entertainment, prestige, and self-improvement. Though organized for entertainment, the *lelemama* dance associations, 1930's-40's, provided women with organizational and leadership experience. Banned in the 1950's because they inflamed ethnic tensions, they were replaced by the Muslim Women's Institute and the Muslim Women's Cultural Association which were founded partly out of a need for prestige and a sense of inferiority to Indian women's organizations. Although their leadership was experienced in *lelemama* activities and their members reflected *lelemama*'s factionalism, their concerns were with social welfare and education. Uninvolved with feminist issues they remain today organizations of, not for, women. Fieldwork and secondary sources; 33 notes.   S. Tomlinson-Brown

155.   Sudarkasa, Niara. WOMEN AND MIGRATION IN CONTEMPORARY WEST AFRICA. *Signs: J. of Women in Culture and Soc. 1977 3(1): 178-189.* Describes the composition and characteristics of the migratory population of West Africa, a substantial portion of which is female. Women are especially prominent among Yoruba traders and craftspeople; the majority are first wives and travel with their husbands. They often achieve more status as joint decision-makers in the family as a result of this arrangement. Some young people migrate to cities to receive an education while doing domestic service in a relative's home. Female migrants often are style setters and social interpreters for their rural sisters. 40 notes.   L. M. Maloney

156.   Thema, B. C. THE CHANGING PATTERN OF TSWANA SOCIAL AND FAMILY RELATIONS. *Botswana Notes and Records [Botswana] 1972 4: 39-43.* Examines the social changes wrought by modernization on the traditional ways of the Tswana people of Botswana since 1930.

157.   Tiberini, Elvira Stefania. NOTE SULL'ABORTO E LA CONTRACCEZIONE TRA GLI NZEMA DEL GHANA [Abortion and contraception among the Nzema of Ghana]. *Africa [Italy] 1980 35(2): 159-170.* The practice of abortion and contraception is mainly based on the use of plants. Traditional sociopsychological legitimate motivations to abort—incest or other violations of tribal rules—have gradually been replaced by socioeconomic motivations.

J/S

158.   Vail, Leroy and White, Landeg. "TAWANI, MACHAMBERO!" FORCED COTTON AND RICE GROWING ON THE ZAMBEZI. *J. of African Hist. [Great Britain] 1978 19(2): 239-263.* By 1935 large-scale recruiting of labor for the mines and farms of southern Africa, coupled with mass migrations to escape administrative oppression, resulted in a severe labor

shortage in Mozambique. Concurrently, Portugal compelled the colonies to increase cotton production. The Sena Sugar Estate, Ltd., the colony's largest employer, required exclusively female cultivation of cotton, leaving men free to work in the company's sugar fields. This policy was adopted by other companies and led to severe oppression which ended only with the abolition of the system in the late 1950's and early 1960's. Based on primary and secondary sources; map, 103 notes.   A. W. Novitsky

159. VanAllen, Judith. "ABA RIOTS" OR IGBO "WOMEN'S WAR"? IDEOLOGY, STRATIFICATION, AND THE INVISIBILITY OF WOMEN. Hafkin, Nancy J. and Bay, Edna G., ed. *Women in Africa: Studies in Social and Economic Change* (Stanford, Ca.: Stanford U. Pr., 1976): 59-85. When thousands of women protested before the native administration centers in the Calabar and Owerri provinces of southeastern Nigeria in 1925, the British found it incomprehensible that women with grassroots leadership could agree on demands and join in concerted action against taxation. In an extension of their traditional methods for settling grievances, the women indicated their dissatisfaction with policies that violated their traditional system of diffuse authority, shared rights of enforcement, and a stable balance of power between men and women. Applying Victorian stereotypes to the Igbo women, the British blamed the men as organizers of the disturbance. Economic and educational reforms spurred by the event applied only to the men. 12 notes.   S. Tomlinson-Brown

160. VanAllen, Judith. AFRICAN WOMEN: "MODERNIZATION," AND NATIONAL LIBERATION. Iglitzin, Lynne B. and Ross, Ruth, ed. *Women in the World* (Santa Barbara, Calif.: Clio Books, 1976): 25-54. Contrary to much social science literature, Western colonization of Africa has hindered equal rights for women. By supplying industrialized countries with raw material without developing industry of its own, Africa has become economically dependent on Western nations. The politicians and skilled and semiskilled workers who benefit economically from Western influences tend to adopt restrictive Western attitudes toward women. Under the system of "female farming," established before colonization, women had been responsible for the growth and sale of crops. Women traders had achieved some independence and formed political groups. The system broke down when colonialists passed on modern farming techniques exclusively to men and began controlling market prices. Although progress toward equal rights is slow and hampered by economic dependence on the Western world in Kenya, Guinea, and Tanzania, political parties in the newly independent nations of Guinea-Bissau, Mozambique, and Angola incorporate women's rights issues in their party philosophies. Secondary sources; 60 notes.   J. Holzinger

161. VanAllen, Judith. MODERNIZATION MEANS MORE DEPENDENCY. *Center Mag. 1974 7(3): 60-67.* Modernization in Africa is causing the women to become more dependent on men.

162. Vaughan, Megan. WHICH FAMILY? PROBLEMS IN THE RECONSTRUCTION OF THE HISTORY OF THE FAMILY AS AN ECONOMIC AND CULTURAL UNIT. *J. of African Hist. [Great Britain] 1983 24(2):*

275-283. There has not been a singular method developed for studying the history of the family in Africa. The primary problem stems from the unit of analysis. A study of the present and past situation in Malawi indicates that the two structures currently explored by historians, lineage and the household, do not satisfy the requirements of research. A new approach is suggested that involves studying organizations, relationships, and institutions that affect the family and its functions. To illustrate this method, *chinjira,* a relationship between women which is not family related, is briefly described. 12 notes.

J. M. Gilbert

163. Verdon, Michel. DIVORCE IN ABUTIA. *Africa [Great Britain] 1982 52(4): 48-66.* During the last century marriage and divorce customs among the Abutia Ewe (one of the numerous "village leagues" of the northern part of the Volta Region of Eweland) have undergone exceptional transformations. By the 1950's traditional marriages had virtually ceased to exist, and church weddings were rare, all forms of alliance between men and women beginning as secret sexual liaisons. Couples both live together and subsequently separate without difficulty. Divorce has long been used, owing to the population drift toward the towns where paid employment is to be found. Thus, living apart for extensive periods has become customary, and the Abutia have changed their definition of the status of marriage. The extensive statistical tables are based on a village called Kloe. Based on field work; 21 tables, 24 ref.

R. Collison

164. Wallace, Tina. WORKING IN RURAL BUGANDA: A STUDY OF THE OCCUPATIONAL ACTIVITIES OF YOUNG PEOPLE IN RURAL VILLAGES. *African R. [Tanzania] 1973 3(1): 133-178.* Analyzes the concepts of formal and informal employment opportunities in a village 17 miles from Kampala. Everyone from 13-25 years of age was contacted with a questionnaire in 1970, and a second one in 1971. In addition, all young people in the village were personally interviewed. Although there are fewer males than females in the village, they hold 64 percent of the jobs. Those who have a formal secondary-school education occupy over 69 percent of the formal jobs, and on an average earn four times the salary of informal workers. Several case studies are presented, based on the educational achievement of the subject. 12 tables, 59 notes, appendixes.

H. G. Soff

165. Weil, Peter M. THE STAFF OF LIFE: FOOD AND FEMALE FERTILITY IN A WEST AFRICAN SOCIETY. *Africa [Great Britain] 1976 46(2): 182-195.* Studies fertility associations among the Mandinka of Gambia. In recent years, Mandinka males have turned almost exclusively to producing cash crops, leaving their wives to grow rice for food in the tidal swamplands. The women thus play a significant role in society, but there are no religious or secular institutions through which they might increase their prestige in consequence. The fertility association consists solely of women who are childless or who have given birth to children who have died. They mimic men, place them in mock subservient positions, and assume male speech and actions. This mock role reversal might mask a desire for status reversal, though proof is lacking, but certainly it enables women to pretend the prestige which they feel is deserved but withheld. 9 notes, ref.

V. L. Human

166. Weinrich, A. K. H. CHANGES IN THE POLITICAL AND ECO-NOMIC ROLES OF WOMEN IN ZIMBABWE SINCE INDEPENDENCE. *Cultures [France] 1982 8(4): 43-62.* Although women have become active in national politics and fought in the liberation army, and legislation has been passed calling for sexual equality, women are discriminated against in education, in employment (most work on farms or as domestic servants), and especially in the family, where bride wealth and polygamy remain.

167. Weis, Lois. WOMEN AND EDUCATION IN GHANA: SOME PROBLEMS OF ASSESSING CHANGE. *Int. J. of Women's Studies [Canada] 1980 3(5): 431-453.* While girls have been admitted to schools in greater numbers and have benefited from the expansion of the educational system in general, girls have been admitted in disproportionate numbers to low status schools and have had greater difficulty in obtaining jobs than have boys. The content of their education differed from that offered boys.

168. Weissleder, W. AMHARA MARRIAGE: THE STABILITY OF DI-VORCE. *Can. R. of Sociol. and Anthrop. 1974 11(1): 67-85.* Marriage, divorce, and remarriage delineate significant status distinctions between the clergy and laity of rural Amhara society. Socio-economic advantages of one group over the other cannot be held accountable for differential divorce rates between the two groups in view of the far-reaching homogeneity that encompasses both. Psychological gratifications, constraints, and pressures appear to be the same in clergy and in laity. In this paper, the incidence of divorce is related not to deterioration of individual marital bonds, but to the playing-out of the societal rationale upon which marriages are based. Divorce is here treated not as a manifestation of the war of men against women, but as a concomitant of the purposive institution of marriage itself.   J

169. White, E. Frances. CREOLE WOMEN TRADERS IN THE NINE-TEENTH CENTURY. *Int. J. of African Hist. Studies 1981 14(4): 626-642.* Yoruba women traders from the Creole communities of Sierra Leone dominated the internal commerce of 19th-century West Africa. They faced opposition from local traders and from male members of the various local communities in which they worked. By the end of the century competition from European firms destroyed much of their commercial power. Based on Colonial Office records; 64 notes.   R. T. Brown

170. White, Susan. WOMEN AND UNDERDEVELOPMENT IN MO-ZAMBIQUE. *Can. Dimension [Canada] 1980 14(6): 38-41.* Discusses the problems of Mozambican women as defined at the 1976 National Conference of the Mozambican Women's Organization (OMM), including illiteracy, unemployment, tribalism, racism, prostitution, and forced marriage among numerous others. Traces women's situation in Mozambique since before the Portuguese invaded in the early 1500's.

171. Wright, Marcia. TECHNOLOGY, MARRIAGE AND WOMEN'S WORK IN THE HISTORY OF MAIZE-GROWERS IN MAZABUKA, ZAMBIA: A RECONNAISSANCE. *J. of Southern African Studies [Great Britain] 1983 10(1): 71-85.* Tonga women living on the fertile Tonga plateau of

southern Zambia traditionally held a secure economic position. They controlled their own grainfields, while men held the tobacco plots. Women commanded the labor of their sons and sons-in-law and even settled and ran some new villages. In recent times, however, the rise of a Western style of farming and capital accumulation among Tonga males has enabled them to assert power within their new polygynous families and erode the earlier independence of many Tonga women. Based on secondary sources; 72 notes.

L. W. Truschel

172. Wright, Marcia. WOMEN IN PERIL: A COMMENTARY ON THE LIFE STORIES OF CAPTIVES IN 19TH CENTURY EAST-CENTRAL AFRICA. *African Social Res. [Zambia] 1975 (20): 800-819.* Brief biographical sketches of three captive women who lived in the Nyasa-Tanganyika corridor in the late 19th century. Narwimba was an older woman, Chisi a young woman, and Meli a child during the period. Women were valued and prime objects in trade and slave raiding; the latter two grew up as slaves to the Bemba. Family and clan ties are discussed as well as male rights to women and offspring. Map, biblio.

H. G. Soff

173. Wrzesinska, Alicja. CONTEMPORANEOUSNESS OF YOUNG AFRICAN GIRLS' ATTITUDES. *Africa [Italy] 1981 36(2): 183-208.* Examines the influence of schools on the attitudes of female students toward marriage and family in Kinshasa, Zaire. Based on a study done in Zaire from 1969 to 1972.

J. Powell

174. —. SYMPOSIUM ON THE CHANGING STATUS OF SUDANESE WOMEN: AHFAD UNIVERSITY COLLEGE FOR WOMEN: OMDURMAN, SUDAN, 23 FEBRUARY-1 MARCH 1979. *Resources for Feminist Res. [Canada] 1980 9(1): 81-94.*

175. —. WOMEN IN AFRICA. *African Econ. Hist. 1978 (5): 62-69.*
Little, Kenneth, *pp. 62-64.*
Lawson, Rowena M., *pp. 65-66.*
Galbraith, Virginia, *pp. 66-69.*
The 11 essays in Nancy J. Hafkin and Edna G. Bay, ed., *Women in Africa: Studies in Social and Economic Change* (Stanford U. Pr., 1976), are stronger as they move away from the contemporary era. Women's activities in Africa have helped sustain and change social systems although beginning with colonization women's status declined. East African women seem to have had more exotic outlets than the market women of West Africa. 2 notes.

W.D. Piersen

3

WOMEN IN THE MIDDLE EAST

176. Abadan-Unat, Nermin. IMPLICATIONS OF MIGRATION ON EMANCIPATION AND PSEUDO-EMANCIPATION OF TURKISH WOMEN. *Int. Migration Rev. 1977 11(1): 31-58.* Examines the impact of the emigration of women from Turkey for foreign employment on the females who stay behind in terms of social and economic issues, especially the idea of emancipation, 1955-75.

177. Abadan-Unat, Nermin. THE MODERNIZATION OF TURKISH WOMEN. *Middle East J. 1978 32(3): 291-306.* Examines the factors since the 1920's that have led to the modernization of Turkish women. There was a slow but constant movement toward emancipation from the 19th century until Kemal Atatürk assumed power in 1923. He introduced bold reforms, such as the Swiss Civil Code of 1926, which emphasized women's equality before the law, strengthening her status within the family. The new law made polygamy illegal, gave the right of divorce to women, made civil marraige obligatory, and gave women the same rights of inheritance as men. The modernization of women has been assisted by urbanization, industrialization, education of women, and their entry into male-dominated professions. New guarantees are now needed to cope with the rapidly modernizing social group of Turkish women. Based on secondary sources; 3 tables, 34 notes.   P. J. Mattar

178. Abrahemian, Ervand. KASRAVI: THE INTEGRATIVE NATION-ALIST OF IRAN. *Middle Eastern Studies [Great Britain] 1973 9(3): 271-295.* Ahmad Kasravi, recognizing the breadth of Iran's problems of tribal social organization, linguistic minorities, and cultural differences, fought for Iran's modernization and national integration 1938-45.

179. Abu-Laban, Baha and Abu-Laban, Sharon McIrvin. EDUCATION AND DEVELOPMENT IN THE ARAB WORLD. *J. of Developing Areas 1976 10(3): 285-304.* Education after national independence often has been viewed as a key to modernization. Often leaders hope to graft a modern educational system upon traditional structures, mass-based education being viewed as a visible accomplishment for new political leaders. Even though education is important in social and economic development, there are many obstacles. Since World War II, education in the Arab world had been gradually secularized, formalized, and universalized (especially at the primary level). Trends are toward more women teachers, large increases in sizes of teaching staffs, huge increases in the number of students, more female students,

and new vocational education opportunities. There is now a great need to expand employment opportunities since people with more education expect to fill "higher" level positions. 6 tables, 26 notes. O. W. Eads, Jr.

180. Ariburun, Perihan. CUMHURIYETIN 50. YILINDA TÜRK KADI-NI .[The Turkish woman on the 50th anniversary of the Republic]. *Belleten [Turkey] 1973 37(148): 481-483.* Describes Kemal Atatürk's attitude to the position of Turkish women in society.

181. Az. THE WOMEN'S STRUGGLE IN IRAN. *Monthly Rev. 1981 32(10): 22-30.* Criticizes the religious dictatorship that took power in Iran after the overthrow of the Shah for its flagrant suppression of Iranian women through enforcement of "Islamic laws" and other "medieval, retrogressive measures" and advocates the formation of an independent women's organization in order to develop the necessary consciousness for the struggle "against imperialism, the remnants of past absolutism, and the present reaction."

182. Baer, Gabriel. WOMEN AND WAQF: AN ANALYSIS OF THE ISTANBUL *TAHRÎR* OF 1546. *Asian and African Studies [Israel] 1983 17(1-3): 9-27.* Women founded nearly one-third of the 2,515 waqf (charitable foundations) in mid-16th century Istanbul (Constantinople), but neither received many benefits from them nor played any significant role in their administration. Women possessed some independent wealth, but generally had a restricted economic role in Ottoman society. Based on an Ottoman register *(Tahrir);* 9 tables, 23 notes. R. T. Brown

183. Calabrese, Maria C. LA POLITICA DI PIANIFICAZIONE FAMIL-IARE IN EGITTO FINO AL 1977 [Family planning policy in Egypt, 1966-77]. *Oriente Moderno [Italy] 1978 58(1-3): 97-107.* Discusses the two plans to deal with overpopulation in Egypt by family planning snce 1966, and asserts that their failure was partly due to religious teaching and the conservative attitudes of the uneducated classes.

184. Cole, Juan Ricardo. FEMINISM, CLASS, AND ISLAM IN TURN-OF-THE-CENTURY EGYPT. *Int. J. of Middle East Studies [Great Britain] 1981 13(4): 387-407.* Discusses the nature of class stratification in turn-of-the-century Egypt, and the debate among those who have written on the position of women in Egypt. By the early 20th century, Egypt was integrated into the world market and possessed all the features of a dependent economy. For the upper middle class, feminism was the solution to problems arising from their needs and responsibilities as agrarian capitalists. For the men of the new lower middle class, even this limited women's emancipation threatened to increase competition for scarce professional positions, and to deny them a traditional source of status as guardians of family honor. 104 notes. R. B. Orr

185. Contu, Giuseppe. LE DONNE COMUNISTE E IL MOVIMENTO DEMOCRATICO FEMMINILE IN EGITTO FINO AL 1965 [Communist women and the women's liberation movement in Egypt up to 1965]. *Oriente Moderno [Italy] 1975 55(5-6): 237-247.*

186. Dodd, Peter C. YOUTH AND WOMEN'S EMANCIPATION IN THE UNITED ARAB REPUBLIC. *Middle East J. 1968 22(2): 159-172.* Discusses the attitudes of young Egyptian males toward the emancipation of women, analyzing those attitudes on the basis of background, social status, and mother's level of education.

187. Dogramaci, Emel. ZIYA GÖKALP AND WOMEN'S RIGHTS. *Welt des Islams [Netherlands] 1978 18(3-4): 212-220.* Ziya Gökalp, the great 20th-century Turkish intellectual, strongly advocated women's rights and education. He studied and wrote about the position of women in pre-Islamic Turkish society and their contributions to social progress. Discusses his views expressed in his poems, articles, and letters. 16 notes.   A. Menicant

188. El Guindi, Fadwa. VEILED ACTIVISM: EGYPTIAN WOMEN IN THE CONTEMPORARY ISLAMIC MOVEMENT. *Mediterranean Peoples [France] 1983 (22-23): 79-89.* The veil cannot be associated with Islam, since its introduction into Egypt was nine or ten centuries before Islam. It distinguished the urban aristocracy from the lower strata of society, and until it was abandoned in 1923 by feminists in Egypt, the veil retained its original elitist character. After the 1973 Arab-Israeli war schoolgirls in Cairo voluntarily adopted a white headscarf as a sign of social and moral conservatism. Gradually, university women in the major Egyptian universities started wearing a standardized robe with headdress, leaving face and hands uncovered. Some donned an additional face veil and gloves. The shift back to a standardized form of public dress for both men and women is one aspect of the Islamic revival.

189. Eliraz, Giora. EGYPTIAN INTELLECTUALS AND WOMEN'S EMANCIPATION, 1919-1939. *Asian and African Studies [Israel] 1982 16(1): 95-120.* Liberal intellectuals took no clear-cut position on the role of women in Egyptian society. 117 notes.   R. T. Brown/S

190. Farooq, S. and Tuncer, B. FERTILITY AND ECONOMIC AND SOCIAL DEVELOPMENT IN TURKEY: A CROSS-SECTIONAL AND TIME SERIES STUDY. *Population Studies [Great Britain] 1974 28(2): 263-276.* "The paper explores the impact of modernization on the fertility levels in Turkey, which started deliberate efforts at economic, social, and political transformation in the early 1920s.... A major finding of the study is that in Turkey, continuing modernization and the concomitant spread of female education will result in a continuing decline in the fertility rate. This negative influence, stable and substantial over time, is largely due to factors other than the usual association between education and opportunity cost of female employment, such as changing attitudes and tastes. Also with the spread of economic and social development influencing the society's norm for average age at marriage and the proportion of women married, the marital rate, though not so significant as education, imparts a direct depressing effect on the aggregate period fertility rate at any given time."   J

191. Faulkner, Constance. WOMEN'S STUDIES IN THE MUSLIM MIDDLE EAST. *J. of Ethnic Studies 1980 8(3): 67-76.* In many respects, the study

of women in the Middle East has resembled women's studies in the West—sparse, eclectic, mainly descriptive, idealized, and reflective of an upper-class urban male bias, while handicapped further by "the virtual impossibility of scholars steeped in the Western social science tradition to deal realistically with the seeming paradoxes of Islamic culture." Reviews the best recent literature in the field and concludes that "despite stated national goals to the contrary, women in Middle Eastern Muslim cultures are worse off today than women in any other area of the world," since essential Islamic values in Moslem families remain intact. 24 notes. G. J. Bobango

192. Ferdows, Adele K. WOMEN AND THE ISLAMIC REVOLUTION. *Int. J. of Middle East Studies [Great Britain] 1983 15(2): 283-298.* Analyzes the writing of Ali Shariati (d. 1977) on the position and role of women in society and the impact of his ideas on Iran after the 1979 revolution. Rejecting the role of women in both Western and traditional societies, Shariati offers the figure of Fatima, daughter of the Prophet Mohammed and wife of Ali, as the personification of women's role. Based on the writings of Ali Shariati; 30 notes. R. B. Orr

193. Gerber, Haim. SOCIAL AND ECONOMIC POSITION OF WOMEN IN AN OTTOMAN CITY, BURSA, 1600-1700. *Int. J. of Middle East Studies [Great Britain] 1980 12(3): 231-244.* Analyzes the social and economic conditions of women in the central Anatolian city of Bursa. Women were far from being equal in the city of Bursa, but their involvement in society and the economy was made possible because the law of inheritance was fully effective concerning them. Based on the court records of 17th-century Bursa housed in the Archaeological Museum of Bursa; 2 tables, 81 notes. R. B. Orr

194. Gerner-Adams, Debbie J. THE CHANGING STATUS OF ISLAMIC WOMEN IN THE ARAB WORLD. *Arab Studies Q. 1979 1(4): 324-353.* Surveys the transformation of the status of the Islamic women from the early feminist movements in the 1930's, to the latest legal, political, and economic developments.

195. Haim, Sylvia G. THE SITUATION OF THE ARAB WOMAN IN THE MIRROR OF LITERATURE. *Middle Eastern Studies [Great Britain] 1981 17(4): 510-530.* Through the study of literature written by women in Arabic and French, the reactions of women themselves to their role in the household and society are examined and this is balanced by Arabic novels written by males who are concerned with the female character and her fate. The study of these sources focuses on the constraints within which women have to develop and the problems which have to be faced when expectations exceed the generally accepted role. Any moves toward female emancipation can only flourish with the approval of the authorities and if both sexes undergo a change in attitudes and demands. Based on fiction, autobiographies, and secondary sources; 9 notes. F. A. Clements

196. Hamman, Mona. WOMEN AND INDUSTRIAL WORK IN EGYPT: THE CHUBRA EL-KHEIMA CASE. *Arab Studies Q. 1980 2(1): 50-69.* Examines the role of women in the Egyptian industrial labor force since the

early 19th century. Describes and analyzes a 1975 experimental literacy program at the Chubra El-Kheima industrial plant, in which the female success rate was much lower than the male.

197. Heussler, Robert. IMPERIAL LADY: GERTRUDE BELL AND THE MIDDLE EAST 1889-1926. *British Studies Monitor 1979 9(2): 3-22.* Review of the career of Gertrude Bell, with particular emphasis on the Middle East. A highly respected scholar and area specialist, she had considerable influence in government, especially at the time of the peace negotiations in 1919 and afterwards. Her moderate, liberal pragmatism was a key factor in the evolution of politics in the Middle East from the war years through the Allied settlement with Turkey in the 1920's. Based on manuscript letters in the library of the University of Newcastle upon Tyne and secondary sources; 48 notes.   R. Howell

198. Jennings, Ronald. THE LEGAL POSITION OF WOMEN IN KAYSERI, A LARGE OTTOMAN CITY, 1590-1630. *Int. J. of Women's Studies [Canada] 1980 3(6): 559-582.* Reports on the legal status of women in Kayseri. Women appeared frequently in court as litigants, had extensive property holdings, inherited and made bequests, bought and sold homes and property, and brought legal claims against men. The court upheld their rights. Based on city judicial records.

199. Jennings, Ronald C. WOMEN IN THE EARLY XVII CENTURY OTTOMAN JUDICIAL RECORDS: THE SHARIA COURT OF ANATO-LIAN KAYSERI. *J. of the Econ. and Social Hist. of the Orient [Netherlands] 1975 18(1): 53-114.* Examines the court's view of the legal position of women and the nature of their participation in aspects of the economic and social order, based on judicial records of the Ottoman court at Kayseri, 1600-1625.

200. Kandiyoti, Deniz. SEX ROLES AND SOCIAL CHANGE: A COM-PARATIVE APPRAISAL OF TURKEY'S WOMEN. *Signs: J. of Women in Culture and Soc. 1977 3(1): 57-73.* Analyzes the sex-role behavior of Turkish women in nomadic tribes, peasant villages, the changing rural environment, small towns, and cities. Influence of the patrilineal extended household is pervasive in all sectors, but less so in towns and cities because of neolocal residence and diminished importance of elders. Though urban women are more likely to head their own households, particularly in families where the men are "guest-workers" in Europe, they play a sharply reduced role in the productive process compared to peasant and nomadic women. The latter do not receive recognition of the value of their labor, so there is no simple decline in women's status in transition to urban wage labor economy. 32 notes.   L. M. Maloney

201. Keddie, Nikki R. THE HISTORY OF THE MUSLIM MIDDLE EAST. Kammen, Michael, ed. *The Past Before Us: Contemporary Historical Writing in the United States* (Ithaca, NY: Cornell U. Pr., 1980): 131-156. US historical interest in the Middle East developed only after political and economic interest, but the area studies tended toward specialization in a single discipline with professors at universities hired by individual departments rather than the area center. The author examines the historiography of leading

experts from pre-14th-century Islam to the present. Western historians are not immune to assumptions of Western superiority; in reaction Third World writers are likely to be as one-sided. Work remains to be done with understanding the positive features of society and culture; the roles of women, peasants, the working class, and nomads; material culture; and elite and folk art as sources of history. 61 notes.

202. Khalifa, A. M. A PROPOSED EXPLANATION OF THE FERTILI-TY GAP DIFFERENTIALS BY SOCIO-ECONOMIC STATUS AND MO-DERNITY: THE CASE OF EGYPT. *Population Studies [Great Britain] 1973 27(3): 431-442.* Theoretically, three types of variables have been examined. The first type contains the structural variables such as socio-economic status; the second demographic variables, such as age at marriage; and the third those concerning contraceptive use. The last are considered as explanatory interven-ing variables. Contraceptive use varies with the structural and the demographic variables. Not all the variation, however, could be explained by the first two types. Using Egyptian data, it was found that there are clear differences in fertility behavior related to all the structural and demographic variables considered. The ideal or preferred family size did not show the same degree of variability; a relatively low family-size preference prevails among most couples in all socio-economic and modernization strata. This means that there is a gap between the behavioral and attitudinal dimensions of fertility. The width of this gap varies with different structural and demographic variables whether single or multiple indicators are used. Considering the frequency of use and use-effectiveness of contraceptives as intervening variables, these gaps can be explained. It was found that differences in use are associated with differences in the gap, although use-effectiveness differences do not conform to exactly the same pattern. J

203. Koning, Karen Lee. REVOLUTIONARY POTENTIAL AMONG ARAB WOMEN TODAY. *Mawazo [Uganda] 1976 4(4): 48-57.* Changes taking place in the role of Arab women in society have paralleled national liberation. Medieval Islamic civilization left women behind veils and walls, isolated from political and cultural life. The author shows the advances made by Arab women through feminist organizations, particularly in Egypt and the Sudan. In the Algerian struggle for independence women were employed out of necessity to aid the war effort but were forced back to economic dependence when the men returned to their jobs at the end of the war. The women's liberation movement has generally continued beyond independence in most Arab states, 1950's-70's. 13 notes. J. J. N. McGurk

204. Kuhnke, Laverne. THE "DOCTORESS" ON A DONKEY: WOMEN HEALTH OFFICERS IN NINETEENTH CENTURY EGYPT. *Clio Medi-ca [Netherlands] 1974 9(3): 193-205.* Given demographic problems, female paramedics were trained to provide simple medical care to women and children otherwise isolated.

205. Loya, Arieh. POETRY AS A SOCIAL DOCUMENT: THE SOCIAL POSITION OF THE ARAB WOMAN AS REFLECTED IN THE POETRY OF NIZĀR QABBĀNĪ. *Int. J. of Middle East Studies [Great Britain] 1975*

6(4): 481-494. Analyzes the position of women in Arab society as reflected in the poems of Nizār Qabbānī, a contemporary Syrian poet. Based on Qabbānī's poems; 27 notes.   R. B. Orr

206.   Mahdavi, Shireen. WOMEN AND THE SHII ULAMA IN IRAN. *Middle Eastern Studies [Great Britain] 1983 19(1): 17-27.* An analysis of the position of women in Iran. Describes the reforms carried out by the Pahlavis, which encompassed the whole population and not any one class. Examines the situation following the Islamic revolution, in which Islamic interpretations of the place of women in society have led to the earlier gains. This reaction may be short-lived, in that many Iranian women, having experienced independence, may not be content to stay at home and accept male domination. Based on Iranian sources; 33 notes.   F. A. Clements

207.   Mahdi, Ali-Akbar. WOMEN OF IRAN: A BIBLIOGRAPHY OF SOURCES IN THE ENGLISH LANGUAGE. *Resources for Feminist Res. [Canada] 1980-81 9(4): 19-24.* Describes the general position of women in modern Iran and their subordination in its patriarchal, Islamic culture. The bibliography mainly involves works written in the 1970's.

208.   Mouelhy, Ibrahim El. LA FEMME ARABE A TRAVERS LES AGES [The Arab woman through the ages]. *Cahiers d'Hist. Égyptienne [Egypt] 1963 9(5-6): 181-186.* Before Mohammed (570-632) Arab women were treated badly. Female infants were often killed. The Koran equated women with men in dignity, rights, and duties. However, during the long religious wars between Moslem factions, women's rights were greatly restricted. The French occupation of 1798, by making wives responsible for their husband's ransoms, raised their status somewhat. In 1919, women participated in the political riots against the English. By 1963 Egyptian women had achieved independence through education and culture. Most, however, preferred to remain at home, raising their children. Islam assures complete freedom and equality to women. 2 illus.   J. Buschen

209.   Özbay, Ferhunde and Shorter, Frederic C. TÜRKIYE'DE AILE PLÂNLAMASI UYGULAMALARINDA 1963 VE 1968 YILLARI ARASINDA GÖRÜLEN DEGIŞMELER [Changes in the application of birth control methods in Turkey, 1963-68]. *Hacettepe Sosyal ve Beşeri Bilimler Dergisi [Turkey] 1970 2(2): 194-211.* Surveys the application of contraceptive methods in Turkey, and shows that between 1963 and 1968 family planning spread throughout the country, though more strikingly in big towns than in rural areas.

210.   Pankhurst, Richard. MAHBUBA, THE "BELOVED": THE LIFE AND ROMANCE OF AN ETHIOPIAN SLAVE-GIRL IN EARLY NINETEENTH-CENTURY EUROPE. *J. of African Studies 1979 6(1): 47-55.* A narrative and analytic account of the adventures and romance between a Silesian aristocrat, Prince Hermann von Pückler-Muskau (1785-1871), and his young Oromo or Galla slave between 1837 and 1840. Pückler-Muskau acquired Mahbuba at the Cairo slave market and took her on his journeys up the Nile and to Syria. He brought her home to Germany in 1840, where she fell ill and

died by the end of the year and was buried in the church of the prince's castle at Muskau. Based on published letters and Ludmilla Assing-Grimelli's biography of the prince; 63 notes. L. W. Truschel

211. Pastner, Carrol McC. ENGLISHMEN IN ARABIA: ENCOUNTERS WITH MIDDLE EASTERN WOMEN. *Signs* 1978 4(2): 309-323. Nineteenth-century authors Sir Richard Burton and Charles Montague Doughty and 20th-century writer Harold Dickson traveled through the Middle East, leaving comments which created a stereotypic Arab woman and which ignored the Bedouin women. Burton saw partial veiling and related customs as somewhat erotic, while Doughty hated the veiling and seclusion of women and saw no rationale for it. Dickson, who lived with the Bedouins, viewed women as children, because vanity was a constant throughout the world. Through a reexamination of both the Victorian and Middle Eastern spheres, the history and anthropology of women can benefit. 70 notes. S. P. Conner

212. Petek-Salom, Gaye and Hüküm, Pinar. APRES KEMAL ATATÜRK, QU'EN EST-IL DE L'EMANCIPATION DES FEMMES? [Where does the emancipation of women stand after Kemal Atatürk?]. *Mediterranean Peoples* [France] 1983 (22-23): 161-180. A historical overview of the status of Turkish women before Turkey became a republic on 29 October 1923, the social changes brought about by Mustafa Kemal Atatürk, and the present situation as abstracted from interviews with 10 Turkish women, immigrants to France, of different social backgrounds and from different geographical areas and religious and ethnic groups.

213. Philipp, Thomas. WOMEN IN THE HISTORICAL PERSPECTIVE OF AN EARLY ARAB MODERNIST (ĞURĞĪ ZAIDĂN). *Welt des Islams* [Netherlands] 1977 18(1-2): 65-83. Ğurği Zaidăn (1861-1914) was a Greek Orthodox born in Beirut. He went to Cairo in 1883 where he began his career as a historical novelist of the Arab *Nahda,* founding the magazine *al-Hilăl* in 1892. In Zaidăn's view women had natural tasks such as family rearing which required their education and social participation. Discusses Zaidăn's views and writings. 27 notes. A. Menicant

214. Saroukhani, Bagher. AGE GAP IN MARRIAGE: A STUDY IN CONTEMPORARY IRAN. *Genus* [Italy] 1979 35(1-2): 265-275. Examines marital age differentials between spouses in Iran, comparing rural and urban differences and variation in *mahr* [bride price] paid, 1956-66.

215. Sayigh, Rosemary. ROLES AND FUNCTIONS OF ARAB WOMEN: A REAPPRAISAL. *Arab Studies Q.* 1981 3(3): 258-274. Describes recent studies of Arab women's social and domestic status, showing a high degree of kin and community action as well as a penetrating political consciousness, thus suggesting an end to the traditional Oriental image of the veiled recluse.

216. Sedghi, Hamideh. AN ASSESSMENT OF WORKS IN FARSI AND ENGLISH ON IRAN AND IRANIAN WOMEN: 1900-1977. *Rev. of Radical Pol. Econ.* 1980 12(2): 37-41. English language works provide valuable information on the history, culture, religion, economy, and society of Iran, but

they fail to examine critically capitalism's development inside Iran and international capital accumulation and investment. Farsi works contain superficial inquiries on urban middle- and upper-class women and also fail to investigate capitalism, particularly women's position in it. Primary sources; 4 notes.   D. R. Stevenson

217.   Sedghi, Hamideh. WOMEN IN IRAN. Iglitzin, Lynne B. and Ross, Ruth, ed. *Women in the World* (Santa Barbara, Calif.: Clio Books, 1976): 219-228. The status of 20th-century Iranian women is changing because the influence of Islam declines while the secular influence of Western countries grows. The Islamic way of life dictated that women were property and inferior in every way to men. "The first noticeable change in the power of Islam" came with the adoption of the constitution of 1906, which was closely modeled on the Belgian constitution of 1830. Although the constitution intended to create a liberal social environment, the changes have been more theoretical than actual. Women cannot penetrate the labor market beyond low-level positions, are barely represented in the National Assembly, and find few educational opportunities. Secondary sources; 32 notes.   J. Holzinger

218.   Sönmez, Emel. TURKISH WOMEN IN TURKISH LITERATURE OF THE 19TH CENTURY. *Welt des Islams [Netherlands] 1969 12(1-3): 1-73.* Describes the social, economic, and educational positions of women in the Ottoman Empire before their emancipation in 1923, mainly as reflected in literature by Namik Kemal (1840-88) and Hüseyin Rahmi Gürpinar (1864-1944). 61 notes.   A. Menicant

219.   Tagher, Jeannette. LES CABARETS DU CAIRE DANS LA SECONDE MOITIÉ DU XIX° SIÈCLE [Taverns in Cairo in the second half of the 19th century]. *Cahiers d'Hist. Égyptienne [Egypt] 1955 7(3): 186-195.* Reproduces contemporary accounts of taverns in Cairo, 1850-1900, to illustrate the decor, types of drinks served, the people who frequented them, and the musicians, storytellers, dancers, and singers who performed in them.

220.   Temelkuran, Tevfik. THE FIRST TEACHER TRAINING COLLEGE FOR GIRLS IN TURKEY. *J. of the Regional Inst. [Iran] 1972 5(1): 37-44.* In 1870 the Istanbul Teacher Training College for Girls was opened to provide women teachers for the high schools for girls that had been opened in 1858. The school was divided into two sections to provide for future teachers of Moslem and non-Moslem schools. The author traces the reasons given for its founding, the preparations made, and the state of the school in 1870 through government documents referring to the school's creation.   E. P. Stickney

221.   Wright, Denis. MEMSAHIBS IN PERSIA. *Asian Affairs [Great Britain] 1983 14(1): 5-14.* Surveys the life and writings of Western women who lived in Persia in the 19th and 20th centuries. Comments on the wives of diplomats and soldiers who were the first on the scene; the spouses of bankers, traders, and missionaries; and certain individual ladies. Comments on the customs and social history of Europeans in Persia. Based on a lecture given at the Royal Society for Asian Affairs in London in June 1982.   S. H. Frank

4

WOMEN IN ASIA

222.   Agnew, Vijay. A REVIEW OF THE LITERATURE ON WOMEN. *J. of Indian Hist.* *[India]* *1977 55(1-2): 307-324.* Reviews the literature on the situation of Indian women, who in the 20th century emerged from their traditional roles into political and social prominence. With few exceptions, they projected an image that was different, radical, and modern. These individuals did not perceive their new political roles in terms which caused them to reject the ideas and values of traditional Hindu womanhood. The women who joined the Indian Congress Party movement for independence were from liberal, wealthy, prestigious families and were a visible example of the new roles being made available to Indian women. Based on secondary sources; 33 notes.

S. H. Frank

223.   Alvarez, J. Benjamin C. and Alvarez, Patricia M. THE FILIPINO FAMILY-OWNED BUSINESS: A MATRIARCHAL MODEL. *Philippine Studies [Philippines]* *1972 20(4): 547-561.* Studies 17 family businesses in Cebu to determine the male-female role and examine the truth of stereotypes respecting issues of authority in business tasks, authority in management process, age, education, hours, and other factors. The Filipina dominates in business as in the home. She wields control, though, at the level of assistant manager or treasurer, thus preserving for the male the public role of leader. Based on questionnaire administered to women only; 9 notes.   D. Chaput

224.   Arvy, Lucie. CLARA LOUISE MAASS (1876-1901) ET LA FIÈVRE JAUNE [Clara Louise Maass (1876-1901) and Yellow Fever]. *Clio Medica [Netherlands]* *1979 13(3-4): 277-282.* Clara Louise Maass studied nursing at the German Hospital in Newark and was a nurse in Florida, Cuba, and the Philippines during the Spanish-American War. While in Havana in 1901 she volunteered to undergo experiments for yellow fever research, submitted to the bite of the culex mosquito, and died. 4 notes, biblio.   A. J. Papalas

225.   Benjamin, N. TWO FAMILY BUDGET SURVEYS IN BRITISH INDIA DURING THE EARLY NINETEENTH CENTURY: A NOTE. *J. of Indian Hist.* *[India]* *1978 56(3): 481-485.* Briefly describes two family budget surveys conducted in British India in 1802. One relates to a laborer's family and the other to a middle-class Hindu family, both in Madras city in 1802. As indicators of general trends, they contribute to the current debate on the trends of the British East India Company in the 19th century. The

information is presented here in tabular form. 2 tables, 6 notes.

D. J. Nicholls

226.   Blair, Harry W. MRS. GANDHI'S EMERGENCY, THE INDIAN ELECTIONS OF 1977, PLURALISM AND MARXISM: PROBLEMS WITH PARADIGMS. *Modern Asian Studies [Great Britain] 1980 14(2): 237-271.* Attempts to formulate a compromise between the pluralist and the Marxist approaches to contemporary Indian history, 1947-77. Neither approach, taken by itself, is sufficient to interpret the State of Emergency of 1975-77, and the 1977 election repudiating Mrs. Indira Gandhi. The two paradigms can be combined, using the pluralist view to explain the electoral and ideological processes of India, and the Marxist class analysis view to explain its underlying economic structure, giving precedence neither to the "superstructure" nor to the "base." 2 fig., 91 notes.

227.   Blumberg, Rae Lesser and Hinderstein, Cara. AT THE END OF THE LINE: WOMEN AND UNITED STATES FOREIGN AID IN ASIA, 1978-80. *Women & Pol. 1982 2(4): 43-66.* US foreign aid programs in Asia have been poorly structured to aid women, and US program evaluation teams have been insufficiently sensitive to women's needs. Based on 49 program evaluation reports.

228.   Brey, Kathleen Healy. THE MISSING MIDWIFE: WHY A TRAINING PROGRAMME FAILED. *South Asian R. [Great Britain] 1971 5(1): 41-54.* Traces the reasons for the failure of the Indian government medical programs to train midwives. The programs assumed that there are indigenous *dais* (midwives) to train; that most Indian births are attended by indigenous *dais*; that these midwives can be recruited and trained; that midwives exercise great influence in their community; and that midwives would actively support family planning. The author documents the failure of each of these assumptions and recommends extensive research before a new program is launched. Based on official government documents and secondary studies; 12 notes.

S. H. Frank

229.   Carroll, Lucy. NIZAM-I-ISLAM: PROCESSES AND CONFLICTS IN PAKISTAN'S PROGRAMME OF ISLAMISATION, WITH SPECIAL REFERENCE TO THE POSITION OF WOMEN. *J. of Commonwealth and Comparative Pol. [Great Britain] 1982 20(1): 57-95.* Analyzes some of the processes and conflicts involved in the current Islamic revolution in Pakistan affecting women. Before the crisis of 1977 the principal law governing the family was the Moslem Family Laws Ordinance (MFLO) of 1961. Many orthodox Moslems found it offensive, but it was protected from judicial scrutiny by the constitutions of 1962 and 1973. In 1979 Shariat benches of the high courts (regulating Islamic law) were established, and they challenged the MFLO on the issue of succession. It was ruled that Shariat benches had no jurisdiction over MFLO; however, the Council of Islamic Ideology, formed in 1973, was henceforth to interpret the law in accordance with Islamic principles. The council consists of 8 to 10 members, only one of whom must be a woman, but its rulings are not always to the advantage of women.

A. Alcock

230. Chattopadhyaya, Kamaladevi. SOME THOUGHTS ON WOMEN'S EDUCATION. *Indian Rev. [India] 1972 (3): 17-21.* Since antiquity the social status of women has declined. The social advancement of women was an important problem faced by independent India. Women lagged behind educationally; at the primary stage girls constituted 50% of the total and at the secondary stage only 25%. The educational system needs changes in curricula and examinations. More attention should be paid to vocational training. Handicrafts, teaching, nursing, and social work are useful avenues of work for women.   Q. Ahmad

231. Chen, L. C.; Ahmed, S.; Gesche, M.; and Mosley, W. H. A PROSPECTIVE STUDY OF BIRTH INTERVAL DYNAMICS IN RURAL BANGLADESH. *Population Studies [Great Britain] 1974 28(2): 277-298.* A group of 209 married, fecund women in rural Bangladesh were studied prospectively for 24 months from 1969 to 1971 to define some of the biological and sociological factors relating to fertility performance. These women were selected from a larger study population of 112,000 that had been followed with a daily house-to-house vital registration programme since 1966. The selected women were interviewed bi-weekly and were asked questions about menstruation, pregnancy, lactation, husband's occupational absences, and monthly urine tests for pregnancy were taken. The results for 193 non-contracepting women revealed that the seasonal pattern of births previously observed in this population could be associated with a corresponding seasonal pattern of conceptions and that this was due to a seasonal trend in fecundability. The highest conception rates were in the coolest months of the year... Overall, the average birth interval was 33 months, with the prolonged lactational amenorrhoea accounting for almost 45 per cent of this interval.   J

232. Cho, Uhn and Koo, Hagen. ECONOMIC DEVELOPMENT AND WOMAN'S WORK IN A NEWLY INDUSTRIALIZING COUNTRY: THE CASE OF KOREA. *Development and Change [Netherlands] 1983 14(4): 515-531.* An examination of how women's economic activities have changed in relation to the pattern of economic development in South Korea in the past two decades.

233. Ch'oe Chae-sok. HAN KUG TOSIKAJOK EUY YOKHAL KUJO [The role structure of the Korean urban family]. *J. of Asiatic Studies [South Korea] 1971 14(1): 15-39.* Examines changes in the Korean urban family in the 1960's through analysis of four family functions in Seoul families: housework, child raising, family budget balancing, and external activities. The traditional division of roles between husband and wife in external activities and housework is no longer as clear as it used to be in the urban family. These changes have been more rapid and clear in the urban than in the rural family. 41 tables, 9 notes.   Y. C. Ro

234. Clair-Louis, Jean. LES DRAMES DE L'UNION INDIENNE D'INDIRA GANDHI [The drama of Indira Gandhi's India]. *Rev. Militaire Générale [France] 1972 (1): 64-80.* In India, Indira Gandhi is attempting to cope with the problems created by the divisive caste system, the rising population combined with insufficient production of food, and the difficult

relations with Pakistan, aggravated by India's support of Bangladesh. To counteract the influence of Peking, she concluded a treaty of friendship with the USSR in 1971. The Bengali refugees who fled from the Pakistan army and found safety in India constitute a special problem for India. Indira Gandhi's greatest problem is how to deal with the centrifugal forces which are blocking the unification of India. 10 notes.   J. S. Gassner

235.   Clark, Alice. LIMITATIONS ON FEMALE LIFE CHANGES IN RURAL CENTRAL GUJARAT. *Indian Econ. and Soc. Hist. Rev. [India] 1983 20(1): 1-26.* During the 19th century, the Leva Kanbi Patidars became the dominant caste in central Gujarat. Two of the practices of this caste were female infanticide and a marriage system characterized by an unusual degree of female subordination. The author uses average sex ratios to estimate the extent of female infanticide. The British were aware of the practice and prohibited it, but they were unable to obtain legal proof in most cases, so their actions against infanticide were minimal. What the Kanbi Patidars gained from the practice was a stable population with minimal fragmentation of their land holdings. This caste gained wealth and resources at a time when other agricultural castes were losing. 5 tables, 58 notes.   J. V. Groves

236.   Cola Alberich, Julio. UN QUINQUENIO DECISIVO EN LA INDIA: 1970-1975 [A decisive five-year period in India: 1970-75]. *Rev. de Pol. Int. [Spain] 1975 (138): 99-121, (139): 139-155, (140): 119-136, (141): 191-207.* The political repercussions of three major events during 1970-75 were the first Indian nuclear test explosion, the annexation of Sikkim, and Prime Minister Indira Gandhi's state of emergency proclamation.

237.   Cuisinier, Jeanne. KARTINI, "MÈRE DES INDONÉSIENNES" (1879-1904) [Kartini, "Mother of Indonesian women" (1879-1904)]. *France-Asie/Asia [France] 1961 17(169): 2475-2478.* The name of Kartini has become a symbol of women's liberation in Java. She was the first to claim the right of education for women of her aristocratic class and for the people of her country. Her only arms in the battle for liberation, however, were love and patience. Based on an introduction to her letters; note.   L. R. Atkins

238.   Culhane, Claire. WOMEN AND VIETNAM. *Can. Dimension 1975 10(8): 4-8.* An on-the-scene account (1967-74) of the conditions of women in Vietnam, focusing on the significant contributions of the Union of Vietnam Women in the hospitals and military and on the Mothers of Combatants Organization.

239.   Davanzo, Julie and Haaga, J. ANATOMY OF A FERTILITY DE-CLINE: PENINSULAR MALAYSIA, 1950-1976. *Population Studies [Great Britain] 1982 36(3): 373-394.* The overall decline in birth rate was not uniform among the Chinese, Indian, and Malay ethnic groups due to differences in breast feeding and contraceptive use.

240.   Devanesan, Savithri. SAROJINI NAIDU. *Indian R. 1972 67(12): 17-23.* Sarojini Naidu (1879-1949), daughter of Dr. Aghorenath Chattopadh-yaya, was raised in Hyderabad and went to England in 1895. While there she

studied literature with the encouragement and guidance of Edmund Gosse and Arthur Symons. She married Govindarajulu Naidu, medical practitioner in Nizam's State (1898). Influenced by Gokhale and Gandhi, she was prominent in Indian politics and was elected first woman president of Indian National Congress. She represented a happy blend of the East and the West.

Q. Ahmad

241. Devi, Annapurna and Pati, N. M. WOMEN IN STATE POLITICS: (ORISSA). *Pol. Sci. Rev. [India] 1981 21[i.e., 20](4): 117-144.* Explains the current role of women in political activities from a historical context and their social demographic status. In the essentially rural area of Orissa, literacy and economic opportunity are limited and below national averages for women. In the period of the Freedom Movement, women participated actively, but since independence, voting and officeholding have been modest in both state and national politics, never amounting to more than 3% for candidacy and a 40% voting rate. Although the major parties articulate a policy of equality, such announcements appear to be mostly lip service in the face of traditional male attitudes. 8 notes, 5 tables.

J. F. Riddick

242. Dewey, Clive. ANNALS OF RURAL PUNJAB. *Modern Asian Studies [Great Britain] 1976 10(1): 131-138.* Reviews Tom G. Kessinger's *Vilyatpur 1848-1968. Social and Economic Change in an North Indian Village* (1974), discussing the reliability of village records as a source for the economic history of modern India, the value of interdisciplinary studies of Indian rural society, and the historical relations in Vilyatpur between landownership, caste, size and structure of households, population growth, and increased agricultural output.

243. Donaldson, P. J. and Nichols, D. J. THE CHANGING TEMPO OF FERTILITY IN KOREA. *Population Studies [Great Britain] 1978 32(2): 231-250.* Indicates that the number of children born to women in the early years of marriage increased among women married 1936-60's, but that overall fertility decreased in Korea by roughly one-third, 1960-70.

244. Dyson, Tim and Moore, Mick. ON KINSHIP STRUCTURE, FEMALE AUTONOMY, AND DEMOGRAPHIC BEHAVIOR IN INDIA. *Population and Development Rev. 1983 9(1): 35-60.* Utilizing data from the beginning of the 20th century, the authors correlate factors of gender relations, regional demography, and geographic variety to provide an understanding of aspects of contemporary Indian society.

245. Elder, R. E., Jr. TARGETS VERSUS EXTENSION EDUCATION: THE FAMILY PLANNING PROGRAMME IN UTTAR PRADESH, INDIA. *Population Studies [Great Britain] 1974 28(2): 249-262.* The article examines the impact of target setting on a Family Planning Programme in the North Indian State of Uttar Pradesh. The author argues that over-concern with target setting has led to a number of negative results including high percentages of marginal cases brought for vasectomy, and low morale on the part of family planning personnel. Trained in extensive education techniques, they have been forced to place quantity above quality once they begin their

work out in the districts. The author provides no easy answer to this tension between targets and extension educators, but the problem which he has raised needs consideration in a developing country concerned with implementing an effective programme of population control.   J

246. Everett, Jana. THE UPSURGE OF WOMEN'S ACTIVISM IN INDIA. *Frontiers: A J. of Women Studies 1983 7(2): 18-26.* Sketches the historical and social context that has shaped the activism of Indian women. Describes the issues on which each activist strand focuses, the strategies they advocate, and the impact of their efforts. Their central accomplishment is that questions of women's oppression and liberation have become part of the political discourse in India.

247. Fernando, Dallas F. S. CHANGING NUPTIALITY PATTERNS IN SRI LANKA 1901-1971. *Population Studies [Great Britain] 1975 29(2): 179-190.* The changing marriage patterns of developing nations are of great importance in view of the tremendous impact such changes may have on fertility change. In this article the changing nuptiality patterns, 1901-71, in Sri Lanka are discussed in detail. The nuptiality transition during this period manifests itself by steady lowering of the females married in the younger age-segments from 1901 to 1971. In view of the serious "marriage squeeze" in 1971 and its continuance till 1981, the proportions of married women may fall further from the levels of 1971 in the younger age segments of the childbearing span. Besides this, the level of spinsterhood may attain higher levels in the coming years.   J

248. Fernando, Dallas F. S. RECENT FERTILITY DECLINE IN CEYLON. *Population Studies [Great Britain] 1972 26(3): 445-453.* The recent declines in fertility in Asia have taken place in countries with a Mongoloid population. The recent fertility decline in Ceylon is interesting in view of the completely different ethnicity of its population. During the period 1963-69 the crude birth rate fell 11%, from 34.1 to 30.4. The analysis indicates that the age structure in 1969 tended to increase the crude birth rate while the marital structure tended to reduce it. Jointly they tended to reduce the birth rate. Besides this marital fertility of women 30-44 declined by 20% during this period while that of women 15-29 did not undergo any appreciable change. In view of the slow pace at which the National Family Planning Program is proceeding it may be safer to assume that the expectations set in the medium projections may be realized by 1978.   J

249. Finnegan, Oliver D., III and Parulan, Dionisio. POLICY GUIDELINES FOR COLLECTIVE BARGAINING AND FAMILY PLANNING. *Studies in Comparative Internat. Development 1973 8(3): 324-333.* Examples from companies in Japan and India, 1952-65.

250. Forbes, Geraldine H. CAGED TIGERS: "FIRST WAVE" FEMINISTS IN INDIA. *Women's Studies Int. Forum 1982 5(6): 525-536.* Between 1900 and World War II, Indian women began to formulate an equal rights ideology which has had profound implications for their nation.

251. Glass, Ruth. EXIT MRS. GANDHI. *Monthly Rev. 1977 29(3): 61-81.*
The attitudes of political elites in India since 1947 allowed Indira Gandhi to
impose emergency rule and, meanwhile, to misjudge the alienation of the
Indian people, which led to her electoral defeat.

252. Greenberger, Allen J. ENGLISHWOMEN IN INDIA. *British Hist.
Illus. [Great Britain] 1978 4(6): 42-51.* Discusses the change in life-style
initiated by the presence of women in Great Britain's colonial India during the
19th century.

253. Gulick, John M. EMILY INNES 1843-1924. *J. of the Malaysian
Branch of the Royal Asiatic Soc. [Malaysia] 1982 55(2): 87-115.* Emily Innes
was author of *The Chersonese with the Gilding Off,* an account of seven years,
1875-82, as the wife of a minor British official in Malaya. Her life and
experiences in the region are recounted including her relationships with Malay
Rajas and villagers and her associations with other British, particularly
Isabella Bird, Bloomfield Douglas, and Hugh Low. Based on newspapers,
public records, the Robertson and Innes letters, and secondary sources; 4
photos. P. M. Gustafson

254. Gupta, Kuntesh. STRUCTURE AND ORGANIZATION OF
INDIAN FAMILY: THE EMERGING PATTERNS. *Internat. J. of Contem-
porary Sociol. 1973 10(4): 163-182.* Discusses the effects of urbanization,
Westernization, and industrialization on families in India.

255. Haldar, Gopal. ISWAR CHANDRA VIDYASAGAR: A RE-ASSESS-
MENT. *J. of the U. of Bombay [India] 1971 40(76): 228-247.* As a social
reformer, Vidyasagar advocated the remarriage of Hindu widows (permitted by
law in 1856), the abolition of polygamy (not achieved until after independence)
and female education. He advocated the study of Sanskrit, Bengali, and
English to improve the vernacular language and initiate modernization in
village schools. He contributed to the development of Bengali literature with
textbooks and good literary examples. He was also responsible for two
important innovations: the introduction of punctuation, and the discovery of
the rhythm of Bengali speech. He was the creator of Bengali prose and the
most important educator of modern India. His social reforms affected only a
small minority, but they reveal his modernism, humanism, and integrity. One
of three lectures in the first Iswar Chandra Vidyasagar Memorial Lectureship
series at the University of Bombay in 1969. J. F. Hilliker

256. Halim, Fatimah. WORKERS' RESISTANCE AND MANAGEMENT
CONTROL: A COMPARATIVE CASE STUDY OF MALE AND FE-
MALE WORKERS IN WEST MALAYSIA. *J. of Contemporary Asia [Swe-
den] 1983 13(2): 131-150.* Investigates industrial relations in West Malaysia in
the 1960's in a case study of male and female workers. The most important
difference between male and female workers was the level of education and
values held about sexual roles. Based on empirical data from two West
Malaysian factories; table, 3 fig., 44 notes. R. B. Orr

257.   Hasan, Rafia. THE ROLE OF WOMEN AS AGENTS OF CHANGE AND DEVELOPMENT IN PAKISTAN. *Human Rights Q. 1981 3(3): 68-75.* Discusses the human rights of women according to Islam and also in Pakistan, with special reference to government programs and voluntary organizations concerned with the status of Pakistani women.

258.   Hirschman, Charles and Aghajanian, Akbar. WOMEN'S LABOUR FORCE PARTICIPATION AND SOCIOECONOMIC DEVELOPMENT: THE CASE OF PENINSULAR MALAYSIA, 1957-1970. *J. of Southeast Asian Studies [Singapore] 1980 11(1): 30-49.* Analysis of women's labor force participation in peninsular Malaya between 1957 and 1970 shows a gradual increase resulting from decline in the agricultural sector but sizable growth in nonagricultural work, especially among younger women. Chinese women appear to have responded most to socioeconomic development, while the most dramatic change was the decline of agricultural work by Indian women as the plantation sector got rid of a substantial proportion of its work force. A strong cultural and ethnic difference may be the Chinese acceptance of single women working in the nonagricultural sector in the towns. Based on census data; 5 tables, 22 notes.   D. J. Nicholls

259.   Husain, Salika Abid. WOMEN WRITERS AND URDU LITERATURE. *Indian Horizons [India] 1974 23(2-3): 5-14.* Traces the role of notable women writers of Urdu literature on the Indian subcontinent during the past century. When women of the middle and upper classes became literate, they wished to use the available media, women's weekly and monthly magazines, to propagate their ideals. Early pioneer writers lacked the political insights of their male counterparts, but they displayed idealism and persistence in their writings. The names of Maulana Altaf Husain Hali and Maulvi Mumtaz Ali were prominent during this period. A brief period of stagnation in Urdu literature followed the upheavals of 1947. The present decade has seen women's novels with their emphasis on their rights and responsibilities come of age. Based on transl. by Mohammed Zakir.   D. J. Wren

260.   In, Sun Yu. THE STATUS OF WOMEN IN TRADITIONAL VIETNAMESE SOCIETY. *Asian & Pacific Q. of Cultural and Social Affairs [South Korea] 1981 13(3): 62-64.* The true role of Vietnamese women depended upon their economic status. Women in wealthy families appear to have been the Confucian stereotype, while women in the lower economic strata were more their husband's equal. They could initiate divorce, inherit property, and engage in business. The husband could not control his wife's property. In the event of divorce, the wife retained her property. Theoretically, men had authority over women, but in practice there was considerable equality in most Vietnamese families.   R. H. Detrick

261.   Iurlova, E. S. BOR'BA KOMMUNISTICHESKOI PARTII INDII ZA PRAVA I INTERESY TRUDIASHCHIKHSIA ZHENSHCHIN [The struggle of the Communist Party of India for the rights and interests of working women]. *Narody Azii i Afriki [USSR] 1981 (2): 110-117.* Describes the Communist Party of India (CPI) from its beginnings in 1925, through the 1930's and 1940's when it organized mass demonstrations of women (many of

whom had studied Marxist-Leninism in jail), to the present day. The Party's organization at all levels is detailed. The December 1953-January 1954 3d Party Congress demanded equal pay for women and equal rights in property, inheritance, marriage, and divorce. In June 1954 the National Federation of Indian Women was formed. Communist women, braving social disapproval, are struggling for their own rights and are strengthening the struggle for democracy and progress. Based on the CPI congress reports and the Indian press; 37 notes.   A. J. Evans

262. Iurlova, E. S. ZHENSKOE OBRAZOVANIE V SOVREMENNOI INDII [Women's education in contemporary India]. *Narody Azii i Afriki [USSR] 1978 (2): 115-122.* Notable success was achieved in the field of women's education in India, 1947-75. Compared with the 1940's, the number of women studying at all levels rose many times by the 1970's, and the number of teachers also increased substantially too. However, the development of women's education has not been consistent throughout the country and there have been enormous regional variations. Caste still discriminates against some groups and the growth of education has not matched the growth of the population. Based on original Indian government statistics and other sources; 45 notes.   J. M. Chambers

263. Iyengar, Shanto. THE DEVELOPMENT OF POLITICAL EFFICA-CY IN A NEW NATION: THE CASE OF ANDHRA PRADESH. *Comparative Pol. Studies 1978 11(3): 337-354.* Examines the sense of political efficacy (the individual's ability to influence government) of children and adolescents in the Indian state of Andhra Pradesh prior to Indira Gandhi's declaration of emergency in 1975.

264. Jacobson, Doranne. INDIAN WOMEN IN PROCESSES OF DEVEL-OPMENT. *J. of Int. Affairs 1976-77 30(2): 211-242.* In modern India, women have received special attention in government and voluntary programs, but as the 1974 report of the Committee on the Status of Women shows, the objectives of these programs have rarely been achieved. Indeed, its data show the persistence of a pattern of systematic discrimination against women in every sector of the Indian society. 170 notes.   V. Samaraweera

265. Jai-Seuk Choi. THE FAMILY PATTERN IN THE EARLY YI DYNASTY: AN ANALYSIS OF THE CENSUS REGISTER ON SAN-EUM. *Chin-Tan Hakpo [South Korea] 1974 37: 133-160.* Discusses clan and family organization, slave ownership, marital patterns, and filial relationships among families during the Yi dynasty as recorded in the San-eum census register in Korea.

266. Jhabvala, R. Prawer. AN EXPERIENCE OF INDIA. *Encounter [Great Britain] 1971 36(2): 3-15.* A first person account of the adventures of the wife of an English newspaper correspondent in India, describing her sexual and other experiences with the Indians.   D. D. Cameron

267. Jones, Connie A. OBSERVATIONS ON THE CURRENT STATUS OF WOMEN IN INDIA. *Int. J. of Women's Studies [Canada] 1980 3(1):*

1-18. Examines the political, social, educational, legal, and economic status of women in India in the 1970's.

268.   Katzenstein, Mary Fainsod. TOWARDS EQUALITY? CAUSE AND CONSEQUENCE OF THE POLITICAL PROMINENCE OF WOMEN IN INDIA. *Asian Survey 1978 18(5): 473-486.* Discusses the anomaly of women in high government positions in India, attributing it to political, rather than religious or social factors. The benefits to Indian women as a group of representation by a few prominent women is insubstantial. Table, fig., 31 notes.
                                                                    J. Tull

269.   Kearney, Robert N. WOMEN IN POLITICS IN SRI LANKA. *Asian Survey 1981 21(7): 729-746.* Discusses the role of women in politics in Sri Lanka since the establishment of universal adult suffrage in the country in 1931. In 1960 Sri Lanka became the first nation in the world to have a woman at the head of government. However, in the parliament, as well as in local politics, women have not been well represented. This is due to the traditional roles that women are taught as children. Primary sources; 5 tables, 33 notes.
                                                                    J. Powell

270.   Klieman, Aaron S. INDIRA'S INDIA: DEMOCRACY AND CRISIS GOVERNMENT. *Pol. Sci. Q. 1981 96(2): 241-259.* So thoroughly unantici- pated, yet seemingly conclusive, was the personal defeat handed Indira Gandhi by the Indian electorate in March 1977 that the only event of comparable political significance was dramatic return to power less than three years later. Mrs. Gandhi's victory at the polls in January 1980 has prompted renewed concern about the likely future course of national politics in India and the prospects for democracy there. By the same token it forces a reconsideration of the earlier 1975-77 period of emergency rule. This article examines the period of emergency rule and the response of India's Parliament, the courts, the public media, the bureaucracy, the army, the states, and the public. Reviews the post-emergency period, with a view to India's political future. Based on primary sources; 16 notes.   J. Powell

271.   Knodel, J. and Prachuabmoh, V. DEMOGRAPHIC ASPECTS OF FERTILITY IN THAILAND. *Population Studies [Great Britain] 1974 13(3): 423-448.* Data from a national rural and urban sample survey are analyzed in order to examine various demographic aspects of fertility in Thailand. Marital fertility rates found for Thailand are among the highest in Asia. Particularly noteworthy is the persistence of high fertility at older ages of childbearing for rural women.... A comparison of current fertility with cumulative fertility strongly suggests that a decline in marital fertility has been under way recently among urban women, especially those residing in the capital, but not at all among rural women. Although it seems safe to assume that the urban fertility decline results in large part from an increasing use of contraception among urban women, those still in the reproductive ages who were using or had previously used birth control were characterized by higher cumulative fertility than women who had never practised contraception. Evidently couples resort to family planning only late in the family building process after they have already achieved or exceeded the number of children they wish to have.   J

272. Krannich, Caryl Rae and Krannich, Ronald L. FAMILY PLANNING POLICY AND COMMUNITY-BASED INNOVATIONS IN THAILAND. *Asian Survey 1980 20(10): 1023-1037.* Thailand is one of the few less developed countries which has a successful family planning program. One important institutional factor contributing to family planning success in Thailand is community-based family planning strategies, whose principles may be relevant for implementing family planning programs in other Third World nations. Based on reports and interviews and secondary sources; 29 notes.

M. A. Eide

273. Kumar, Radha. FAMILY AND FACTORY: WOMEN WORKERS IN THE BOMBAY COTTON TEXTILE INDUSTRY, 1919-1939. *Indian Econ. and Soc. Hist. Rev. [India] 1983 20(1): 81-110.* Women constituted a high proportion of the work force in the cotton industry in Bombay between 1919 and 1939. However, after 1929 there was a steady decline in their number. There have been several explanations for this decline: 1)that men's wages were considered family wages and women's only supplementary; 2)that women were less securely attached to the labor force than men; 3)that the Maternity Benefit Act prevented women from working at night so they were less desirable employees; and 4)that rationalization and retrenchment in the industry meant that women's jobs were discontinued. The author presents evidence to show that the last is the correct explanation. Based on government reports, private contemporary sources, and secondary works; 11 tables, 2 graphs, 69 notes.

J. V. Groves

274. Leonard, Karen. WOMEN IN INDIA: SOME RECENT PERSPEC-TIVES. *Pacific Affairs [Canada] 1979 52(1): 95-107.* With independence in 1947 and the subsequent promulgation of the Indian constitution came the promise of equality for all citizens, women as well as other formerly subordinate categories such as the untouchables. Unfortunately, the lives of the majority of Indian women have not been significantly enhanced in terms of literacy, educational opportunity, economic viability, or public health. Compares the official government studies with scholarly research. Secondary sources; 64 notes.

S. H. Frank

275. Limqueco, Peter. NOTES ON A VISIT TO VIETNAM. *J. of Contemporary Asia [Sweden] 1976 6(4): 405-423.* Interviews with former Vietnamese soldiers, drug addicts, prostitutes, political prisoners, revolutionary soldiers, and officials of the Vietnamese government illustrate the horrors of war and the changes that have occurred since peace.

K. W. Berger

276. Maitreyan. SAROJINI NAIDU: THE NIGHTINGALE OF INDIA. *Indian Rev. [India] 1976 (11): 13-15.* A poet, orator, freedom-fighter and champion of women's rights and communal harmony, Sarojini Naidu (1879-1949) had a multifaceted personality. A Brahman, she married a non-Brahman, and fought against barriers of religion and caste. Her English poetry, of which several collections have been published, reflect the spirit of Oriental culture. She often spoke in light vein about Gandhiji, but respected him deeply.

Q. Ahmad

277.   Manderson, Lenore. THE DEVELOPMENT AND DIRECTION OF FEMALE EDUCATION IN PENINSULAR MALAYSIA. *J. of the Malaysian Branch of the Royal Asiatic Soc. [Singapore] 1978 51(2): 100-122.* The first girls' school opened at Penang in 1817 and government vernacular schools were created in the Straits Settlements from 1855, mainly for Europeans but later for Eurasians, Chinese, and Indians. The first Malay girls' school opened in 1833 in Johore Bahru and by 1895 Perak had six. Malay, Chinese and Tamil elites tended to patronize English-medium schools run by missions. The curricula were biased toward traditional female occupations. In 1938, women's literacy was still only 10% but since 1957 enrolment has increased and by 1959 32%, and by 1974, 44% of all pupils were girls. 74 notes.   E. Sarkisyanz/S

278.   Manderson, Lenore. THE SHAPING OF THE KAUM IBU (WOMEN'S SECTION) OF THE UNITED MALAYS NATIONAL ORGANIZATION. *Signs: J. of Women in Culture and Soc. 1977 3(1): 210-228.* The period prior to and immediately after Malayan independence was one of rapid social change which permitted women as well as men to participate in public affairs. However, the Kaum Ibu (Women's Association) changed from a group of relatively independent women's associations to a single adjunct of the United Malays National Organization, reflecting thereby the continued acceptance of the view that women's roles must remain supportive. 41 notes.

L. M. Maloney

279.   Marková, Dagmar. THE IMPACT OF CONTEMPORARY URBANIZATION ON THE LIFE OF INDIAN WOMEN. *Arch. Orientální [Czechoslovakia] 1982 50(2): 143-161.* A review of the changing roles of women in urban areas of India. Available statistics reveal that the changes have been less than dramatic; in some respects there has been a return to earlier practices. The sharpest changes have come in those areas dominated by economic necessity—employment and the increased use of birth control. The lowest rates of change have come in areas still dominated by religion. In sum, change has been sporadic and hesitating, nor can major changes be expected until India has been swept by a major socioeconomic transformation. 86 notes.
V. L. Human

280.   Marr, David. THE 1920S WOMEN'S RIGHTS DEBATES IN VIETNAM. *J. of Asian Studies 1976 35(3): 371-389.* A review of the dawning of the women's liberation movement in Vietnam during the 1920's. Though not always intentionally, French colonial authorities began gradually to change the subservient status of women. Women enrolled in schools, and women's magazines were published. Both traditionalists and radicals made their views known, but the moderates clearly held sway during the 1920's. The moderates wanted change, but slowly. Women proved unwilling to wait. As the depression decade of the 1930's dawned, the moderates lost influence and more extreme views took hold. 69 notes.   V. L. Human

281.   McCarthy, Florence E. BENGALI WOMEN AS MEDIATORS OF SOCIAL CHANGE. *Human Organization 1977 36(4): 363-370.* Assesses the role of women in social change within Bengali villages as one of mediation (incorporation of progressive technology and ideas within the bounds of

traditional social structure) rather than one of mobilization (change instituted by going outside of the traditional social structure), 1960's-70's.

282. Mitra, Manoshi. WOMEN IN COLONIAL AGRICULTURE: BIHAR IN THE LATE 18TH AND 19TH CENTURY. *Development and Change [Netherlands] 1981 12(1): 29-54.* Presents evidence on work patterns of women of low socioeconomic status in the agrarian society of Bihar in the 18th and 19th centuries and on the ways in which their status was adversely affected by a qualitative change in the profitability of agriculture engendered by the impetus to commercialization of British colonial policy.

283. Mohan, Raj Pa. ABORTION IN INDIA. *Social Sci. 1975 50(3): 141-143.* "The liberalization of Indian abortion laws in 1971 was profoundly influenced by the consciousness of pressing and critical population problems, otherwise such a liberal attitude would never have attained the status of law in a country which has been so steeped in tradition and orthodoxy."

284. Morris-Jones, W. H. WHOSE EMERGENCY—INDIA'S OR INDIRA'S? *World Today [Great Britain] 1975 31(11): 451-461.* Indira Gandhi's assumption of dictatorial powers in response to mounting opposition against her accorded with her penchant for bold and ruthless action. The question is whether she is too experienced a politician not to perceive the dangers of self-imposed isolation for herself as well as for India.　　　　　　　　　J

285. Mortimer, Joanne Stafford. ANNIE BESANT AND INDIA 1913-1917. *J. of Contemporary Hist. [Great Britain] 1983 18(1): 61-78.* Freethinker, champion of women's rights, socialist, and theosophist, Annie Besant worked for her social ideals in India from 1907 to 1913. Then she turned to politics, agitated for self-government, organized national movements, and finally in 1917 at age 70 was elected president of the Indian National Congress at Calcutta. Based on published primary and secondary sources; 45 notes.　　　　　　　　　　　　　　　　　　　M. P. Trauth

286. Mukherjee, Mukul. IMPACT OF MODERNIZATION ON WOMEN'S OCCUPATIONS: A CASE STUDY OF THE RICE-HUSKING INDUSTRY OF BENGAL. *Indian Econ. and Soc. Hist. Rev. [India] 1983 20(1): 27-46.* In Bengal, the job of husking the paddy rice was reserved for women. Women husked the rice in one of two ways: by hand pounding or by *dhenki*. Husking rice was one of the few means women had of earning income outside of the household. Although they were normally paid in rice, the addition to family incomes was substantial. When rice mills took over the manufacture of milled rice, women lost their major source of outside employment, family incomes declined, and the nutritive value of the rice was impaired. Based on government reports and secondary works; 14 tables, 61 notes.　　　　J. V. Groves

287. Mya Sein, Daw. TOWARDS INDEPENDENCE IN BURMA: THE ROLE OF WOMEN. *Asian Affairs [Great Britain] 1972 59(3): 288-299.* Traces the role of women in the history of Burma, especially in the struggle for independence. Notes the traditional lack of unfair discrimination against women in Burmese society, and the influence of Buddhism on the roles of

women. Reevaluates the actions of the Burmese queens Alenanmadaw and Supayalat as the principal precipitators of the British expansion into Upper Burma. Narrates the nationalist and suffragette activities of Daw Kwin Myaing and Daw Hla May in the Burmese independence movement. Based on a lecture to the Royal Central Asian Society, London, 10 May 1972.   S. H. Frank

288. Nadarajah, T. THE TRANSITION FROM HIGHER FEMALE TO HIGHER MALE MORTALITY IN SRI LANKA. *Population and Development Rev. 1983 9(2): 317-325.* Traditionally higher male infant mortality and improvements in maternal death rates reversed the male-female mortality ratios in about 1963 in Sri Lanka.

289. Nicholas, Ralph W. THE GODDESS SĪTALĀ AND EPIDEMIC SMALLPOX IN BENGAL. *J. of Asian Studies 1981 41(1): 21-45.* The rise of Sītalā as the Goddess of Smallpox occurred after the 12th century and she became particularly important in Bengal villages in the 18th century. Her relationship to the disease did not displace naturalistic treatment but complemented it. With the decline of smallpox Sītalā continues to hold an important position the one around which the villages rally in order to bring about reunification after a period of disorder. Hindu scriptures, British Colonial reports, Bengal Sanitary Commission reports; 2 fig., 12 notes, 86 ref.
P. M. Gustafson

290. Novelo Vignal, Adriana. LA PARTICIPACION DE LA MUJER VIETNAMITA EN LA LIBERACION NACIONAL Y EL SOCIALISMO [The role of Vietnamese women in national liberation and socialism]. *Estudios de Asia y Africa [Mexico] 1982 17(3): 491-515.* One of the main goals in the Vietnamese national revolution has been the awakening of class consciousness and political participation among women. Organizations that have involved women in the struggles for independence and reunification have included the Anticolonialist Women's Association in the 1930's, the Women's Association for National Liberation in the 1940's, and the Vietnamese Women's Union. Women have enjoyed equal rights legally since the 1946 constitution, but traditional views, especially within the family, have proved very difficult to change. 9 notes.   C. Pasadas-Ureña

291. Omvedt, Gail. WOMEN AND RURAL REVOLT IN INDIA. *J. of Peasant Studies [Great Britain] 1978 5(3): 370-403.* Women's major productive role (outside of the home) in agriculture and the crucial part which women play in peasant revolts have been more or less ignored by social scientists. In this paper an attempt is made to analyse the interconnections between class and sexual oppression, and between women's movements and class struggle, in rural India: with class structure, the nature of society, and the development of social movements looked at from the viewpoint of women themselves. With the use of two key concepts, work participation and mode of production, it is argued that in India, increasingly during the last decade, capitalism has developed in the countryside, and that, with the changing social relations of production, there has emerged a mass-based and militant women's movement, whose objective basis has been the militancy of women of the rural poor. This

is illustrated for a variety of Indian states, but especially for the state of Maharashtra. J

292. Papanek, Hanna. PURDAH: SEPARATE WORLDS AND SYMBOL-IC SHELTER. *Comparative Studies in Soc. and Hist. [Great Britain] 1973 15(3): 289-325.* Examines the purdah system of secluding women within the specific context of Pakistani, Bengali, and Indian society. Purdah is not a single clear-cut institution but varies in accordance with other social features. The discussion of symbolic shelter centers on problems of impulse control, the role of women as demonstrators of status, and in religious observance, honor and family pride, and the arrangement of marriages. Based on field work of the author, primary, and secondary sources; 86 notes. M. M. McCarthy

293. Pearson, Gail. RESERVED SEATS—WOMEN AND THE VOTE IN BOMBAY. *Indian Econ. and Soc. Hist. Rev. [India] 1983 20(1): 47-66.* In 1931, after the Gandhi-Irwin pact was signed, the Indian National Congress reentered negotiations on a constitution for India. One of the issues to be decided was the representation of women. The most important question to be decided was whether women would have special seats reserved for them in parliament. In Bombay, the nationalist women opposed reserved seats. Since there was to be a property qualification for voting, they also opposed wives voting on the property of their husbands. They favored a literacy test instead. The constitution of 1935 provided for reserved seats for women, but these were abolished at independence. Based mostly on government records and contemporary periodicals; 91 notes. J. V. Groves

294. Quintos, Floy C. THE "SWEET STRANGER" BECOMES A FILIPI-NA. *Asian & Pacific Q. of Cultural and Social Affairs [South Korea] 1981 13(2): 86-89.* Celebrates the posthumous recognition given in 1977 to Josephine Leopoldine Bracken by the Bayaning Filipino Foundation and puts to rest several myths concerning Josephine and her common-law husband, Jose Rizal. Reprinted from "Panorama," Sunday Magazine of the Bulletin *Today.* R. H. Detrick

295. Rahim, M. A. MAHAM ANAGA, THE NURSE-PRIME MINISTER OF AKBAR. *J. of the Asiatic Soc. of Bangladesh [Bangladesh] 1974 19(2): 37-51.* Maham Anaga, whose antecedents are not fully known, was not a wet-nurse of Akbar who ruled from 1556 to 1605, but superintendent of his nurses. (Anaga in Turkish means a wet nurse, but not always). She acquired much influence over Akbar and virtually became the prime minister during 1560-61. The misdemeanors of her son, Adham Khan, annoyed Akbar and indirectly caused the decline of her influence. 44 notes. Q. Ahmad

296. Rausa-Gomez, Lourdes and Tubangui, Helen R. REFLECTIONS ON THE FILIPINO WOMAN'S PAST. *Philippine Studies [Philippines] 1978 26(1-2): 125-141.* Examines foreign written observations on the occupations, role in the family and business, beauty, and morals of Filipino women. Most quotes are by 19th-century Spaniards and 20th-century Americans. The Filipina was unusual in Asia. She was visibly subordinate in the household, but wielded much subtle social and economic power. D. Chaput

297.   Ray, Rajat K. MAN, WOMAN AND THE NOVEL: THE RISE OF A NEW CONSCIOUSNESS IN BENGAL, 1858-1947. *Indian Econ. and Social Hist. Rev. [India] 1979 16(1): 1-31.* The novel was a literary form introduced into India by the British, but during the Bengal Renaissance a number of talented Indian novelists, using Indian content, developed an indigenous fiction. A major theme of this fiction was man-woman relationships despite the difficulty of the context of Hindu marriage customs. Examines Bengali fiction in the light of indigenous criteria, and selects several novels and evaluates them in their treatment of male-female relationships. 20 notes.
J. V. Groves 1940D 1900H

298.   Reddy, M. Atchi. FEMALE AGRICULTURAL LABOURERS OF NELLORE, 1881-1981. *Indian Econ. and Soc. Hist. Rev. [India] 1983 20(1): 67-80.* In the Nellore district of Andhra Pradesh, there were more free female farm servants than there were male, at least prior to 1951. Farm work included many different operations, a number of which required only light labor, within the strength of women. Moreover, there were virtually no barriers to entry. Most of the article is devoted to *maletas,* i.e., female farm servants paid a fixed annual or seasonal payment in addition to their daily wages. *Maletas* were used to gather the casual laborers in the morning and to distribute food at mealtimes. Normally, they were employed only by farmers who farmed at least 20 acres. Men tended to be paid more than women, but they also did the heavier work. 4 tables, 29 notes, government reports, private contemporary sources and secondary works.
J. V. Groves

299.   Rele, J. R. and Kanitkar, Tara. RESIDENCE BACKGROUND AND FERTILITY IN GREATER BOMBAY. *Population Studies [Great Britain] 1974 28(2): 299-308.* The residence background of wives who migrate to metropolitan areas plays an important role in determining their fertility. From the data collected during 1966, relating to 7,872 currently married women of Greater Bombay, an attempt was made to establish differentials in marital fertility by residence background of the wives. This was categorized into three groups—non-migrants, urban migrants and rural migrants. The variable that has emerged as the most influential in creating fertility differentials is education of the wife, which is shown to be negatively associated with the level of fertility.
J

300.   Richman, Paula and Fisher, Michael. SOURCES AND STRATEGIES FOR THE STUDY OF WOMEN IN INDIA. *J. of Ethnic Studies 1980 8(3): 123-141.* Analyzes writings about women in India based on indigenous, precolonial texts and explores the changes in women's condition brought by the conquest and domination of the subcontinent by Moslems and Europeans. The exogenous rulers such as missionaries, civil servants, and travelers added new types of source material. Examines models for women created by Indian society as it sought to reform and reassert itself during the late 19th and early 20th centuries—the "nationalistic and republican" period—and summarizes the basic approaches to Indian women's study over the years, calling for new sets of questions to be asked of the materials, questions probing the actual nature of the women's world.
G. J. Bobango

301. Rindfuss, Ronald R. and Morgan, S. Phillip. MARRIAGE, SEX, AND THE FIRST BIRTH INTERVAL: THE QUIET REVOLUTION IN ASIA. *Population and Development Rev. 1983 9(2): 259-278.* In Asia since the 1950's, shorter intervals between marriage and childbirth may be explained by pre-marital conception and coital frequency due to romantic rather than family-arranged marriage.

302. Rudolph, Susanne Hoeber and Rudolph, Lloyd I. AUTHORITY AND THE TRANSMISSION OF VALUES IN THE RAJPUT JOINT FAMILY. Albin, Mel, ed. *New Directions in Psychohistory: The Adelphi Papers in Honor of Erik H. Erikson* (Lexington, Mass.: Heath, 1980): 143-160. Examines the joint family of the Indian noble Amar Singh through his extensive diaries written between 1872 and 1942. The common beliefs that the nuclear family was a necessary condition or even a cause of modernization and adaptation and that the traditional joint family was oriented toward conservation are challenged. The analysis prompts an assessment of the way effect and authority are organized and distributed, bearing consequences for superego and ego formation, and the forms and fate of noncompliance, evasion, and rebellion in the joint family. Secondary sources; 7 notes.   J. Powell

303. Sahgal, Nayantara. THE MAKING OF MRS. GANDHI. *South Asian Rev. [Great Britain] 1975 8(3): 189-210.* Traces the connections between the upbringing of Indira Gandhi and her style of leadership as prime minister of India. The only child of Jawaharlal Nehru, Mrs. Gandhi grew up in a household of adults who were in the vanguard of India's fight for independence. When she became prime minister, she assumed, like most Indians, that she would provide a continuity with Nehru's policies, Initially reserved, Mrs. Gandhi enjoyed tremendous popularity following the 1969 Congress Party crisis, the 1972 Pakistan war, and her party's overwhelming triumph in the state elections. She proved to be politically tough, shrewd in political manipulations, and forceful in repeated public confrontations. In dealing with serious economic problems and charges of election fraud, she did not hesitate to make frequent use of extraparliamentary devices. India's democracy, long nurtured by Prime Minister Nehru, was seriously curtailed by his daughter. From a paper delivered at the University of London in March, 1974. Secondary sources; 15 notes.   S. H. Frank

304. Sahgal, Nayantara. NEHRU'S QUIET DAUGHTER. *Wilson Q. 1982 6(5): 160-170.* Discusses Indira Gandhi's personality and political career since 1966.

305. Santha, K. S. THE EXPLOITATION OF THE BEGUMS OF AWADH BY THE EAST INDIA COMPANY, A CASE HISTORY OF MALIKA-I-JAHAN, SECONDARY WIFE OF MUHAMMAD ALI SHAH. *Q. Rev. of Hist. Studies [India] 1980-81 20(2-3): 19-25.* The difficulties encountered by Malika-i-Jahan, a secondary wife of Muhammad Ali Shah, demonstrate the abuse and manipulation experienced by the begums during the rule of the East India Company. The correspondence between the East India Company, the begums, and the nawabs provides evidence of this exploitation. Based on primary sources; 18 notes.   W. T. Walker

306. Serruys, Henry. TWO REMARKABLE WOMEN IN MONGOLIA: THE THIRD LADY ERKETÜ QATUN AND DAYICING-BEYIJI. *Asia Major [Great Britain] 1975 19(Part 2): 191-245.* Discusses the lives of two well-known women in Mongolian history: the "Third Lady" Erketü Qatum, who used her influence in favor of peaceful relations with China, 1570-1612; and Dayicing-Beyiji (d. 1625), a powerful woman known for her devout Buddhism.

307. Smith, Peter C. ASIAN MARRIAGE PATTERNS IN TRANSI-TION. *J. of Family Hist. 1980 5(1): 58-96.* In a wide ranging historical and cross-national analysis the author studies the impact of industrialization on Asian marriage. Notable alterations, including a rising age at marriage, have occurred, although it is still unclear whether this shift marks an enduring change to an individual-based model of marriage. 11 tables, 5 fig., 55 notes, biblio.   T. W. Smith

308. Staudt, Kathy. POLITICS AND PHILIPPINE WOMEN: AN EX-PLORATORY STUDY. *Philippine J. of Public Administration [Philippines] 1973 17(4): 466-484.* Western generalizations concerning the political attitudes and participation of women in general are not necessarily applicable to Filipino women in particular. In this exploratory study of responses by Filipino students in the University of Wisconsin, the following generalizations have been found to be inapplicable: that women are more conservative and personalistically oriented than men; that they idealize the political system more; that they have less political interest and aspirations; and that there is a negative attitude about women entering politics. These findings can be explained by the fact that, traditionally, the Filipino woman has held important positions in the community. Whatever decline in her social position was wrought by Western colonization has been restored by the war, by education, and by trends towards sexual equality. It is true that she has yet to achieve absolute equality with the Filipino male, but, where her participatory and leadership roles in the community are concerned, she seems to be far ahead of her Western counterparts.   J

309. Stein, Dorothy K. WOMEN TO BURN: SUTTEE AS A NORMA-TIVE INSTITUTION. *Signs 1978 4(2): 253-268.* Neither 19th-century India nor Great Britain provided an honorable social role for widows. The Hindu widow or *sati* was reminded of the evil nature which was unleashed after her husband's control ended, so she submitted herself to the funeral pyre. English attempts to suppress suttee or widow suicide brought attention to the plight of Hindu women, resulting in the Remarriage Bill and the Age of Consent Bill. In England, unmarried women of good breeding were also considered a social problem. While the problem was actively discussed, it remained unremedied. 38 notes.   S. P. Conner

310. Stoler, Ann. CLASS STRUCTURE AND FEMALE AUTONOMY IN RURAL JAVA. *Signs: J. of Women in Culture and Soc. 1977 3(1): 74-89.* Women in Java have retained a large degree of social and economic autonomy due to their importance in agriculture. Dutch colonialism did not push women out of rice production or lead to sharper division of labor. But demographic

pressures and technological change have increasingly stratified the village economy, with different effects for women in different classes. Defines female autonomy and social power with reference to access to strategic resources within the domestic and social sphere. Sexual inequality must be examined within the context of class inequality, even in peasant society, because both gender and class determine access to strategic resources. Table, graph, 45 notes.   L. M. Maloney

311.   Strange, Heather. EDUCATION AND EMPLOYMENT PATTERNS OF RURAL MALAY WOMEN 1965-1975. *J. of Asian and African Studies [Netherlands] 1978 13(1-2): 50-64.* A report on fieldwork in the Malay coastal villages of Trengganu that showed social change through growth of educational and employment opportunities for women. 9 notes, biblio.   R. T. Brown

312.   Subbaraj, B. K. THE STORY OF A DIAMOND. *Indian Rev. [India] 1975 71(7): 31-34.* Outlines the history of the Besant Theosophical College in Madanapalle, India, 1915-75, where its founder Dr. Annie Besant applied theosophy to education.

313.   Ta, Van Tai. THE STATUS OF WOMEN IN TRADITIONAL VIET-NAM: A COMPARISON OF THE CODE OF THE LE DYNASTY (1428-1788) WITH THE CHINESE CODES. *J. of Asian Hist. 1981 15(2): 97-145.* A comparison of the Lê Dynasty code with Chinese dynastic codes indicates that although the Lê code included many items from Chinese codes there still was an attempt by the Vietnamese to break away from some aspects of Confucian influence. The Lê code gave Vietnamese women a status superior to their Chinese counterparts. They were somewhat better protected by criminal law and had numerous personal and property rights that their husbands had to respect. Over the centuries, despite civil code changes, the Vietnamese have remained loyal to portions of the Lê code. Elements of the code are included in the 1959 law on marriage and family, which was retained by the unified Socialist Republic of Vietnam. Biblio. of Chinese, English, French, and Vietnamese sources; glossary of Chinese terms; 137 notes.
R. H. Detrick

314.   Tambiah, H. W. THE FAMILY: THE "GEDERA" OF THE SIN-GHALESE, AND THE "KUDUMBAM" OF THE TAMILS AND MUS-LIMS. *J. of the Sri Lanka Branch of the Royal Asiatic Soc. [Sri Lanka] 1975 19: 1-16.* Compares the family structure of the Singhalese, Tamils, and Moslems of Ceylon and notes the decline of the family structure under foreign rule, 16th-19th centuries.

315.   Thakur, Ramesh. THE RETURN OF THE HELMSWOMAN. *Queen's Q. [Canada] 1980 87(4): 693-708.* Discusses the 1980 victory of Indira Gandhi. The rival Indian politicians lost because the coalition had failed to perform effectively, the result both of the virulent factionalism within its ranks and of its obsessive desire to humiliate Gandhi. Her widespread popularity and ability to enforce discipline within her party led to her victory. While Gandhi assured the Indian public that she would not invoke emergency powers, both

the judiciary and the press edged back toward the substance of emergency. 9 notes.   L. V. Eid

316.   Thakurdas, Frank. A POLITICAL DISSENTER'S DIARY. *Gandhi Marg [India] 1979 1(5): 282-286.* A review article of Krishnabai Nimbkar's *A Political Dissenter's Diary 1970-1978,* 2 vols., (Poona, India: Int. Book Service, 1978, 1979), in which the author, an activist and anti-Communist physician, airs her criticism of Indira Gandhi and her political convictions and beliefs.

317.   Thompson, Frank. A FEMINIST FOCUS IN INDIAN PAINTING. *Atlantis [Canada] 1982 8(1): 67-77.* Much modern painting in India has been representational and reflects social concerns and awareness of artists. Feminist focus outlined in this article relates directly to women in their social situations or in the uniqueness of their persons. Artists discussed included painters Amrita Sher-Gil, Nikhil Biswas, Bijan Chowdhury, Isha Muhammed, Bikash Bhattacharjee, Nalini Malani, Veena Bhargava, and sculptor Meera Mukharjee. 8 photos, 33 notes.   S. E. Bellingham

318.   Trautmann, Thomas R. MARRIAGE AND RANK IN BENGALI CULTURE. *J. of Asian Studies 1980 39(3): 519-524.* Reviews Ronald Inden's *Marriage and Rank in Bengali Culture,* a cultural explanation, based on the philosophical · monism of the Bengali, of the caste system and the place marriage plays in it. Objects that the theoretical perspective hides the oppositions in the system. Culture is not autonomous, and so needs sociological and historical analysis for fuller understanding.   P. M. Gustafson

319.   Truong Thi Kim Lien; Vo Thi To Nga; Cao The Que Houng; and Truong Hong Lien. DONNE NELLE PRIGIONI DI THIEU [Women in Thieu's prisons]. *Ponte [Italy] 1973 29(1): 49-60.* Details cases of torture in South Vietnamese prisons, 1969-70.

320.   Turley, William S. WOMEN IN THE COMMUNIST REVOLUTION IN VIETNAM. *Asian Survey 1972 12(9): 793-805.* The prominent role of women in North Vietnam's government and in the Communist Party give credence to their claims about women's achievements in the system, 1930-72.

321.   Werner, Jayne. WOMEN, SOCIALISM, AND THE ECONOMY OF WARTIME NORTH VIETNAM, 1960-1975. *Studies in Comparative Communism 1981 14(2-3): 165-190.* Although the role of women changed during the war against the French, the greatest change occurred during the war against the United States from 1965 to 1973. Necessity rather than the Party's commitment to social equality led to this change. Women's participation in the economy and political bodies increased substantially. The Party had required in 1967 an increase in female participation in the labor force and Party work. Full equality has not yet been achieved. 55 notes.   D. Balmuth

322.   Yayori, Matsui; Sharnoff, Lora, transl. SEXUAL SLAVERY IN KO-REA. *Frontiers 1977 2(1): 22-30.* Discusses the *kisaeng,* Japanese guided tours to South Korea for the purpose of visiting prostitutes; from colonization in 1910 the business continued through the Japanese military occupation before

and during World War II, and has received continued Korean government support since 1945.

323. Yoon, Soon Young. WOMEN'S STUDIES IN KOREA. *Signs 1979 4(4): 751-762.* Since the opening of the Ewha Women's University in Seoul in 1977, more progress toward an international identity of women's studies has developed. Research indicates that Korean programs must deal with the traditional-modern identity crisis and international studies must realize that there are multiple routes to liberation. To Korean researchers, evolutionist theories are more acceptable because the problem of women's studies did not develop from a men versus women dichotomy but from a conflict between feudalism and capitalism or socialism. 22 notes.   S. P. Conner

5

WOMEN IN THE PACIFIC REGION

324.   Gailey, Christine Ward. PUTTING DOWN SISTERS AND WIVES: TONGAN WOMEN AND COLONIZATION. Etienne, Mona and Leacock, Eleanor, ed. *Women and Colonization: Anthropological Perspectives* (New York: Praeger, J. F. Bergin Publ., 1980): 294-322. The formation of a state structure in Tonga in response to 19th-century colonization efforts resulted in the loss of social authority and personal autonomy for Tongan women. Both rank and gender determined status in this kinship-organized society which placed sisters above brothers in the sibling group. The author analyzed early travelers' accounts, missionary and colonial officers' journals, written records of Tongan oral histories, myths, and legends, colonial office records, and 20th-century ethnographic reports to present an overview of the impact of Western colonization on Tongan society and the consequences for the role of women. Photo, 7 notes, ref.   S

325.   Hooper, Paul F. FEMINISM IN THE PACIFIC: THE PAN-PACIFIC AND SOUTHEAST ASIA WOMEN'S ASSOCIATION. *Pacific Hist. 1976 20(4): 367-378.* The Pan-Pacific Women's Association was instrumental in establishing women's activities in the Pacific Basin. Its first meeting in 1928 established the transcultural nature of the organization. Not a militant group, PPSEAWA has worked quietly and deliberately to correct political, social, and economic problems affecting the area. Primary and secondary sources; 3 illus., 31 notes.   G. L. Olson

326.   Johnson, Walter and Tupouniua, Sione. AGAINST FRENCH NUCLEAR TESTING: THE A.T.O.M. COMMITTEE. *J. of Pacific Hist. 1976 11(4): 213-216.* The ATOM Committee (Against Testing of Mururoa) of Fiji was formed to protest French nuclear pollution of the Pacific. The Fiji Young Women's Christian Association, the Fiji Council of Churches, and the University of the South Pacific Students' Association sponsored the public meeting on 28 May 1970 at the Suva Town Hall. In June 1971 the governments of Fiji, Tonga, Western Samoa, the Cook Islands, and Nauru sent a joint protest to France. The French cancelled the balance of the 1971 tests but in March 1972 the French announced resumption of the tests. A series of meetings and conferences culminated in a conference in April 1975 sponsored by 34 international and 16 Fiji groups. These meetings were unusual because aboriginal peoples, and not governments, academics, nor the church dominated them. 8 notes.   E. P. Stickney

327. Langmore, D. A NEGLECTED FORCE: WHITE WOMEN MIS-SIONARIES IN PAPUA 1874-1914. *J. of Pacific Hist. [Australia] 1982 17(3): 138-157.* One third of the missionaries serving in Papua from 1874 to 1914 were women of the Roman Catholic Sacred Heart Mission, the Methodist Mission, and the London Missionary Society. In addition, there were numerous wives associated with the latter two organizations. Apart from their teaching, nursing, and social work, these four groups of women helped to raise the status of native women. These forms of work brought the women into closer contact with natives than their male counterparts occupied with more pastoral duties, such as preaching and bible study. Primary sources; 75 notes.   H. S. Shields

328. Reay, Marie. RITUAL MADNESS OBSERVED: A DISCARDED PATTERN OF FATE IN PAPUA NEW GUINEA. *J. of Pacific Hist. [Australia] 1977 12(1-2): 55-79.* Temporary dissociation, or *Komugl Tai,* occurs in many individuals among the groups of the Western Highlands of Papua New Guinea. The Kuma believe that *Komugl Tai* results from ingesting certain varieties of mushrooms. The phenomenon, an annual occurrence, begins near the Chimbu border and travels in a western direction from group to group. Affected males experience dissociation for about two hours, while females are often affected for 24 to 48 hours. Dissociation among females is known as *Ndadl,* and may be interpreted as a rite drawing attention to the differences between the sexes, as it caricatures the male/female dichotomy of dominance and dependence. Based on personal field work and published secondary sources; 33 notes.   D. R. McDonald

6

WOMEN IN LATIN AMERICA AND THE WEST INDIES

330. Aho, William R. SEX CONFLICT IN TRINIDAD CALYPSOES 1969-1979. *Revista/Review Interamericana [Puerto Rico] 1981 11(1): 76-81.* Calypsoes in Trinidad are generally negative toward women and their role in female-male relations. Such an attitude is unfair to women in Trinidad and Tobago. Based on the lyrics of 311 calypso songs from Trinidad and Tobago; table, 2 notes, biblio.   J. A. Lewis

331. Alarcón, Haydée. A CHILEAN WOMAN SPEAKS. *Monthly Rev. 1977 29(1): 58-62.* A Chilean dentist who participated in public health reform during the Popular Unity period, 1970-73, recalls the political imprisonment and torture of women following the coup d'etat of 1973.

332. Alegría, Fernando. APORTE DE LA MUJER AL NUEVO LEN-GUAJE POETICO DE LATINOAMERICA [Women's contribution to the new language of Latin American poetry]. *Revista/Review Interamericana [Puerto Rico] 1982 12(1): 27-35.* The founders of the Modernist movement in Latin American literature did not include any female writers, yet women writers did exist, and they had no sense of being a group apart. 9 notes.
                                                          J. A. Lewis

333. Alemán, José Luis. LA PROSTITUCIÓN: SUS DETERMINANTES ECONÓMICOS [Prostitution: its economic determinants]. *Estudios Sociales [Dominican Republic] 1974 7(4): 201-210.* Discusses and defines the problem of prostitution in Santo Domingo in the 1960's and 1970's, stressing the economic factors causing prostitution in the Dominican Republic and in Latin America as a whole.

334. Alexandraki, C. SERVICES RENDERED BY ICM TO MIGRANT AND REFUGEE WOMEN. *Int. Migration [Netherlands] 1981 19(1-2): 225-240.* Discusses the primary services of the Intergovernmental Committee for Migration to female national migrants and refugees emigrating under its sponsorship, 1956-80, with special attention to refugee women, women relocated under family reunion schemes, unsponsored single Greek women who were moved under the government-assisted programs of Australia, Canada, and New Zealand, with the agreement of the Greek government and ICM, and

professional women emigrating to Latin American countries under the Selective Migration Program. Primary sources; 4 tables, 2 notes.   J. Powell

335.   Andreas, Carol. THE CHILEAN WOMEN: REFORM, REACTION, AND RESISTANCE. *Latin Am. Perspectives 1977 4(4): 121-125.* Though not specifically feminist in nature, Popular Unity reforms enacted in Chile in 1970-73 benefited women by providing socialized medical care and day care centers, broadening employment prospects, and encouraging local political participation.

336.   Archetti, Eduardo and Stølen, Kristi Anne. KVINNEARBEID, ARV OG KAPITALISERING [Women's work, inheritance and capitalization]. *Tidsskrift for Samfunnsforskning [Norway] 1980 21(2): 139-159.* Family farms in Argentina have undergone a capitalization process during recent decades from traditional labor intensive units based on family labor into capital intensive units based primarily on mechanical equipment. This paper analyzes changes in farm women's situation caused by this mechanization process over three generations, including changes in female participation in production and in community activities, changes in the patterns of inheritance, and marginalization of women in the more capitalist context.   J/S

337.   Arenal, Electa. TWO POETS OF THE SANDINISTA STRUGGLE. *Feminist Studies 1981 7(1): 19-27.* Poetic volumes *Sobrevivo* [I Survive] by Claribel Alegría and *Linea de fuego* [Firing Line] by Gioconda Belli, which recaptured elements of the people's war against Somozas' dictatorship, received the 1978 poetry prize of the prestigious Casa de las Americas in Havana. Alegría and Belli filled the role of "spokespoet" for a period of revolution and reconstruction, a role few women poets have fulfilled. Alegría's volume is characterized by a distilled and abstracted simplicity which interweaves complex historical and personal themes. Belli's volume expresses the fragility and fleetingness of life, woman's erotic sensuality amidst strife, and the ongoing resistance of a united people. 7 notes.   P. D. Hinnebusch

338.   Arizpe, Lourdes. MUJERES MIGRANTES Y ECONOMÍA CAMPESINA; ANÁLISIS DE UNA COHORTE MIGRATORIA A LA CIUDAD DE MÉXICO, 1940-1970 [Migrant women and farm economy: the analysis of a migrant group in Mexico City, 1940-70]. *Am. Indígena [Mexico] 1978 38(2): 303-326.* Analyzes a small sample of women migrants to Mexico City to determine whether their transfer was due to peasant family strategy or to purely personal decision. Latin American women have migrated more than men, which appears to confirm the migration law formulated by Ernst Georg Ravenstein in 1885. While true for the majority of cases studied in Latin America, it has not applied in other regions of the world such as African countries south of the Sahara and Islamic countries, or to overseas European migrations in the last century and a half. Thus, it is impossible to establish general nonhistoric laws for a phenomenon derived from capitalism without knowing how capitalism works in individual economies.   J/S

339.   Arizpe, Lourdes. WOMEN IN THE INFORMAL LABOR SECTOR: THE CASE OF MEXICO CITY. *Signs: J. of Women in Culture and Soc.*

1977 3(1): 25-37. Discusses the relation of women to the informal labor sector, those intermittent, part-time, unpaid, or noncontractual jobs outside the formal occupational structure. Women workers remain locked in this sector, and domestic service provides the government with an excuse for not attempting to improve female employment. Women with the same schooling as men experience higher unemployment rates; but while middle- and upper-class women may choose not to work, poor women are forced to; their job options must be examined within a class context. Immigrant women's options are most restricted; they are found almost exclusively in the informal labor sector. 3 tables, 27 notes.   L. M. Maloney

340. Arrom, Silvia Marina. MARRIAGE PATTERNS IN MEXICO CITY, 1811. *J. of Family Hist. 1978 3(4): 376-391.* A high proportion (about 25%) of adults were unmarried in Mexico City in 1811. The mean age for men was 24.2 and for women 22.7. These statistics matched the classic Western European marriage pattern. This pattern, however, was not uniform through all classes of society. The Spanish matched the pattern more closely than the castes or Indians. Based on the manuscript census of Mexico City in 1811; 4 tables, 18 notes, biblio.   T. W. Smith

341. Arrom, Silvia Marina. TEACHING THE HISTORY OF HISPANIC-AMERICAN WOMEN. *Hist. Teacher 1980 13(4): 493-507.* Discusses approaches to the teaching of Latin American women's history. Analyzes Latin America's stratified class structure, the role of the Catholic Church, its legal system, and sex-role differentiation. In Latin America machismo and marianismo have been the key to women's power rather than oppression. Based on a syllabus used for such a course taught in the spring of 1979 at Yale University; annotated biblio.   S. H. Frank

342. Aviel, JoAnn Fagot. POLITICAL PARTICIPATION OF WOMEN IN LATIN AMERICA. *Western Pol. Q. 1981 34(1): 156-173.* Examines education and economic status as factors contributing to the amount and type of political participation by women in Latin America, 1960-79. Women's role in the family, although typically perceived as an obstacle to participation, also serve as a rationalization for leadership as well as a catalyst for mobilization against the regime. Mainly secondary sources; 2 tables, 82 notes.   J. Powell

343. Azicri, Max. WOMEN'S DEVELOPMENT THROUGH REVOLUTIONARY MOBILIZATION: A STUDY OF THE FEDERATION OF CUBAN WOMEN. *Int. J. of Women's Studies [Canada] 1979 2(1): 27-50.* Discusses the achievements of the Federation of Cuban Women (FMC) which works within the political framework established under the revolution in the areas of education, labor, and politics to achieve social equality for women in Cuba.

344. Baily, Samuel L. MARRIAGE PATTERNS AND IMMIGRANT ASSIMILATION IN BUENOS AIRES, 1882-1923. *Hispanic Am. Hist. Rev. 1980 60(1): 32-48.* Prior to World War I about 50% of the inhabitants of Buenos Aires, Argentina, were foreign-born, largely Italians and Spaniards. Homogamous marriages were preferred when spouses of the same national

origin were available. The large number of marriages among Argentines after 1908 actually reflects intragroup marriages among second generation Italians or Spaniards. For Buenos Aires, cultural pluralism is a more appropriate concept than the melting pot. The author evaluates Franco Savorgnan's "Matrimonial Selection and the Amalgamation of Heterogeneous Groups" in International Union for the Scientific Study of Population, *Cultural Assimilation of Immigrants* (London, 1950), pp 59-67. Based on the *Anuario estadístico de la ciudad de Buenos Aires, 1882-1923;* 8 tables, 21 notes.

B. D. Johnson

345. Bambirra, Varia. WOMEN'S LIBERATION AND THE CLASS STRUGGLE. *R. of Radical Pol. Econ. 1972 4(3): 75-84.* Reviews women's liberation in Chile. The Left has not really taken a stand, while bourgeois comment is generally irrelevant. Liberation must come through the industrialization of the domestic economy, and the leftist parties are the crucial tools. From *Punto Final.*

C. P. de Young

346. Barnett, Sheila. NOTES ON CONTEMPORARY DANCE-THEATRE IN JAMAICA 1930-1982. *Jamaica J. [Jamaica] 1982 (46): 80-93.* Chronicles major events and recognizes such contributors to Jamaica's dance theater as Ivy Baxter and Eddy Thomas.

347. Barradas, José Pérez de. RITOS MUISCAS DE LA FECUNDIDAD Y DE LA MUERTE [Rites of fertility and death among the Muiscas]. *Razon y Fabula [Colombia] 1973 (32): 81-94.* Contrasts the evidence suggested by archaeological research with that yielded by Spanish chroniclers regarding the customs and mores of the Muiscas in the 16th century, an Indian tribe who lived in the Andean Plains of Cundinamarca and Boyacá in Colombia.

348. Barrios de Chungara, Domitila and Viezzer, Moema. LET ME SPEAK! *Monthly Rev. 1979 30(9): 42-54.* Presents excerpts from *Let Me Speak!* by Domitila Barrios de Chungara, wife of a Bolivian tin miner and leader of the Housewive's Committee of the Siglo XX Mines, a participant in the struggles of the mining community with mine administrators and their CIA and United States Embassy "advisors."

349. Berleant-Schiller, Riva. MATING IS MARRIAGE IN THE CARIBBEAN. *Montclair J. of Social Sci. and Humanities 1972 1(1): 66-79.* Discusses marriage customs and family organization in the Caribbean.

350. Blanco, Iris. LA MUJER EN LOS ALBORES DE LA CONQUISTA DE MEXICO [Women at the time of the conquest of Mexico]. *Aztlán 1980 11(2): 249-270.* Examines the position of women in native society at the time of the Spanish conquest. Although sources of information are limited, and carry the biases of the writers, it is possible to survey women's status, education, division of labor, and social expectations. Aztec women were reclusive, expected to be virgins at marriage, and to embrace the responsibilities of motherhood. Weaving was a main occupation but women were also involved in many other fields of endeavor. The Spanish conquest resulted in

important changes in how the role of women in the new society would be defined. 35 notes.

A. Hoffman

351. Blay, Eva Alterman. THE POLITICAL PARTICIPATION OF WOMEN IN BRAZIL: FEMALE MAYORS. *Signs 1979 5(1): 42-59.* Between 1972 and 1976, 60 women mayors were elected in Brazil. Although statistics are difficult to gather, the phenomenon warrants explanation because politics in Brazil have always been a male domain. Since 1964, however, municipalities have exercised less power, particularly in areas where women are now assuming leadership roles. These women are typically less educated, of a lower socioeconomic status, younger, and with less political experience than their male counterparts. Based on statistical evidence, interviews, and secondary sources; 6 tables, 21 notes.

S. P. Conner

352. Bogantes Hidalgo, Olivet. FAMILIA Y ESTRUCTURA SOCIAL EN AMERICA LATINA [Family and social structure in Latin America]. *R. de la U. de Costa Rica [Costa Rica] 1971 (30): 87-93.* Analyzes the social structure of Latin America, concluding that it impedes the normal functioning of family unity, especially in the lower social strata, which are the most numerous and miserable of the population. Biblio.

J. P. P. (IHE 84821)

353. Bolinaga de Dúo, María Begoña. SIMÓN BOLÍVAR Y LAS MUJERES [Simón Bolívar and women]. *Bol. Hist. [Venezuela] 1977 (43): 44-61.* Simón Bolívar was not the conqueror of women as mere objects of pleasure. He first saw women as mothers and he had special thoughts for his mother Concepción Bolívar, Inés Mancebo de Miyares who fed him when a baby, and his black nurse Hipólito. He also had a close relationship not only with his wife, María Teresa, but after her death with his consecutive lovers Fanny de Villars, Josefina Machado, Manuelita Sáenz, Bernardina Ibáñz, Joaquina Garaicoa, Benedicta Nadal, and Jeannette Hart. He found in each one a real and loyal friend as can be proved through the legislation he passed dignifying the role of women. 20 notes.

L. Makin

354. Bolles, A. Lynn. IMF DESTABILIZATION: THE IMPACT ON WORKING CLASS JAMAICAN WOMEN. *TransAfrica Forum 1983 2(1): 63-76.* Studies some of the effects which the International Monetary Fund program had from May 1978 to March 1979 on the productive and reproductive activities of a group of urban female industrial workers and their households in Kingston.

355. Breslow, Nancy. FRIDA KAHLO: A CRY OF JOY AND PAIN. *Américas (Organization of Am. States) 1980 32(3): 33-39.* Examines the life and paintings of Mexican artist Frida Kahlo (1910-54), wife of Diego Rivera.

356. Briceño, Jacqueline C. de. EL CULTO DE MARÍA LIONZA [The Cult of María Lionza]. *América Indígena [Mexico] 1970 30(2): 359-374.* Analyzes the María Lionza cult, which recently was extended and intensified in Venezuela and which includes a wide social base. Probably arising in Yaracuy state, the cult spread to other states and cities, including Caracas. It

has arisen out of social and cultural oppression, and its evolution is not unlike that of other cults of North and South America. J/S

357. Briceño Perozo, Mario. BARBARITA [Barbarita]. *Bol. de la Acad. Nac. de la Hist. [Venezuela] 1981 64(255): 577-579.* Among the defenders of Trujillo, Venezuela in the war of independence was Barbara de la Torre, young daughter of Vicente de la Torre, military leader of the republican forces. She commanded a platoon and was condemned to die after the initial defeat of the rebel forces in 1815. Her father, however, voluntarily substituted for her before the firing squad. Her fortunes after the achievement of independence are recounted. Ref. J. V. Coutinho

358. Brundenius, Claes. SOME NOTES ON THE DEVELOPMENT OF THE CUBAN LABOR FORCE 1970-1980. *Cuban Studies 1983 13(2): 65-77.* Previous studies of the Cuban labor force have underestimated the growth in the number of workers by overlooking the large number of women now entering the labor market. Previous studies have also underestimated the real level of unemployment. Based on the 1979 census; 8 tables, 10 notes. J. A. Lewis

359. Brzezinski, Steven. CHURCH VERSUS STATE: FAMILY PLANNING IN COLOMBIA, 1966-1972. *J. of Church and State 1976 18(3): 491-502.* Examines the conflict between civil and Catholic religious authorities in Colombia over birth and population control methods. This has been the major issue between the Catholic Church and the state, causing a steady decline in the Church's power, although the Church did interfere with the government's program between 1966 and 1972. There is a chart showing the development of *Profamilia* clinics, 1965-71. 24 notes. E. E. Eminhizer

360. Buenaventura-Posso, Flora and Brown, Susan E. FORCED TRANSITION FROM EGALITARIANISM TO MALE DOMINANCE: THE BARI OF COLOMBIA. Etienne, Mona and Leacock, Eleanor, ed. *Women and Colonization: Anthropological Perspectives* (New York: Praeger, J. F. Bergin Publ., 1980): 109-133. The Bari, also known as the Motilones, are one of the least acculturated indigenous groups in Colombia. Numbering between 1,500 to 1,800 today, the Bari until recently maintained their traditional social organization in spite of 400 years of exposure to colonial elements. The recent cultural transformation has its basis in the Motilon Development Plan which was devised by a North American missionary in 1961. The egalitarian structure of Bari society has gradually changed through the creation of male chief roles, usurpation of women's traditional healing role, exploitation of female labor, breakdown of the communal residential unit, and neglect of women's participation in ceremonies and rituals. Photo, 8 notes, ref.

361. Buendía N., Jorge. EL SACRIFICIO DE LAS CUATRO HEROINAS DE PASTO [The sacrifice by the four heroines of Pasto]. *Repertorio Hist. de la Academia Antioqueña de Hist. [Colombia] 1971 27(218): 238-241.* Recounts the sentencing of four heroic women (Luisa Góngora, Andrea Velasco, Domitila Sarasti, and Dominga Burbano) for freeing imprisoned independence leaders. Discusses their personalities, pointing out that their heroism has not

been given due credit. Based on unpublished documents from the General Archive in Bogota.   J. G. R. (IHE 87964)

362. Burkett, Elinor C. IN DUBIOUS SISTERHOOD: RACE AND CLASS IN SPANISH COLONIAL SOUTH AMERICA. *Latin Am. Perspectives 1977 4(1-2): 18-26.* Analyzes the author's experiences in researching the "female experience" in early Latin American history. All women share certain commonalities but the data tends to support an alternative perspective. Despite similarities, more significant differences among women are found when women are considered as members of particular social classes and these differences are important for understanding women's experience.   J. L. Dietz

363. Burkett, Elinor C. INDIAN WOMEN AND WHITE SOCIETY: THE CASE OF SIXTEENTH-CENTURY PERU. Lavrin, Asunción, ed. *Latin American Women* (London: Greenwood Pr., 1978): 101-128. In precolonial Peru, a woman's position was determined by Inca society's fixed political aristocracy. There was a sharp division of labor according to sex, and although women's work in the household was essential to community survival, women were subordinated to men. The Spanish Conquest affected Indian men and women differently. While men became subservient, those women who came into direct contact with Spanish colonial society gained new opportunities. In Arequipa they dominated the marketplace, ran shops, and provided the bulk of household labor. They disposed of property, made contracts, and fought for legal rights. Because social conventions restricted intermarriage, many remained single, forming close associations with other indigenous women but keeping separate from Indian men. Revision of a previous article (see abstract 24A:3481). Based on notarial records, court cases, royal licenses, inquisition papers, and secondary sources; 66 notes.   S. Tomlinson-Brown

364. Burkett, Elinor C. LA MUJER DURANTE LA CONQUISTA Y LA PRIMERA EPOCA COLONIAL [Women during the conquest and the initial colonial period]. *Estudios Andinos 1976 5(1): 1-35.* Considers the impact of 16th-century Spanish colonization on native women in the Andes region of South America. The Spanish sought to consolidate their conquest by intermarriage. Native women thus served as cultural links between Spanish and Indian society. New laws protected the welfare of native women and granted them greater economic rights than in Incan times. Women migrated to urban areas where many sold goods. In contrast to native women, Indian men enjoyed little access to Spanish society and continued in subservient roles. Sexual factors mitigated racial prejudice during the colonial period, and resulted in social fluidity for women. 50 notes.   J. L. White

365. Bush, Barbara. DEFIANCE OR SUBMISSION? THE ROLE OF THE SLAVE WOMAN IN SLAVE RESISTANCE IN THE BRITISH CARIBBEAN. *Immigrants & Minorities [Great Britain] 1982 1(1): 16-38.* Historians have traditionally ascribed a minor role to slave women in Caribbean slave resistance. Examination of 17th- and 18th-century Caribbean slave women's noncooperation, and role in slave uprisings demonstrates their active role in the struggle against servitude. Resistance among the slaves was unified through forms of West African religious ritual, and women, especially old women, were

often powerful priests in these religious societies. Because of their central position in slave families, women transmitted through oral tradition the attitude of resistance to their children. Primary sources; 106 notes.

J. Powell

366. Caicedo, Bernardo J. EL SUPUESTO RAPTO DE MANUELITA SAENZ [The alleged ravishing of Manuelita Sáenz]. *Bol. del Arch. General de la Nacion [Venezuela] 1981 71(240-241): 130-135.* Manuelita Sáenz, Bolívar's last lover, has long been the subject of historical novels. Certain writers have alleged that she was carried away from a Venezuelan convent and then abandoned by an officer in the service of Spain. The author points out the confusion in the historical information on her background and argues that her alleged ravisher never even existed. 2 notes. J. V. Coutinho/S

367. Camp, Roderic Ai. WOMEN AND POLITICAL LEADERSHIP IN MEXICO: A COMPARATIVE STUDY OF FEMALE AND MALE POLIT-ICAL ELITES. *J. of Pol. 1979 41(2): 417-441.* As a result of the 1910 revolution, women in the Yucatán received the right to vote in local elections in 1922, and Chiapas granted women political equality in 1925. While women's groups had been organized in the 1920's, and expanded in subsequent decades, women were not granted the right to vote in municipal elections throughout Mexico until 1946 and in off-year elections for national deputies in 1955. Women have consistently scored lower than men in political knowledge and interest, but discrepancies have decreased as education increased. Politically, women have been most successful as candidates for the Chamber of Deputies and Senate, but have received few administrative posts and play a very small role among the political elite. Female political leaders are no younger than men, come from middle and upper-class families and are frequently natives of urban areas which provide greater educational opportunities. 6 tables, 43 notes. A. W. Novitsky

368. Campo del Pozo, Fernando. ALONSO DE OJEDA Y SU ESPOSA ISABEL, ALGUNOS DATOS BIOGRAFICOS DE AMBOS E HISTORIA DE SUS RESTOS [Some biographical data on Alonso de Ojeda and his wife Isabel de Ojeda]. *Bol. de la Acad. Nac. de la Hist. [Venezuela] 1982 65(257): 131-157.* Alonso de Ojeda (1472-?1515), companion of Columbus, Vespucci, and other navigators, was the discoverer of the lake of Maracaibo and the very embodiment of the spirit of his time. His wife was an Indian woman of the neighborhood of Barra in Venezuela. Based on primary material in the archdiocesan archive of Caracas; map, 68 notes, document regarding the remains of Ojeda and his wife. J. V. Coutinho

369. Cancian, Francesca; Goodman, Louis Wolf; and Smith, Peter H., ed. INTRODUCTION. *J. of Family Hist. 1978 3(4): 314-317.* Introduces a special issue on the family in Latin America, sponsored by the Joint Committee on Latin American Studies of the American Council of Learned Societies and the Social Science Research Council. T. W. Smith

370. Candelaria, Cordelia. LA MALINCHE, FEMINIST PROTOTYPE. *Frontiers 1980 5(2): 1-6.* Examines the cultural significance of pre-Columbian

traitor Malintzin, known as Doña Marina by the padres of Hernando Cortés and as La Malinche by the Aztecs, and her role in the Spanish Conquest of Mexico.

371. Capellin, Paola. ESTRUCTURA PRODUCTIVA CAPITALISTA Y TRABAJO FEMENINO: LAS CONDICIONES DE EXISTENCIAS DE LA FUERZA DE TRABAJO FEMENINO EN BRASIL [Capitalist production structure and women's labor: the conditions of the existence of the female labor force in Brazil]. *Demografía y Economía [Mexico] 1978 12(1): 37-45.* Discusses-the twofold contribution of working-class women to Brazil's capitalist economy in the 1970's: salaried labor and domestic work.

372. Carlos, Manuel L. and Sellers, Lois. FAMILY, KINSHIP, STRUC-TURE, AND MODERNIZATION IN LATIN AMERICA. *Latin Am. Res. Rev. 1972 7(2): 95-124.* Examines the socioeconomic and cultural environments of the nuclear and extended families in urban and rural areas of Latin America, 1968-74.

373. Casal, Lourdes. REVOLUTION AND *CONCIENCIA:* WOMEN IN CUBA. Berkin, Carol R. and Lovett, Clara M., ed. *Women, War & Revolution* (New York: Holmes & Meier, 1980): 183-206. The status of women in prerevolutionary Cuba was characterized parodoxically by advances in legal equality and by discrimination in the labor force in terms of concentration in low-paying and low-status jobs, limited varieties of jobs, and labor divisions in the family. Discusses the changes affecting women since the revolution in labor, education, community service, legislation, politics, and ideology. Also briefly mentions the Federation of Cuban Women (FMC), formed in 1960, and its role in mobilizing women into the political mainstream.

374. Chandler, David L. FAMILY BONDS AND THE BONDSMAN: THE SLAVE FAMILY IN COLONIAL COLOMBIA. *Latin Am. Res. Rev. 1981 16(2): 107-131.* Slave life in Colombia, an area of slow economic development, was comparatively mild. Male-female ratios became more equal over the years. Slave families were viable units. Slaves were able to accumulate property and purchase their freedom. Both state and Church accorded protection to the slave, and bondsmen used the office of Protector of the Poor and the court system to defend their rights. Based on inventories from mines and haciendas, notarial and other legal documents from national archives of Colombia and Ecuador; 8 tables, 3 fig., 51 notes.   J. K. Pfabe

375. Cherpak, Evelyn. THE PARTICIPATION OF WOMEN IN THE INDEPENDENCE MOVEMENT IN GRAN COLOMBIA, 1780-1830. Lavrin, Asunción, ed. *Latin American Women* (London: Greenwood Pr., 1978): 219-234. Women of all classes contributed significantly to the independence movement in Gran Colombia, 1780-1830. Some participated personally in espionage or in combat, disguised as men. Others supported the cause through traditional women's roles as nurses and hostesses or through economic contribution of supplies or money. Many suffered great personal and financial losses. However, this participation was not matched with a movement to expand women's privileges or to challenge traditional roles. When the crisis

had passed, women were expected to return to their proper sphere. Based on archival sources, judicial petitions, primary, and secondary sources; 60 notes.

S. Tomlinson-Brown

376. Chinchilla, Norma Stoltz. INDUSTRIALIZATION, MONOPOLY CAPITALISM, AND WOMEN'S WORK IN GUATEMALA. *Signs: J. of Women in Culture and Soc. 1977 3(1): 38-56.* Documents changes in female occupational patterns in Guatemala from the advent of monopoly capitalism based on foreign, particularly United States, investment, in three stages: 1920-44, 1944-54 and 1954-73. Poor, uneducated women are increasingly confined to the informal labor market, particularly in the cities, where they are overwhelmingly employed as domestics. Meanwhile middle- and upper-class women are entering white-collar jobs, but women professionals are almost exclusively elementary school teachers and nurses. 8 tables, 17 notes.

L. M. Maloney

377. Chinchilla, Norma Stoltz. MOBILIZING WOMEN: REVOLUTION IN THE REVOLUTION. *Latin Am. Perspectives 1977 4(4): 83-102.* General overview of the possibilities for women's movements within socialist revolutions in Latin America.

378. Ciski, Robert. JOSEPH OBREBSKI, THE WEST INDIAN SOCIAL SURVEY, AND THE ETHNOLOGY OF THE WEST INDIAN FAMILY. *Phylon 1980 41(4): 345-355.* Joseph Obrebski (1905-67), Polish-born anthropologist, did research on rural Jamaica, 1947-48, collecting data on the social and economic structure of rural black Jamaican society, particularly concerning the variety of coexisting family types and the prevalence of certain socially disruptive features. His work has not received sufficient attention. Based on primary materials in the archives of the University of Massachusetts, Amherst; 13 notes.

J. V. Coutinho

379. Clendinnen, Inga. YUCATEC MAYA WOMEN AND THE SPANISH CONQUEST: ROLE AND RITUAL IN HISTORICAL RECONSTRUCTION. *J. of Social Hist. 1982 15(3): 427-442.* Search for common men and women has been pursued with varying success in different eras and areas; the discovery of "the common woman" in Latin America has been particularly difficult. It seems that the depopulation of much of Yucatan before and soon after the Spanish conquest and colonization had a definite impact on the status of women. Prior to discovery in 1517 subjugation seems to have characterized the status of women; in the years following effective colonization after 1540, subjugation was compounded by frequent separation from men and domination by the male-oriented Catholic Church. 55 notes.

C. M. Hough

380. Cobas, José A. MODERNISMO Y USO DE ANTICONCEPTIVOS EN GUATEMALA: ANÁLISIS DE DOS MODELOS CAUSALES [Modernism and the use of contraceptives in Guatemala: two causal models]. *Estudios Centro Americanos [El Salvador] 1975 30(315): 23-39.* Defines and contrasts two causal models of modernism and contraceptive use in Guatemala today, using graphs and charts to illustrate the theoretical base of the analysis.

381.   Cole, Johnnetta B. WOMEN IN CUBA: THE REVOLUTION WITH-IN THE REVOLUTION. Lindsay, Beverly, ed. *Comparative Perspectives of Third World Women: The Impact of Race, Sex, and Class* (New York: Praeger, 1980): 162-178. Compares conditions for women in prerevolutionary Cuba with conditions after the 1959 revolution until 1979, focusing on the literacy campaign, the transformation of health care, the availability of work, housing, and women's participation in sports. While the revolution has changed the position of women, there are still prejudices and sexist attitudes that need changing.

382.   Costa, Iraci del Nero da. A ESTRUCTURA FAMILIAL E DOMICI-ÁRIA EM VILA RICA NO ALVORECER DO SÉCULO XIX [Family and household structure in early 19th-century Vila Rica]. *Rev. do Inst. de Estudos Brasileiros [Brazil] 1977 19: 17-34.* Analyzes census statistics published by Herculano Gomes Mathias in *Recenseamento na Capitania de Minas Gerais (Vila Rica—1804)* (1969), and establishes the size and composition of families and households.

383.   Couturier, Edith. WOMEN IN A NOBLE FAMILY: THE MEXI-CAN COUNTS OF REGLA, 1750-1830. Lavrin, Asunción, ed. *Latin American Women* (London: Greenwood Pr., 1978): 129-149. An examination of the women of an elite Mexican family over four generations reveals the variety of roles possible in the culture. The Countess of Miravelle, María Micaela Romero de Terreros, María Josefa Rodriguez, and the third Countess of Regla were noteworthy for their economic and social independence. As widows or single women, they were influential as executors of wills, guardians of minors, inheritors of property, or enterprising business women. Even these women were bound by strict social prohibitions and were largely restricted to their extended family. Although the other four women lived traditional lives as wives, mothers, and consumers, their marriages had political and economic signifi-cance. In spite of their circumscribed lives, they were pivotal as marriageable pawns, childbearers, advisors, and heiresses. Based on letters, business records, legal suits, and secondary souces; table, fig., 61 notes.

S. Tomlinson-Brown 1800H

384.   Craton, Michael. CHANGING PATTERNS OF SLAVE FAMILIES IN THE BRITISH WEST INDIES. *J. of Interdisciplinary Hist. 1979 10(1): 1-35.* Discredits the theory that the nuclear family could not exist in slavery, summarizes present evidence, and discusses developmental models. The trienni-al census returns of British West Indian slaves are invaluable in comparing slave family patterns. Samples are analyzed from three prominent slave-holding families. Four influences worked against the development of family systems: the breakup of the old slave quarters, the persistence of impersonal plantations, accelerated urbanization, and the spread of respectability. At abolition the more fortunate ex-slaves formed their own villages and developed a healthy peasant society. Evaluates slavery by how much it allowed family lives to proceed unhindered. Based on British government documents, Bahamas gov-ernment documents, Bahamas archives, census returns, and letters; illus., map, 9 tables, 5 graphs, 39 notes.   E. R. Campbell

385. Craton, Michael. JAMAICAN SLAVE MORTALITY: FRESH
LIGHT FROM WORTHY PARK, LONGVILLE AND THE THARP
ESTATES. *J. of Caribbean Hist. [Barbados] 1971 3: 1-27.* Revision is called
for in accepted notions of life expectancy among Jamaican plantation slaves. In
shipment, 20 percent died, 30 percent of the survivors died in the next three
years, but the remainder probably lived to be 30 or 40. Equalization of the sex
ratio and elimination of the Africa-born explain natural population increase of
slaves. Based on Parliamentary Papers, Tharp Papers, *Worthy Park Plantation
Books;* 11 tables, 38 notes.   M. Rippy

386. Crummett, Maria de los Angeles. EL PODER FEMENINO: THE
MOBILIZATION OF WOMEN AGAINST SOCIALISM IN CHILE. *Latin
Am. Perspectives 1977 4(4): 103-113.* Composed of upper-class women, El
Poder Femenino sought to overthrow the government of Salvador Allende
which threatened to deprive them of their elite status.

387. Cubitt, Tessa. LATIN AMERICAN WOMEN. *J. of Latin Am. Studies
[Great Britain] 1980 12(1): 169-184.* This review of seven books on Latin
American women published between 1977 and 1979 considers the works as
empirical contributions, examples of the "life history" technique, and as
contributions to a theoretical framework for women's studies. Latin American
women must be considered in terms of the class society of peripheral
capitalism. The books together reveal that the opportunities women have in
Latin America are limited as a result of the economic structure present.
Secondary sources; 21 notes.   M. A. Burkholder

388. Cubitt, Tessa. THE PARTICIPATION OF WOMEN IN THE LATIN
AMERICAN LABOUR FORCE. *J. of Area Studies [Great Britain] 1983 (7):
13-18.* Data taken in 1960 and 1975 indicate that the proportion of women in
the Latin American labor force has decreased except in skilled areas.

389. Cutright, Phillips; Hout, Michael; and Johnson, David R. STRUCTUR-
AL DETERMINANTS OF FERTILITY IN LATIN AMERICA: 1800-1970.
Am. Sociol. Rev. 1976 41(3): 511-527. Reviews theoretical arguments that
structural modernization reduces fertility rates, discussing related empirical
work. Tests the view that Latin American fertility has not responded to
increasing modernization because the Catholic Church is a powerful pronatalist
institution. Characteristics of Spanish rule before 1830 and 19th century
immigration patterns determined the level of modernization and Catholic
institutional strength in 1900. Modernization reduced crude birth rates in 1910
and later years and also depressed illegitimate and marital fertility. A strong
negative effect of Catholic strength on illegitimacy was counterbalanced by its
strong positive impact on marital fertility.   J

390. Cypess, Sandra Messinger. VISUAL AND VERBAL DISTANCES:
THE WOMAN POET IN THE PATRIARCHAL CULTURE. *Revista/
Review Interamericana [Puerto Rico] 1982 12(1): 150-157.* The changing role
of the female in Latin American society can be traced in the feminist poetry of
the region. 10 notes.   J. A. Lewis

391. DaCosta, Iraci del Nero. VILA RICA: CASAMENTOS (1727-1826) [Vila Rica: marriages, 1727-1826]. *Rev. de Hist.* *[Brazil]* *1977* *55(111): 195-208.* Surveys marriage trends in Vila Rica, Minas Gerais. Examines correlations between the number of marriages and statistics relating to the importation of gold, the comparative social class of the parties, color, previous marriages, legitimacy of birth, seasonal variations, and place of birth. Based on statistics from the register of the Paróquia de Nossa Senhoraada Conceição de António Dias. 17 tables, 2 notes.   R. O. Khan

392. daSilva, Maria Beatriz Nizza. EDUCAÇÃO FEMININA E EDUCA-ÇÃO MASCULINA NO BRASIL COLONIAL [Female and male education in colonial Brazil]. *Rev. de Hist.* *[Brazil]* *1977* *55(109): 149-154.* Examines the statutes of the Recolhimento de Nossa Senhora da Glória do lugar da Boavista de Pernambuco, and of the Seminário Episcopal de Nossa Senhora da Graça da Cidade de Olinda de Pernambuco. Establishes the conditions of entry, organization and curriculum, particularly comparing educational practice for girls and for boys. The influence of Fénelon's *Traité sur l'éducation des filles* and the more extensive and higher level curriculum offered to boys are stressed, and especially the pronounced differences between male and female education in Brazil compared to Portugal, where aristocratic girls had more education. 10 notes.   R. O. Khan

393. Deere, Carmen Diana. CHANGING SOCIAL RELATIONS OF PRO-DUCTION AND PERUVIAN PEASANT WOMEN'S WORK. *Latin Am. Perspectives 1977 4(1-2): 38-47.* Analyzes the changes in the degree of exploitation of peasant women under various modes of production. The author's central hypothesis is that the development of the productive forces in the transition from servile to capitalist relations of production is progressive in terms of nature, duration, and intensity of women's work. Examines women's work obligations on haciendas, in capitalist enterprises, and on independent peasant holdings in light of the development of capitalism in agriculture. Based on primary sources and interviews.   J. L. Dietz

394. Deere, Carmen Diana. THE DIFFERENTIATION OF THE PEAS-ANTRY AND FAMILY STRUCTURE: A PERUVIAN CASE STUDY. *J. of Family Hist. 1978 3(4): 422-438.* This study relates changes in the family structure of Peruvian peasants to macroeconomic changes in the production system as the old hacienda system gave way to agrarian capitalism. It appears that there was more patriarchal control in peasant households internal to the hacienda system rather than in those external to it. Proletarianization of the peasants favored nuclearization of the peasant households. Table, 5 notes, biblio.   T. W. Smith

395. Deiner, John T. EVA PERON AND THE ROOTS OF POLITICAL INSTABILITY IN ARGENTINA. *Civilisations [Belgium] 1973/74 23/24(3/4): 195-212.* Eva Peron from 1945 to 1952 helpd transform Argentine politics by her activities with the workers, women, and the poor. She made them feel they were a part of the Argentine political system and they made demands on the system and received benefits from it. Eva Peron was a charismatic political

figure who managed to generate strong empathy for others. 27 notes.

H. L. Calkin

396. Deschamps Chapeaux, Pedro. EL NEGRO EN LA ECONOMÍA HA-BANERA DEL SIGLO XIX: LAS COMADRONAS O PARTERAS [The Negro in the Havana economy of the 19th century: the midwives]. *Rev. de la Biblioteca Nac. "José Martí" [Cuba] 1970 12(3): 49-62.* Discusses the profession of midwifery in Havana, 1820-45, which was practiced largely by free mulatto women, giving statistics taken from periodicals of that era and detailing the lives of several of the midwives.

397. De-Sola Ricardo, Irma. MARIA TERESA RODRIGUEZ DEL TORO Y ALAYZA DE BOLIVAR [María Teresa Rodríguez del Toro y Alayza de Bolívar]. *Rev. de la Soc. Bolivariana de Venezuela [Venezuela] 1981 38(132): 86-92.* Reviews the short relationship between Simón Bolívar and María Teresa who had only been married eight months when she died of yellow fever.

398. DeTejeira, Otilia Arosemena. THE WOMAN IN LATIN AMERICA: PAST, PRESENT, FUTURE. *Américas (Organization of Am. States) 1974 26(4): S1-S16.* A special supplement on the role of women in Latin American history.

399. Dey, Susnigdha. VICTORIA OCAMPO: HISTORY OF AN ARGENTINE PASSION. *Indian Horizons [India] 1980 28(4): 39-43.* Victoria Ocampo (1890-1979) a member of the Argentine Academy of Letters, is remembered for her interest in Indian culture. Her journal *Sur* provided the literary world with commentaries on the lives and works of such prominent Indian figures as Mahatma Gandhi and Rabindranath Tagore. In recognition for her contributions, Vishwa Bharati University bestowed its highest honor of "Desikottama" on her in 1967.

D. J. Wren

400. Diggs, Irene. COLONIAL SEXUAL BEHAVIOR. *Negro Hist. Bull. 1974 37(2): 214-216.* Examines marriage patterns among the Spanish, African slaves, and Indians in Latin America during the 16th and 17th centuries.

401. Dirks, Robert and Kerns, Virginia. MATING PATTERNS AND ADAPTIVE CHANGE IN RUM BAY, 1823-1970. *Social and Econ. Studies [Jamaica] 1976 25(1): 34-54.* Relates mating patterns and economic activity in a British Virgin Islands community. During periods of prosperity the marriage rates increase, while extralegal unions are more common in less prosperous times. This is an adaptation to changing economic situations within the context of the cultural norms. 6 tables, fig., 7 notes, biblio.

E. S. Johnson

402. Dougnac Rodríguez, Antonio. ESTATUTO DEL HIJO ILEGÍTIMO EN EL DERECHO INDIANO [Statute of the illegitimate child in Indian law]. *Rev. de Estudios Historico-Juridicos [Chile] 1978 (3): 113-132.* Examines the variety of marriage contracts and laws governing the legitimacy of children in the face of the large number of illegitimate children in Chile in the 17th and 18th centuries.

403.   Early, John D. POPULATION INCREASE AND FAMILY PLAN-NING IN GUATEMALA. *Human Organization 1975 34(3): 275-288.*

404.   Ebanks, G. Edward; George, P. M.; and Nobbe, Charles E. PATTERNS-OF SEX-UNION FORMATION IN BARBADOS. *Can. R. of Sociol. and Anthrop. 1974 11(3): 23-246.* This study, based on a sample of 4199 lower socioeconomic status women interviewed on the island of Barbados in 1971, examines patterns of sex-union formation. Three types of sex unions are identified—visiting, commonlaw, and married. The overwhelming majority of all partnerships is initiated and terminated as a visiting union. A large number of partnerships progresses from one union type to only one other, with the most frequent being visiting to commonlaw and visiting to married. In general, when there is a change-of-union status within a partnership it is in the direction of a more stable type of union. The findings of this study support those of a 1956 study in Jamaica.   J

405.   Edmonds, Juliet. CHILD CARE AND FAMILY SERVICES IN BARBADOS. *Social and Econ. Studies [Jamaica] 1973 22(2): 229-248.* De-scribes various family services, from family planning clinics to education of the mentally retarded, in Barbados. Notes the successes and problems of each program. 13 notes.   E. S. Johnson

406.   Escobar, Gabriel. ANÁLISIS PRELIMINAR DEL PARENTESCO Y LA FAMILIA DE CLASE MEDIA DE LA CIUDAD DEL CUZCO [Preliminary analysis of family relationships and the middle-class family of the city of Cuzco]. *Rev. del Museo Nac. [Peru] 1974 40: 331-340.* A descriptive analysis of the middle class in Cuzco since roughly 1945. The middle classes' ability to maintain a stable traditional structure in comparison with other classes rests upon the extended family. Adults in the 20 to 30 recognizable extended middle-class families in Cuzco regularly maintain close ties with parents, grandparents, siblings, and in-laws. The extended family commonly resides in close proximity. It uses positions held to aid other members of its group. God parentage is used primarily to reinforce family ties. Today's middle-class families are smaller and less well-to-do financially then were their predecessors in 1945. Based on Richard P. Schaedel's *La demografía y los recursos humanos del sur del Perú* (1967) and two family genealogies; biblio, appendix.   M. A. Burkholder

407.   Estrada, Marcos. CATALINA GODOY, SOLDADO DE LA TROPA DE LINEA EN LA LUCHA POR LA ORGANIZACION NACIONAL [Catalina Godoy, a soldier with front-line troops fighting for the national government]. *Bol. de la Acad. Nac. de la Hist. [Argentina] 1965 38(2): 161-180.* Describes the character and military activities of Catalina Godoy of San Juan province, Argentina, wife of Natalio Godoy of the First Cavalry Regiment. Testimonials written by José Silvana Daza, second lieutenant in the cavalry, and by other army officers, are partly reproduced here: the regiment was engaged in putting down the rebellion of Ricardo López Jordán in the province of Entre Ríos, and Catalina's conduct in the engagements and later Indian uprisings was exceptionally valorous. 12 notes, biblio.   R. O. Khan

408. Fernandez Larrain, Sergio. CARTAS DE FE Y PATRIOTISMO DE CONDELL A SU ESPOSA [Letters of faith and patriotism from Condell to his wife]. *Rev. Chilena de Hist. y Geografía [Chile] 1979 (147): 125-183.* Letters of Carlos Condell, one of the heroes of the Battle of Iquique, and a leader in Chile's naval campaign during the War of the Pacific. Provides insights into the war as well as information on his personal life and his postwar naval career.   W. F. Sater

409. Fleming, Carrol B. LADIES OF THE SKULL AND CROSSBONES. *Américas (Organization of Am. States) 1978 30(9): 23-26.* Provides an account of the lives of women pirates Mary Read and Anne Bonny who plagued the West Indies before being captured and sentenced to the gallows. Both were reprieved because of pregnancy. Based on Captain Charles Johnson's *The General History of the Robberies and Murders of the Most Notorious Pirates* (1724).

410. Flinn, William L. FAMILY LIFE OF LATIN AMERICAN URBAN MIGRANTS: THREE CASE STUDIES IN BOGOTA. *J. of Inter-Am. Studies and World Affairs 1974 16(3): 326-349.* Bogotá, Colombia has grown from a city of 500,000 in 1950 to one of 3.6 million in 1974. Half of the city's population is composed of migrants who live in small communities that spring up around the core city. Within these communities there is a stable family life, and most migrants are better off than people living in rural areas. This partially explains the continuing flow of people into the cities. Based on Colombian government reports, newspaper accounts, and secondary sources; 14 tables, biblio.   J. Thomas

411. Flora, Cornelia B. WOMEN IN LATIN AMERICA: A FORCE FOR TRADITION OR CHANGE? *Secolas Ann. 1976 7: 68-78.* Tradition has provided Latin American females with power in the home. They will not willingly give up this power for a change unless alternative forms of feminine power seem possible. Secondary sources; 42 notes.   J. A. Lewis

412. Forero, Manuel José. ELOGIO DE DOÑA MARIA CLEMENCIA CAYCEDO, FUNDADORA DEL COLEGIO DE LA ENSEÑANZA [Eulogy of Doña María Clemencia Caycedo, founder of the College of Teaching]. *Bolet,n de Hist. y Antigüedades [Colombia] 1973 60(700): 127-134.* Evocation of María Clemencia Caycedo, who in 1765 proposed founding a convent at Bogotá with the special mission of teaching girls; the first stone was laid five years later, and the convent school attracted a socially distinguished clientele.
                                                              D. Bushnell

413. Foster, David William. BIBLIOGRAPHY OF WRITINGS BY AND ABOUT VICTORIA OCAMPO (1890-1979). *Inter-American Rev. of Biblio. 1980 30(1): 51-58.* Victoria Ocampo (1890-1979) was a focal point of Argentine culture. As founder and editor of the journal *Sur* and director of the press Sur, her influence was far-reaching. This checklist is of her monographs and collections of essays, review articles of her works, and criticism of her works found in monographs, collections of essays, and academic journals. Writings about *Sur* are also listed.   B. D. Johnson

414.   Fuller, Gary. ON THE SPATIAL DIFFUSION OF FERTILITY DECLINE: THE DISTANCE-TO-CLINIC VARIABLE IN A CHILEAN COMMUNITY. *Econ. Geography 1974 50(4): 324-332.*

415.   Gabaldón, José Rafael. MUJERES DE AMERICA [Women of America]. *Bol. de la Acad. Nac. de la Hist. [Venezuela] 1983 66(261): 113-124.* Sketches of three Spanish American women: Maria de la Concepción Palacios y Sojo de Bolívar y Ponte, Simón Bolívar's mother; Maria Teresa Toro y Alaiza, Bolívar's wife of a few months, who died soon after she arrived in Venezuela; and Luisa Cáceres de Arismendi, wife of an independence hero, who was imprisoned by the Spaniards and gave birth to a son in jail. Speech delivered in Buenos Aires in 1940 at the Consejo de Mujeres de la Republica Argentina.   J. V. Coutinho

416.   Gallagher, Ann Miriam. THE INDIAN NUNS OF MEXICO CITY'S *MONASTERIO* OF CORPUS CHRISTI, 1724-1821. Lavrin, Asunción, ed. *Latin American Women* (London: Greenwood Pr., 1978): 150-172. Although the Catholic Church was interested in preparing Indian women as Christian wives and mothers, it did not consider them worthy to embrace a monastic life. Not until 1724, when nuns and chaplains spoke in their behalf, was the Corpus Christi convent founded. The women admitted were members of the Indian nobility, though not necessarily wealthy, free from involvement with idolatry, and racially pure. Most had been educated at home in Christian doctrine, Latin, and the domestic arts. Despite early attempts to keep the Indian women in subservient positions, they gradually assumed control of the nunnery. The *monasterio* was significant in that it demonstrated that Indians could pursue a religious life. Based on private manuscript collections, documents concerning information about applicants, and other primary, secondary sources; 2 tables, 83 notes.   S. Tomlinson-Brown

417.   Gallo, María Gowland de. AMANDA LABARCA, CHILEAN EDU-CATOR. *Américas (Organization of American States) 1975 27(8): 12-16.* Chronicles the activities of Amanda Labarca, a woman educator in Chile, 1917-75; Labarca was concerned with upgrading education for all Chileans, but primarily with the improvement of the status of women.

418.   García de D'Agostino, Olga. VISION FRANCESA DE LA ARGEN-TINA (1850-1880) [French views of Argentina, 1850-80]. *Bol. del Inst. de Hist. Argentina y Americana [Argentina] 1982 17(27): 93-133.* During this period several French entrepreneurs, doctors, engineers, and tourists visited Argentina and left accounts of their journeys. The author describes their views on the daily life of the inhabitants, housing, clothing, food, position of women, occupations, and entertainment, as well as their opinions on the character of the people. 134 notes.   J. V. Coutinho

419.   Garrett-Schesch, Pat. THE MOBILIZATION OF WOMEN DURING THE POPULAR UNITY GOVERNMENT. *Latin Am. Perspectives 1975 2(1): 100-104.* Refutes claims made by David Belnap in a 1974 Los Angeles *Times* article which held that women in Chile were overwhelmingly pro-Allende.

420. Garriga, María M. López. ESTRATEGIAS DE AUTOAFIRMACIÓN EN MUJERES PUERTORRIQUEÑAS [Strategies of self-affirmation in Puerto Rican women]. *Rev. de Ciencias Sociales [Puerto Rico] 1978 20(3-4): 257-286.* Analyzes a sample of 80 Puerto Rican women from both middle and working-class backgrounds in an attempt to understand their use of manipulative strategies to circumvent patriarchal authority in the family. Although it was suggested that women from different social classes reacted differently, the results of the study did not bear out this hypothesis. J/S

421. Gautier, Arlette. LES ESCLAVES FEMMES AUX ANTILLES FRANCAISES 1635-1848 [Female slaves in the French Antilles, 1635-1848]. *Hist. Reflections [Canada] 1983 10(3): 409-433.* Female slaves in Martinique, Guadeloupe, and Haiti often fulfilled sex-specific roles: seamstresses, maids, and laundresses. Whereas men did heavy labor, women's tasks in the field were less strenuous. Masters adopted varying strategies regarding female slaves as procreators. Some chose to support family contexts and reproduction; most, however, sought quick profit and cared less about successful natality. Relations with white masters sometimes provided advantages for female slaves. Based on archival, primary, and secondary sources; 86 notes. M. Schumacher

422. Gilfeather, Katherine Anne. WOMEN RELIGIOUS, THE POOR, AND THE INSTITUTIONAL CHURCH IN CHILE. *J. of Interamerican Studies and World Affairs 1979 21(1): 129-155.* The Catholic Church in Chile has stressed service in the marginal urban and rural areas in an effort to reach the poor. With a diminishing number of clergy, many native and foreign religious women have left their intended work to serve the marginal areas during the 1960's and 1970's. These women reflect in microcosm the Church's struggles to faithfully continue its spiritual work. These women have confronted frustrations and tensions which at times were generated by the Church. Ref. T. D. Schoonover

423. Grisanti, Angel. IMPOSTERGABLE UNA BIOGRAFIA DE LA MADRE DEL LIBERTADOR [A biography of the mother of Bolívar not to be disregarded]. *Rev. de la Soc. Bolivariana de Venezuela [Venezuela] 1981 38(129): 78-80.* Comments on a book written by Simón Bolívar's mother in which she tells of the ways she administered the affairs of the family after the death of her husband.

424. Guérin-Gonzáles, Camille. WOMEN IN LATIN AMERICA: FOUR VIEWS. *New Scholar 1982 8(1-2): 593-597.* Elsa M. Chaney's dissertation "Women in Latin American Politics: The Case of Peru and Chile" (U. of Wisconsin 1971), Gilberto Freyre's, *The Mansions and the Shanties: The Making of Modern Brazil* (1963), Ann M. Pescatello's *Power and Pawn: The Female in Iberian Families, Societies, and Cultures* (1976), and Carolina Maria de Jesus, *Child of the Dark: The Diary of Carolina Maria de Jesus* (1962) explore feminist issues: man's world; woman's sphere; the mother as unrecognized cultural leader; women in race and culture. D. K. Pickens

425. Guy, Donna J. WOMEN, PEONAGE, AND INDUSTRIALIZATION: ARGENTINA, 1810-1914. *Latin Am. Res. Rev. 1981 16(3): 65-89.*

Changes in women's work in Argentina reveal the impact of modernization on females. At the time of independence, women's cottage industries were a foundation of interior province economies; they remained so until the 1870's. Peonage laws attempted to regulate female morality and keep them in productive employment. Modernization of the coastal and especially interior provinces reduced employment possibilities for women. The main demand for female labor was in growing cities, particularly in unskilled, nonmechanical tasks. Immigrant women initially had greater opportunities. Protective legislation discouraged expansion of industries that relied on female labor. As a result, women were directed into household work. Based on provincial laws, archival records, and national censuses; 2 tables, 58 notes.   J. K. Pfabe

426. Guzmán, Ricardo Franco. EL REGIMEN JURIDICO DE LA PROS-TITUCION EN MEXICO [The legal regulation of prostitution in Mexico]. *Rev. de la Facultad de Derecho de México [Mexico] 1972 22(85-86): 85-134.* Reviews Mexican laws on prostitution, considering arguments for its abolition and the question of jurisdiction.

427. Hahner, June E. FEMINISM, WOMEN'S RIGHTS, AND THE SUF-FRAGE MOVEMENT IN BRAZIL. *Latin Am. Res. Rev. 1980 15(1): 65-111.* Brazilian feminism originated in the mid-19th century with a small group of pioneer feminists who expressed dissatisfaction with female roles. Some women participated in the abolition movement, but not in policymaking roles. Journals and newspapers disseminated feminist ideas, urging an improved position in the family and access to better education and careers. After the late 1880's, suffrage became the focal point, and the women's movement, led by professional women and relatives of the elite, became more conservative and thus more acceptable. Suffrage was achieved in 1932. Based on feminist journals and newspapers and Brazilian government documents; 134 notes.
J. K. Pfabe 1900H

428. Hahner, June E. THE NINETEENTH CENTURY FEMINIST PRESS AND WOMEN'S RIGHTS IN BRAZIL. Lavrin, Asunción, ed. *Latin American Women* (London: Greenwood Pr., 1978): 255-285. Dissatisfied with the traditional roles assigned to them, some Brazilian women founded newspapers and journals preaching women's rights in the second half of the 19th century. Early journals also provided social and fashion news and although the importance of education for self-realization and social improvement was stressed, writers expressed ambivalence about women's role. Family concerns were usually given precedence. By the end of the century, as greater numbers of women were educated and had taken jobs, magazines began to cover national world news. They expressed concern about women's legal status, family relations, the abolition of slavery, and the right to vote, thus laying the groundwork for women's economic, social, and legal status in the 20th century. 125 notes.   S. Tomlinson-Brown

429. Hahner, June E. RESEARCHING THE HISTORY OF LATIN AMERICAN WOMEN: PAST AND FUTURE DIRECTIONS. *Inter-American Rev. of Biblio. 1983 33(4): 545-552.* Surveys problems and tasks in Latin

America, following the model of women's studies in Europe and the United States. 15 notes.   J. V. Coutinho

430. Hall, Linda B. VISIONS OF THE FEMININE: THE DUAL GOD-DESSES OF ANCIENT MEXICO. *Southwest Rev. 1978 63(2): 133-141.* Explores the duality attached to feminine models in Mexico which dates from pre-Columbian times, yet have bearing on both historical and contemporary Mexican culture.

431. Hall, N. A. T. ANNA HEEGAARD—ENIGMA *Caribbean Q. [Ja-maica] 1976 22(2-3): 62-73.* A biographical sketch of Anna Heegaard, a free colored woman who was the consort of Peter von Scholten, the last governor of the Danish West Indies, from 1828 to 1848. Heegaard was a major influence on Scholten's policies and thus on the course of the history of the Danish Virgin Islands, a veritable "sleeping partner" in promoting emancipation and the amelioration of the living conditions of Negroes. Primary sources; 58 notes.
                                                              R. L. Woodward, Jr.

432. Hareven, Tamara K. POSTSCRIPT: THE LATIN AMERICAN ES-SAYS IN THE CONTEXT OF FAMILY HISTORY. *J. of Family Hist. 1978 3(4): 454-457.* The family not only responds to change but also initiates it. Modernization does not replace a uniform preindustrial family system with a postindustrial family system, but leads to certain changes and certain continua-tions, with many variations. Changes in family systems often differ by class, region, race, or other major social divisions. Biblio.   T. W. Smith

433. Harkness, Shirley and Flora, Cornelia B. WOMEN IN THE NEWS: AN ANALYSIS OF MEDIA IMAGES IN COLOMBIA. *Rev. Interamerica-na [Puerto Rico] 1974 4(2): 220-238.* Using the newspapers *El Tiempo* and *El País*, the authors found the Colombian press projecting four stereotypes of women: the saintly mother, the beauty queen, the altruist, and the politician. Each stereotype had its own peculiar attributes, though it was possible for one person to combine the characteristics of several categories. Primary and secondary sources; 2 tables, biblio.   J. A. Lewis

434. Harrison, Polly F. IMAGES AND EXILE: THE CUBAN WOMAN AND HER POETRY. *Rev. Interamericana [Puerto Rico] 1974 4(2): 184-219.* Analyzes the poetry of several Cuban women of the 19th and 20th centuries from an anthropological perspective, focusing on the constancy and change of imagery, symbolism, and values. The centrality of the exile condition in Cuba makes exile (the sea) an elaborating symbol and root metaphor. Primary and secondary sources; 59 notes.   J. A. Lewis/S

435. Hart, John. WORKING-CLASS WOMEN IN NINETEENTH CEN-TURY MEXICO. Mora, Magdalena and DelCastillo, Adelaida R., ed. *Mexi-can Women in the United States: Struggles Past and Present* (Los Angeles: U. of California Chicano Studies Res. Center, 1980): 151-157. Discusses the nature of incipient labor activities in 19th-century Mexico, socialist influences, and the participation of working-class women. The industrialization of Mexico during the latter half of the 19th century resulted in an influx of rural workers

to urban areas, many of whom were women employed in the manufacture of textiles. Although women were not allowed formal participation in leadership, they were among the first to join labor movements. It was not until 5 March 1876 that women were allowed to participate as delegates to the first Congreso General Obrero de la República. Three years later, Carmen Huerta was elected president of the Congreso. Secondary sources; 35 notes.   J. Powell

436. Henry, Frances and Wilson, Pamela. THE STATUS OF WOMEN IN CARIBBEAN SOCIETIES: AN OVERVIEW OF THEIR SOCIAL, ECONOMIC AND SEXUAL ROLES. *Social and Econ. Studies [Jamaica] 1975 24(2): 165-198.* Summarizes the role of women in the Caribbean over the past 30 years. Women's roles vary with the economy in which they live and the type of household in which they reside, but in all cases the role is subservient to that of men. 59 notes.   E. S. Johnson

437. Hernández Michel, Susana. ALGUNAS CARACTERISTICAS DE LA MUJER MEXICANA DE CLASE MEDIA [Some characteristics of middle-class Mexican women]. *Rev. Mexicana de Ciencia Pol. [Mexico] 1971 17(65): 99-105.* Although the place of Mexican middle-class women is largely in the home, there is still room, and even a demand, for their participation in the economic, social, and political life of the country.

438. Herrera, Luz Alicia. TESTIMONIES OF GUATEMALAN WOMEN. *Latin Am. Perspectives 1980 7(2-3): 160-168.* Interviews with two Guatemalan women, one an unmarried peasant woman struggling to keep her family together, the other an upper-class university graduate who has experienced social and personal consciousness raising.   J. F. Vivian

439. Herrera-Sobek, Maria. MOTHERS, LOVERS, AND SOLDIERS: IMAGES OF WOMAN IN THE MEXICAN *CORRIDO. Keystone Folklore 1979 23(1-2): 53-77.* Describes the images of women in Mexican *corridos*, story-telling folksongs that record violent crimes, battles, heroic deeds, and unrequited love, focusing on several examples to trace the evolution of the depiction of women in such roles as unfaithful wife, soldiers, mothers, personification of evil, lovers, sex objects, and the liberated women of the 1970's from the origins of the genre in the period of the Spanish Reconquest.

440. Herrmann, Eleanor Krohn. BELIZEAN NURSING EDUCATION IN THE 19TH CENTURY. *Belizean Studies [Belize] 1979 7(4): 16-24.* Relates the history of the training of professional nurses from Governor Sir Alfred Moloney's proposal through the arrival of nurse Marian Edith Beresford from England to instruct three student nurses at the Belize Hospital in Belize City until the experiment was officially declared successful by the Medical Department of British Honduras.

441. Herrmann, Eleanor Krohn. ORAL HISTORY: CLEOPATRA WHITE. *Belizean Studies [Belize] 1982 10(6): 1-4.* In this interview a certified midwife and award-winning social worker reveals the sensitivity to her people that made her a leader in Gales Point Village, Belize.

442.   Higman, B. W. AFRICAN AND CREOLE SLAVE FAMILY PAT-
TERNS IN TRINIDAD. Crahan, Margaret E. and Knight, Franklin W., ed.
Africa and the Caribbean: The Legacies of a Link (Baltimore: Johns Hopkins
U. Pr., 1979): 41-64. Analyzes a census of slaves in Trinidad undertaken in
1812-13, only 15 years after the English acquired it and introduced extensive
sugar culture, with its dependence on slavery. Compares family forms—
isolated individuals, nuclear or extended family, mother-centered units—
according to place of birth, urban or plantation residence, and size of
slaveholding. Most African slaves were isolated from any formal family system.
African ethnic groups lost their identity almost immediately through intermarriage. African and Creole (American-born) families contrasted strongly. A
matrifocal tendency developed as the Creole population grew, but for the
African-born the extended family remained the norm. From a paper delivered
to the Latin American Studies Association, 1977, and a version originally
published in *Family History* (Summer 1978); map, 6 tables, graph, 36 notes.

443.   Higman, B. W. HOUSEHOLD STRUCTURE AND FERTILITY ON
JAMAICAN SLAVE PLANTATIONS: A NINETEENTH-CENTURY EX-
AMPLE. *Population Studies [Great Britain] 1973 27(3): 527-550.* The structure of the slave households on two Jamaican sugar estates and a livestock pen,
with a total population of 864 slaves in 1825, is established. The modal
household type approximated the elementary family, and half the slaves lived
in such units. These households were dominated by Africans, whereas the
Creoles lived in more complex, extended units. Africans were also predominant
in the single-member households since they lacked the ramifications of kinship
of the Creoles. Slaves of colour lived in households dominated by mothers,
grandmothers and aunts, and lacking male slave mates. Polygynists are
identified among both Africans and Creoles. The 'grandmother family' is found
to be very rare. The nuclear family was more important than is commonly
thought, and it is suggested that the degree of instability of unions may also
have been smaller. Fertility is measured for the period 1817-32. The most
fertile women were those living in households approximating the elementary
family, though women living with their children and without a male mate were
almost as fertile. Those living with adults who were not identifiable kin were
the least fertile. These findings conform with the modern consensus that
marital instability and casual mating within West Indian family structure
depress fertility.   J

444.   Higman, B. W. THE SLAVE FAMILY AND HOUSEHOLD IN THE
BRITISH WEST INDIES, 1880-1834. *J. of Interdisciplinary Hist. 1975 6(2):
261-287.* An analysis of slave families and households in Barbados, Jamaica,
and Trinidad in the early 19th century. The dominance of the nuclear unit was
not a chance occurrence, but rather a constant model. The characterization of
the slave family as matrifocal, unstable, and promiscuous fits the Caribbean no
better than it fits North America. Based on published sources; 9 tables, 44
notes.   R. Howell

445.   Hiriart, Rosario. AMERICA'S FIRST FEMINIST. *Américas (Organization of Am. States) 1973 25(5): 2-7.* Life history of Sor Juana Ines de la

Cruz, a member in the Order of St. Jerome and a leading literary figure in Mexico, 1668-95.

446. Hiriart, Rosario. LYDIA CABRERA AND THE WORLD OF CUBA'S BLACKS. *Américas (Organization of Am. States) 1980 32(3): 40-42.* Examines the fiction of Lydia Cabrera which focused on the African presence in Cuba and was particularly concerned with religious beliefs.

447. Hoberman, Louisa S. HISPANIC AMERICAN WOMEN AS POR-TRAYED IN THE HISTORICAL LITERATURE: TYPES OR AR-CHTYPES? *Rev. Interamericana [Puerto Rico] 1974 4(2): 136-147.* The historical literature of Latin America does not support the interpretation that women played only a passive role in the history of that area. Instead, the Latin American female participated in all the areas traditionally thought of as exclusively male-dominated and, at the same time, has maintained her traditional role in the home. Secondary sources; 54 notes.   J. A. Lewis

448. Hollander, Nancy Caro. SI EVITA VIVIERA. *Latin Am. Perspectives 1974 1(3): 42-57.* The role of women in the Peronism of Argentina.

449. Hollander, Nancy Caro. WOMEN WORKERS AND THE CLASS STRUGGLE: THE CASE OF ARGENTINA. *Latin Am. Perspectives 1977 4(1-2): 180-193.* Analyzes the political organization of working women that occurred in the Peronist movement in the 1940's. While early capitalist development brought women into the labor force, futher expansion led to the substitution of immigrant European workers for women. The case raises important political questions about the role of women in populist coalitions; Peronism actually served to reinforce the oppression of women under capitalist development.   J. L. Dietz

450. Homar, Susana. INFERIORIDAD Y CAMBIO: LOS PERSONAJES FEMENINOS EN LA LITERATURA PUERTORRIQUEÑA [Inferiority and change: female characters in Puerto Rican literature]. *Rev. de Ciencias Sociales [Puerto Rico] 1978 20(3-4): 287-303.* Analyzes the development of female characters in Puerto Rican literature. Suggests that as women play a more active role in Puerto Rican society now than they did in the 19th and early 20th centuries, so this is reflected in the work of contemporary writers. Studies the works of two authors René Marqués and Luis Rafael Sánchez, noting their attitude toward women, and comments on the emergence of women as authors.   J/S

451. Huasi, Julio. VIOLETA DE AMERICA [Violeta of America]. *Casa de las Américas [Cuba] 1971 11(65-66): 91-104.* Discusses the life and work of Violeta Parra (1917-67), Chilean poet of revolution in Latin America.

452. Hum, D.; Lobdel, R.; and Spencer, Barbara. PLANTATIONS, STA-PLE EXPORTS AND SEASONALITY OF BIRTHS IN JAMAICA: 1880-1938. *Social and Econ. Studies [Jamaica] 1977 26(1): 63-85.* Relates seasonality of births by parish to the nature of agricultural output and the mode of production. There is greater seasonality in the birth pattern for

commercial production regardless of whether that commercial production is one on plantations or by small farmers. 2 tables, 2 figs., 13 notes.

E. S. Johnson

453. Hunter, Yvonne. THE SISTERS OF MERCY IN BELIZE. *Belizean Studies [Belize] 1983 11(1): 1-15.* Discusses the history, growth, and development of the Sisters of Mercy in Belize, including obstacles to growth, establishment of the St. Catherine Convent, and key administrators of the order.

454. Jaquette, Jane S. FEMALE POLITICAL PARTICIPATION IN LATIN AMERICA. Iglitzin, Lynne B. and Ross, Ruth, ed. *Women in the World* (Santa Barbara, Calif.: Clio Books, 1976): 55-74. Women have the vote in all Latin American countries, but registration of eligible women voters is generally lower than that of men. While more women vote in urban areas, the majority of people in all areas and classes believe politics is for men. Economic inequalities and class exploitation concern women more than political issues or sexual inequalities. It is easier for middle- and upper-class women to enter politics because servants are able to take care of their families. Moreover, there is "no stigma attached to a professional career for the woman." Women in politics tend to concentrate on such "feminine" issues as education, health, and social welfare. Elimination of sex role differences could cause women to lose political power since the "mother-role" in Latin American politics is a strong force. Secondary sources; 45 notes. J. Holzinger

455. Jehenson, Myriam Yvonne. FOUR WOMEN IN SEARCH OF FREEDOM. *Revista/Review Interamericana [Puerto Rico] 1982 12(1): 87-99.* Alfonsina Storni, Delmira Agustini, Juana de Ibarbourou, and Gabriela Mistral—four important female poets of the 20th century in Latin America—sought freedom through their writing, yet none achieved it. 25 notes. J. A. Lewis

456. Jelin, Elizabeth. MIGRATION AND LABOR FORCE PARTICIPATION OF LATIN AMERICAN WOMEN: THE DOMESTIC SERVANTS IN THE CITIES. *Signs: J. of Women in Culture and Soc. 1977 3(1): 129-141.* Concerns the migration of Latin American women from rural to urban areas and their occupational and domestic alternatives in the cities. Women migrate in greater numbers than men, and the elastic market for domestic service—since there is "no end to housework"—absorbs most of them. After a period spent in domestic service, some women enter other fields, but a large proportion marry and continue life as unpaid domestic workers. These phenomena of domestic service, differential labor-force participation and women's work are seen as part of the larger pattern of the organization of households and must be studied in that context. 37 notes. L. M. Maloney

457. Jones, H. R. METROPOLITAN DOMINANCE AND FAMILY PLANNING IN BARBADOS. *Social and Econ. Studies [Jamaica] 1977 26(3): 327-338.* Family planning has been more effective in the metropolitan areas where permanent clinics are established than in rural areas where there are only field workers. Based on data from the Barbados Family Planning Association for 1960 and 1970; 4 maps, 4 tables, 7 ref. E. S. Johnson

458. Kanner, Leopoldo. PROCERIDAD Y NIÑEZ DE DAVID PEÑA [The childhood and distinguished lineage of David Peña]. *Bol. de la Acad. Nac. de la Hist. [Argentina] 1965 38(2): 181-198.* Discusses the colonization and inhabitants of northeastern Argentina and describes the experiences of the Fernandez de la Corte and the de la Peña families ca. 1795-1879. Presents the historical background to the childhood of David Peña, discusses his birthplace, genealogy, and major figures of his family stressing the role of his female relatives. Publishes some of the family correspondence, including that with General Justo José Urquiza. 11 notes, biblio, 3 appendixes.   R. O. Khan

459. Katra, William H. EVA PERÓN: MEDIA QUEEN OF THE PERONIST WORKING CLASS. *Revista/Review Interamericana [Puerto Rico] 1981 11(2): 238-251.* Eva Perón effectively portrayed herself to Argentina's masses as passive, servile, and antirational, attributes that endeared her to people with precisely these traits. Based on secondary sources; 30 notes.   J. A. Lewis

460. Kettle-Williams, Jay. WOMAN-MADE LANGUAGE: THE CASE OF PARAGUAY. *J. of Area Studies [Great Britain] 1983 (7): 19-24.* Decimation of the male population in two major wars since 1865 and the presence of "men's words" and "women's words" in Guarani may account for the language's persistence.

461. King, Marjorie. CUBA'S ATTACK ON WOMEN'S SECOND SHIFT. *Latin Am. Perspectives 1977 4(1-2): 106-119.* Focuses on the efforts of the Cuban state to liberate women from the "second shift" that awaits them at home after working outside the home in social production. Addresses the theoretical question of the relation of women's participation in social production, freedom from domestic drudgery, and the attainment of full equality for women. The problem is not just one of socializing housework or legislating the sharing of housework among men and women, but of struggling to eliminate old ways of thinking about the roles of men and women. The author describes the difficulties Cuba has encountered in this campaign as well as the significant advances.   J. L. Dietz

462. Kinzer, Nora Scott. SEXIST SOCIOLOGY. *Center Mag. 1974 7(3): 48-59.* Discusses sexism inherent in most sociological works dealing (or not dealing) with Latin American women.

463. Knaster, Meri. WOMEN IN LATIN AMERICA: THE STATE OF RESEARCH, 1975. *Latin Am. Res. Rev. 1976 11(1): 3-74.* Lists and assesses the various research activities, with an emphasis on publications after 1970, in the field of women in Latin America and includes a substantial bibliography of women in Latin America.

464. Kuznesof, Elizabeth Anne. THE ROLE OF THE FEMALE-HEADED HOUSEHOLD IN BRAZILIAN MODERNIZATION: 1765 TO 1836. *J. of Social Hist. 1980 13(4): 589-614.* The increase in the number of households headed by women in a city like São Paulo, and information from other Brazilian and Chilean research, suggest that this occurred as household and neighborhood centered economic activity was replaced by activity geared to

agricultural exports. São Paulo censuses for 1765, 1802, and 1836 reveal an increase from 28.9% in 1765 to 44.7% in 1802, and a slight drop to 39.3% in 1836. As subsistence farming was rivaled and then replaced by more urban occupations in São Paulo and as plantations arose elsewhere, male workers were drawn away. The rise of household textile manufacturing provided economic support for female heads of households in the early 19th century, but as it declined, less lucrative urban employment remained the only support of the female-headed household. Factory work did not become widespread until the end of the century. 6 tables, 40 notes.   M. Hough

465. Kyle, Patricia A. and Francis, Michael J. WOMEN AT THE POLLS: THE CASE OF CHILE, 1970-1971. *Comparative Pol. Studies 1978 11(3): 291-310.* Analyzes women's voting patterns from data collected in Chile's 1970 election.

466. LaDuke, Betty. CHILE: EMBROIDERIES OF LIFE AND DEATH. *Massachusetts Rev. 1983 24(1): 33-40.* Reports on the women embroiderers of Chile. There are two groups who have received international recognition: the women of rural Isla Negra and the urban women of Santiago. Describes how the embroideries are made and the subjects chosen. Their endeavors, which are approved by the government, and assisted by the prestige of museum exhibits, find a ready market at home and abroad. Sometimes the women select a common theme, each making a panel which are then sewn together to make a tapestry mural, called *arpilleras* in Spanish. The Isla Negra technique employs wool embroidery which completely covers the surface. Their work portrays idealized rural scenes, using their art as an escape from reality. The Santiago women, however, use fabric collages portraying their interpretation of their current political and social reality, representing a symbolic confrontation of art with life. Illus., 5 photos, note.   E. R. Campbell

467. Lamur, Humphrey E. DEMOGRAPHIC PERFORMANCE OF TWO SLAVE POPULATIONS OF THE DUTCH SPEAKING CARIBBEAN. *Bol. de Estudios Latinoamericanos y del Caribe [Netherlands] 1981 (30): 87-102.* One of the few exceptions to the general Caribbean pattern of declining slave populations in the 19th century is the demographic performance of slaves in the Netherlands Antilles. A comparison between Curaçao and Surinam suggests that the fertility rate of the former was twice as high as that of the latter. It is likely that this differential is caused by differences in the average birth interval between the two populations. This demographic variable, in turn, is probably related to differences in both the nature of slavery and the labor conditions on the plantations. Nutrition is another factor that may have contributed to the differences in fertility. Biblio., ref., 8 tables.
R. L. Woodward, Jr.

468. Lavrin, Asunción. IN SEARCH OF THE COLONIAL WOMAN IN MEXICO: THE SEVENTEENTH AND EIGHTEENTH CENTURIES. Lavrin, Asunción, ed. *Latin American Women* (London: Greenwood Pr., 1978): 23-60. The image of the colonial Mexican woman was a creation of men who extolled her role as wife and mother but regarded her as secondary. However, the acceptance of this role varied widely and applied primarily to the upper

classes. Though legislative regulations were restrictive, women were often active legal partners with their husbands or acted as independent legal persons in financial matters. Wills and dowries reveal women's role in cementing kinship relationships and show their importance as heiresses and controllers of property. Widows exercised great freedom, with direct control of their dowry, *arras,* and half their husband's estate. Although women participated in multiple roles, their primary role was protector of marriage and the family. Archival and litigation records, contemporary prescriptive literature, and secondary sources; 85 notes.   S. Tomlinson-Brown

469.   Lavrin, Asunción and Couturier, Edith. LAS MUJERES TIENEN LA PALABRA: OTRAS VOCES EN LA HISTORIA COLONIAL DE MEXICO [The women have the floor: other voices from the colonial history of Mexico]. *Hist. Mexicana [Mexico] 1981 31(2): 278-313.* Women have played a subordinate role in Mexican historiography. Sources for this study of the personal and social roles of women include legal documents from the civil and ecclesiastical courts and private letters. Male-female relationships reveal hitherto unexplored aspects of personal life as well as aspects of colonial society. Based on primary material in several Mexican and one US archives; 27 notes, biblio.   J. V. Coutinho

470.   Lavrin, Asunción. SOME FINAL CONSIDERATIONS ON TRENDS AND ISSUES IN LATIN AMERICAN WOMEN'S HISTORY. Lavrin, Asunción, ed. *Latin American Women* (London: Greenwood Pr., 1978): 302-332. The history of Latin American women has been approached in two ways: women have been defined according to sources which reflect cultural norms, such as legislative and educational material, or in terms of individual biographies of exceptional women. Historians must amplify this limited picture by seeking a definition of the ideals that served as guidelines for behavior and by studying behavior in its historical reality. Important areas for consideration are prescriptive and educational literature written for women, the impact of the law on women's lives, and women's roles in politics, the work force, feminism, and women's associations. Questions about the differences between rural, urban, white, Indian, and black families and the changes in them resulting from the formation of a new society also merit attention. 70 notes.
                                                           S. Tomlinson-Brown

471.   Lavrin, Asunción. WOMEN IN CONVENTS: THEIR ECONOMIC AND SOCIAL ROLE IN COLONIAL MEXICO. Carroll, Berenice A., ed. *Liberating Women's Hist.* (Chicago: U. of Illinois Pr., 1976): 250-277. Convents established in New Spain expressed and reinforced the social order of the ruling minority. Their social function was to provide shelter for unmarried women from the economic and social elite and to offer them an education in reading, writing, and the womanly arts. As financial units, convents exercised an important function by offering credit to landowners and merchants, and because of their extensive properties, they were considered as important as the most powerful masculine orders. Based on legal records and secondary sources; table, 77 notes.   S. Tomlinson-Brown

472. Leal, Magdalena Leon de and Deere, Carmen Diana. ESTUDIO DE LA MUJER RURAL Y EL DESARROLLO DEL CAPITALISMO EN EL AGRO COLOMBIANO [Rural women and the development of capitalism in agrarian Colombia]. *Am. Indígena [Mexico] 1978 38(2): 341-381.* Elaborates on the general characteristics of capitalism's development process, its significance in four different regions of Colombia, and the division of labor by sex. The analysis of capitalist development in these regions illustrates three forms of regional integration within the national economy: production for the international market, capitalistic production in response to internal market development, and the function of providing manual labor. Each form of integration has had its special agrarian structure and an internal process of change in production relationships, with important repercussions for the rural economy.
J/S

473. Leante, César. *CECILIA VALDÉS, ESPEJO DE LA ESCLAVITUD* [*Cecilia Valdés,* mirror of slavery]. *Casa de las Américas [Cuba] 1975 15(89): 19-25.* Discusses the Cuban novel *Cecilia Valdés* (1882), by Cirilio Villaverde, giving a detailed look at the novel's reflection of Cuban slavery and its position on racism in its time.

474. Leite, Miriam Lifchitz Moreta. A BRAZILIAN FEMINIST AND HER CONTRIBUTION TO THE PACIFIST CAUSE. *Women's Studies Int. Forum 1983 6(4): 371-373.* Between the wars, Maria Lacerda de Moura was a pioneering Brazilian voice in feminism and pacifism, who was driven into seclusion for her activism.

475. León, Luis A. LA MUJER INDÍGENA EN LA RÉGIMEN LABORAL INCÁSICO Y COLONIAL DEL REINO Y DE LA REAL AUDIENCIA DE QUITO [The Indian woman and the labor regime of Incan and colonial Quito]. *Am. Indígena [Mexico] 1975 35(3): 539-556.* A thorough revision of works on Indian women and the regime in the ancient towns of Ecuador. Pottery, the textile industry, and agricultural activities give an idea of labor life before the Inca Empire. Information about the Empire, however, must begin with the *quipucamayos* and the reports from chroniclers on the Spanish conquest. Finally, the colonial period must be examined from the point of view of the establishment of mitas, systems of tribute, repartimientos, encomiendas, and other personal services which cruelly exploited the Indians, involving directly and indirectly the Indian women. Based on the information of contemporary chroniclers and historians.
J

476. León de Leal, Magdalena. PERSONAS INTERESADAS EN LA PROBLEMÁTICA FEMININA EN PERÚ, ARGENTINA, BRASIL Y VENEZUELA [Persons interested in the feminine problem in Peru, Argentina, Brazil, and Venezuela]. *Latin Am. Res. Rev. 1979 14(1): 134-144.* Provides a listing of persons and institutions involved in research on women in Latin America, with a description of projects completed or in process. Includes a list of governmental and nongovernmental organizations working for women's rights. Based on visits and interviews in 1976; 2 appendixes.
J. K. Pfabe

477.   León de Leal, Magdalena and Deere, Carmen Diana. RURAL WOM-
EN AND THE DEVELOPMENT OF CAPITALISM OF COLOMBIAN
AGRICULTURE. *Signs 1979 5(1): 60-77.* Four case studies of Colombian
rural areas show the heterogeneity of the sexual division of labor. Fredonia
became a coffee producer in the late 19th century, while El Espinal and
Sincelejo expanded their internal markets in the 20th century. In Garcia
Rovira, the economy was weakened so that by 1955 men were required to find
additional proletarian jobs while women assumed larger agrarian roles. Regardless of the particular pattern, women must always provide the family
labor. Based on the Rural Women Research Project, Colombian Association
of Population Studies; 5 notes.   S. P. Conner

478.   Leridon, H. and Charbit, Y. PATTERNS OF MARITAL UNIONS
AND FERTILITY IN GUADELOUPE AND MARTINIQUE. *Population
Studies [Great Britain] 1981 35(2): 235-246.* Statistics from a 1975-76 survey.

479.   Levine, Linda Gould. MARÍA LUISA BOMBAL FROM A FEMI-
NIST PERSPECTIVE. *Rev. Interamericana [Puerto Rico] 1974 4(2): 148-161.*
Although one of Chile's most famous female novelists, María Luisa Bombal
(1910-) develops many of her works around weak female characters. These
fictional women have no life of their own but depend on male acceptance for
their very existence. Bombal's characters deviate from the traditional stereotypes of Latin American women only in their unusual sexual passions. Primary
and secondary material; 20 notes.   J. A. Lewis

480.   Lewin, Linda. SOME HISTORICAL IMPLICATIONS OF KINSHIP
ORGANIZATION FOR FAMILY-BASED POLITICS IN THE BRAZIL-
IAN NORTHEAST. *Comparative Studies in Soc.and Hist. [Great Britain]
1979 21(2): 262-292.* Examines the relationship between the descent system
and preferred marital patterns as they illustrate the integral relationship
between kinship and the political role of power families (or *parentalas)* in
northeastern Brazil, 1889-1930.

481.   Lewis, Jean Battey. ALICIA ALONSO AND THE CUBAN NA-
TIONAL BALLET. *Américas (Organization of Am. States) 1978 30(9):
49-53.* Gives a biography of Cuban ballerina Alicia Alonso, who has enjoyed
international fame as a ballerina and director of the National Ballet of Cuba
since the 1940's.

482.   Lewis, Paul H. THE FEMALE VOTE IN ARGENTINA, 1958-1965.
Comparative Pol. Studies 1971 3(4): 425-442. Analysis of female voting and
voting behavior in Argentina, 1958-65, indicates that women have greater
interest in the electoral process than men, tend to be more conservative than
men (except working class women who tend to be more radical), and switch
partisan support with about the same regularity as men.

483.   Lindstrom, Naomi. FEMINIST CRITICISM OF LATIN AMERI-
CAN LITERATURE: BIBLIOGRAPHIC NOTES. *Latin Am. Res. Rev.
1980 15(1): 151-159.* Describes several facets of Latin American literature: 1)
sex-role analysis; 2)the impact of feminism in the 1970's, particularly the

promotion of female authors and enterprises dedicated solely to women's literature; and 3)feminist criticism outside of specialized feminist publishing sources. Biblio.   J. K. Pfabe

484. Little, Cynthia J. EDUCATION, PHILANTHROPY, AND FEMI-NISM: COMPONENTS OF ARGENTINE WOMANHOOD, 1860-1926. Lavrin, Asunción, ed. *Latin American Women* (London: Greenwood Pr., 1978): 235-253. Rapid urbanization, increased foreign immigration, and economic changes altered the traditional role of Argentina's women, 1860-1926. In response to the social dislocation of the immigrant population, women participated in philanthropic ventures such as the Society of Beneficence, a socially-approved outlet for the nonworking, educated woman. Under the influence of Domingo Faustino Sarmiento (1811-88), vocational schools were established to educate skilled workers for the commercial and agricultural sectors. Educated women became interested in the eradication of social ills, stressing reforms aimed to alter women's attitudes about themselves. Though their approach was moderate and ladylike and did not change mainstream attitudes, they drew attention to women's debased legal and political status and poor living and labor conditions, leading to the civil code reforms in 1926. Based on newspapers, other primary and secondary sources; 7 notes.
S. Tomlinson-Brown

485. Little, Cynthia J. PAULINA LUISI: URUGUAYAN FEMINIST AND REFORMER OF MORALS. *Tr. of the Conference Group for Social and Administrative Hist. 1976 6: 91-104.* Discusses the efforts of Uruguayan physician, surgeon, and feminist activist, Paulina Luisi, against the prostitution laws in Montevideo and Buenos Aires from the early 1900's until her death in 1950.

486. Little, Cynthia Jeffress. MORAL REFORM AND FEMINISM: A CASE STUDY. *J. of Inter-Am. Studies and World Affairs 1975 17(4): 386-396.* A Uruguayan physician, Pauline Luisi (1875-1950) was dedicated to both moral reform and feminism. She fought for women's rights and for the establishment of one sexual moral standard. She worked to destroy white slavery and alcoholism while at the same time urging the acceptance of women in institutions of higher education. Her own career served as a model for other women because she was Uruguay's first woman bachelor's degree holder, its first woman physician and surgeon, and a member of the Uruguayan diplomatic corps. She believed that women possessed a moral superiority and that feminine values, if adopted by society, could alleviate the major social ills of the time. Based on Uruguayan newspapers, organization documents, and secondary sources.   J. R. Thomas

487. Lobo, Francisco Bruno. DUAS PIONEIRAS—MADAME DUROCH-ER, RITA LOBATO [Two pioneering women: Madame Durocher and Rita Lobato]. *Rev. do Inst. Hist. e Geog. Brasileiro [Brazil] 1980 (328): 53-56.* At a time when Brazilian women were not allowed to enter the professions, Marie Josephine Mathilde Durocher (1809-93) and Rita Lobato Velho Lopes (b. 1867) were the first exceptions. The former was a midwife, author of many

publications, and a leader in her profession. The latter was a physician, active though not prominent among her colleagues. Refs.   J. V. Coutinho

488.   Lobo, Francisco Bruno. RITA LOBATO: A PRIMEIRA MÉDICA FORMADA NO BRASIL [Rita Lobato: the first woman doctor to graduate in Brazil]. *Rev. de Hist. [Brazil] 1971 42(86): 483-485.* Biography of Dr. Rita Lobato de Freitas (b. 1867), the first woman to receive a medical degree from a Brazilian university. The Leôncio de Carvalho reform of 1879 considerably modified Brazilian higher education, permitting the matriculation of women. Rita Lobato matriculated in 1884 and graduated in 1887.   P. J. Taylorson

489.   Lomnitz, Larissa and Pérez-Lizaur, Marisol. KINSHIP STRUCTURE AND THE ROLE OF WOMEN IN THE URBAN UPPER CLASS OF MEXICO. *Signs 1979 5(1): 164-168.* Five generations of the family of Carlos Gómez (1825-76), a merchant of Puebla, Mexico, indicate that family cohesion and strong kinship ties remain even when socioeconomic differences within the family have been greatly magnified over the generations. Women serve as "centralizing" agents in the network of communication, and in more recent years, they have also assumed a greater role in the family businesses. Based on participant observation.   S. P. Conner

490.   Lomnitz, Larissa Adler and Perez Lizaur, Marisol. THE HISTORY OF A MEXICAN URBAN FAMILY. *J. of Family Hist. 1978 3(4): 392-409.* This remarkable genealogical study traces the Gomez family over more than a century. It shows how the family members defined relationships and carried on social and economic exchanges. In nonunilinear kinship systems such as prevail in Mexico there are few formalized rules of interaction between relatives and these have to be forged on the individual family level. Table, 3 notes, biblio.
                                                      T. W. Smith

491.   MacDonald, John Stuart and MacDonald, Leatrice D. TRANSFORMATION OF AFRICAN AND INDIAN FAMILY TRADITIONS IN THE SOUTHERN CARIBBEAN. *Comparative Studies in Soc. and Hist. 1973 15(2): 171-198.* The Negro family ideology of the southern Caribbean was formed because of slavery and semi-paternalistic peonage, while East Indian family ideology was formed despite bondage in bureaucratic agriculture. Both drew on the respective principles of family organization from their cultures of origin. Based on censuses of Barbados, Grenada, and Trinidad and Tobago, field work, and other primary and secondary material; 9 tables, 10 notes, biblio., 2 appendixes.   M. M. McCarthy

492.   Macías, Anna. FELIPE CARRILLO PUERTO AND WOMEN'S LIBERATION IN MEXICO. Lavrin, Asunción, ed. *Latin American Women* (London: Greenwood Press, 1978): 286-301. Felipe Carrillo Puerto, socialist governor of Yucatan, 1922-24, was the center of the Mexican women's liberation movement. His predecessor, Salvador Alvarado, had been a feminist advocate, implementing significant reforms in jobs, education, and political participation. Although not close friends, the two shared similar ideas on social and economic issues. Carrillo Puerto consolidated his predecessor's reforms and sought to free women from the Church, interest them in political affairs,

and liberate them from their exclusive concern with domestic life. His radical views on marriage, divorce, and birth control, however, convinced conservatives that feminism was dangerous, causing Mexican feminists to disassociate themselves from him in 1923. Newspaper articles, other primary, and secondary sources; 73 notes. S. Tomlinson-Brown

493. Macias, Anna. WOMEN AND THE MEXICAN REVOLUTION, 1910-1920. *Americas (Acad. of Am. Franciscan Hist.) 1980 37(1): 53-82.* In the Mexican Revolution a significant number of women—especially schoolteachers—made their mark as precursors, propagandists, or other activists. President Venustiano Carranza's collaborator Hermila Galindo was just one of those who combined service to the revolutionary cause with campaigning for women's rights that brought few immediate accomplishments but catalyzed further efforts. Many more women served as *soldaderas* or "soldiers' women"; some were female soldiers. Also important was the role of women in opposition to the revolution, particularly its anticlerical aspects. Based on contemporary press accounts, oral history, and secondary sources; 134 notes. D. Bushnell

494. MacLachlan, Colin M. MODERNIZATION OF FEMALE STATUS IN MEXICO: THE IMAGE OF WOMEN'S MAGAZINES. *Rev. Interamericana [Puerto Rico] 1974 4(2): 246-257.* The mass media, especially women's magazines, offer insights into the status of women in Mexico. The role of the Mexican female has changed in recent times, but *machismo* (the cult of male dominance) still plays a decisive part in the conduct of women. Recent changes have come from the force of foreign examples rather than domestic pressure. Primary and secondary sources; 39 notes. J. A. Lewis

495. Madeira, Felicia R. and Singer, Paul. STRUCTURE OF FEMALE EMPLOYMENT AND WORK IN BRAZIL, 1920-1970. *J. of Inter-Am. Studies and World Affairs 1975 17(4): 490-496.* Technological changes have altered the social division of work in Brazil and have enabled women to aspire to careers beyond homemaking. But the jobs available for women are linked to the development level of the nation and educational opportunities for women. Up to 1940, 70% of the Brazilian work force was in agriculture, where women had many opportunities to perform productive activities without leaving the home. During that period, women who did work in urban centers were employed as housemaids and seamstresses, which did not conflict with their traditional training. City and country women participated in work only as aids to men. Since 1940, however, there have been deep changes due to increased industrialization. There are more opportunities for women in banking, textile factories, and social services. There are still too few jobs open to women, but the future appears to hold promise. J. R. Thomas

496. Magón, Ricardo Flores. A LA MUJER (TO WOMEN). Mora, Magdalena and Del Castillo, Adelaida R., ed. *Mexican Women in the United States: Struggles Past and Present* (Los Angeles: U. of California Chicano Studies Res. Center, 1980): 159-162. Translates Ricardo Flores Magón's article, originally published in his newspaper, *Regeneración.* He opposed the degradation of women in Mexico and called for revolution. J. Powell

497.   Mahieu, José Agustín. FEMININE TYPES AND STEREOTYPES IN MEXICAN AND LATIN AMERICAN CINEMA. *Cultures [France] 1982 8(3): 83-95.* Discusses the status of women as directors, actresses, scriptwriters, stenographers and technicians in Mexican and Latin American cinema.

498.   Manyoni, Joseph R. METHODS IN CARIBBEAN ANTHROPO-LOGICAL RESEARCH: A RE-CONSIDERATION. *Anthropologica [Canada] 1982 24(2): 167-191.* Describes the effect of the Catholic Church, the Anglican Communion, and European colonialism on marriage and family patterns in Caribbean plantation society from the late 17th to the early 19th centuries.

499.   Markmann, Hans-Jochen. ERGÄNZUNGSMATERIALIEN FÜR DEN UNTERRICHT: DONNA MARINA UND DIE BEGEGNUNG VON CORTEZ UND MONTEZUMA 1519 [Supplementary material for instruction: Donna Marina and the meeting of Cortes and Montezuma 1519]. *Geschichtsdidaktik [West Germany] 1979 4(1): 87-89.* Points out the lack of information about and the historical importance of Malinche, also known as Tenepal, the Aztec princess who became Hernando Cortes's translator, diplomatic advisor and mistress.

500.   Martín-Baró, Ignacio. LA IMAGEN DE LA MUJER EN EL SALVA-DOR [Images of women in El Salvador]. *Estudios Centroamericanos [El Salvador] 1980 35(380): 557-568.* Analyzes attitudes toward women of 800 men and women in El Salvador between the ages of 14 and 40. Macho attitudes were most prevalent among the least educated and those unable to overcome the demands of the dominant culture. Biblio.

R. L. Woodward, Jr.

501.   Martínez Guayanes, María A. LA SITUACIÓN DE LA MUJER EN CUBA EN 1953 [The situation of women in Cuba in 1953]. *Santiago [Cuba] 1974 (15): 195-226.* Discusses the social status and professional and socioeconomic problems of women in Cuba in the 1950's.

502.   Mattelart, Michele. CHILE: EL GOLPE DE ESTADO EN FEMENI-NO O CUANDO LAS MUJERES DE LA BURGUESÍA SALEN A LA CALLE [Chile: the women's coup d'etat or when the women of the bourgeoisie hit the street]. *Casa de las Américas [Cuba] 1975 15(88): 75-90.* Studies the role women played in the overthrow of the Allende government (1970-73). Shows how the reactionaries successfully utilized women in the coup d'etat and suggests the need for leftists to learn from this experience. Depicts the role of women in the anti-Allende movement as organizers and participants in street demonstrations, as supporters of strikes by miners and truck drivers, and as organizers of women from all socioeconomic classes to combat the socialist government. Women in *barrio* agencies and cultural centers proved effective organizers of women in poorer classes. Reactionaries spread propaganda by the mass media about the evils of communism. Past conservative governments had a poor record in granting women political and civil rights but they realized that women were an important tool for the coup d'etat, without giving up their

reactionary views of a woman's place. Based on newspaper sources.

H. J. Miller

503. Mellafe, Rolando. TAMAÑO DE LA FAMILIA EN LA HISTORIA DE LATINOAMERICA, 1562-1950 [Family size in Latin American history, 1562-1950]. *Histórica [Peru]* 1980 4(1): 3-19. Discusses some methodological possibilities regarding a neglected subject in Latin American studies. After constructing a chronological table of family size with data drawn from diverse geographical sources, the author recommends further research based on demographic and kinship factors, economic organization, and class and ethnic affiliation. Table, biblio. J. V. Coutinho

504. Mendelson, Johanna S. R. THE FEMININE PRESS: THE VIEW OF WOMEN IN THE COLONIAL JOURNALS OF SPANISH AMERICA, 1790-1810. Lavrin, Asunción, ed. *Latin American Women* (London: Greenwood Pr., 1978): 198-218. Influenced by Enlightenment ideas, popular periodicals in Latin America increasingly dealt with the condition of women as an issue. The *Mercurio Peruano* (1791-95), *Telégrafo Mercantil* (1801-02), *Diario Mexico* (1805-07), and *Semanario Económico de Mexico* (1810-11) describes upper-class women as protectors of cultural heritage. Since occupation was considered below their station, roles were limited to motherhood, childrearing, or membership in a religious order. On the other hand, except for the *Mercurio Peruano*, the magazines accepted the right of women to education. Women's improved position was justified as a benefit to the colony rather than in terms of self-improvement. Although the numerous articles about women reflect a significant change in attitudes toward them since the 17th century, women's role remained restricted and largely unchallenged. Contemporary periodicals and secondary sources; table, 51 notes. • S. Tomlinson-Brown

505. Mikell, Gwendolyn. WHEN HORSES TALK: REFLECTIONS ON ZORA NEALE HURSTON'S HAITIAN ANTHROPOLOGY. *Phylon* 1982 43(3): 218-230. Zora Neale Hurston, a black female anthropologist during the 1920's and 1930's, faced the dilemma of speaking for herself while retaining the objectivity required of academic scholarship. Her book, *Tell My Horse,* documents her enthusiasm for Caribbean culture and for the Africanisms she found in Haitian peasants. She attempted to identify with the people and yet maintain an intellectual separation from them. A. G. Belles

506. Miller, Beth. PERUVIAN WOMEN WRITERS: DIRECTIONS FOR FUTURE RESEARCH. *Revista/Rev. Interamericana [Puerto Rico]* 1982 12(1): 36-48. Women writers in Peru have been relatively ignored by scholars compared to those in Argentina and Mexico, yet Peruvian female writers merit attention and ought to receive it. 28 notes. J. A. Lewis

507. Miranda, Glaura Vasques de. WOMEN'S LABOR FORCE PARTICIPATION IN A DEVELOPING SOCIETY: THE CASE OF BRAZIL. *Signs: J. of Women in Culture and Soc.* 1977 3(1): 261-274. In Brazil, economic development did not lead to higher levels of women's participation in the labor market during 1940-70. The process of dependent capitalist development is responsible both for a lower level of women's participation in agriculture and

for a lower level of absorption in urban development. This situation is not caused by industrialization itself but by industrial finance capital and advanced technology which is capital-intensive. In Brazil the situation is aggravated by the concentration of industrial activity in a few regions. Unequal regional development leads to different female participation rates in economic activity because regions are in different stages of development. 9 tables, 23 notes.

L. M. Maloney

508. Miranda Hevia, Alicia. INTRODUCCIÓN A LA OBRA NOVELES-CA DE CARMEN NARANJO [Introduction to the novels of Carmen Naranjo]. *Cahiers du Monde Hispanique et Luso-Brésilien [France] 1981 (36): 121-129.* Carmen Naranjo was born in Cartago, Costa Rica in 1930, began publishing in 1966, and was ambassador and cabinet minister in the social democratic governments of the 1970's. Both her work and her writing have aimed at national liberation. 4 notes, biblio.   D. R. Stevenson

509. Montezuma Hurtado, Alberto. LA SIN VENTURA DOÑA BEATRIZ [The unfortunate Doña Beatriz]. *Bol. Cultural y Biblio. [Colombia] 1982 19(4): 93-99.* Doña Beatriz, wife of Pedro de Alvarado, suffered when her husband died and shortly thereafter died herself following a volcanic eruption in Guatemala.

510. Mújica, Elisa. MARÍA MARTÍNEZ DE NISSER, ESCRITORA Y SOLDADO [María Martínez de Nisser, writer and soldier]. *Bol. Cultural y Bibliografico [Colombia] 1979 16(5): 166-169.* María Martínez de Nisser's diary of her experience as a soldier during the revolution in Antioquia in 1840-41 was published in 1843. The year she was hailed a heroine also marked the beginning of her return to obscurity once the special circumstances of war returned her to the role of a 19th-century Colombian woman.

511. Muriel, Josefina. EN TRONO A UNA VIEJA POLÉMICA: EREC-CIÓN DE LOS DOS PRIMEROS CONVENTOS DE SAN FRANCISCO EN LA CIUDAD DE MÉXICO. SIGLO XVI [An old controversy: the building of the first two convents of Saint Francis in Mexico City in the 16th century]. *Estudios de Hist. Novohispana [Mexico] 1978 (6): 7-38.* Traces the origins of the building of the first two Franciscan convents in Mexico City, providing details of their location, previous land ownership, and use until 1524.

512. Nash, June. AZTEC WOMEN: THE TRANSITION FROM STATUS TO CLASS IN EMPIRE AND COLONY. Etienne, Mona and Leacock, Eleanor, ed. *Women and Colonization: Anthropological Perspectives* (New York: Praeger, J. F. Bergin Publ., 1980): 134-148. With the arrival of the Spaniards in 1519 the Aztec empire, still in its formative stages, underwent transformation from a kinship-based society with little social stratification to a class-structured empire. The changing regulations on marriage, inheritance, labor recruitment, and production reflect the conflict between the crown, the Catholic Church, and the colonists in claiming control over women's reproduction. The patriarchal right of the male to determine the status of a woman's offspring was strengthened by crown and Church rulings and overshadowed

the creative role of Indian women in the formation of the emergent mestizo culture with the stigma of illegitimacy.

513. Navarro, Marysa. THE CASE OF EVA PERÓN. *Signs: J. of Women in Culture and Soc. 1977 3(1): 229-240.* Traces the rise of Eva Perón (1919-52) and explains how she used her position as Juan Perón's wife to establish her own unique power position. She operated especially through control of the ministry of labor, which had been the original basis of her husband's influence, and through the Fundación Eva Perón. Nevertheless, her power and leadership remained dependent on him and showed no sign of rivalry. 22 notes.

L. M. Maloney/S

514. Navarro, Marysa. RESEARCH ON LATIN AMERICAN WOMEN. *Signs 1979 5(1): 111-120.* Reviews Latin American social science literature of the 1970's on women, citing the major centers of scholarly activity. Latin American scholars are typically not feminists, but they use the "structural dependency" approach developed by Fernando Henrique Cardoso and Enzo Faletto *Dependency and Development in Latin America*, Majory Urquidi, transl., (U. of California Pr., 1979). Because capitalism does not define all labor relations in Latin America, work and nonwork must be redefined using a noncapitalist approach. The household provides an important basis for study. 26 notes.

S. P. Conner

515. Nevadomsky, Joseph. WEDDING RITUALS AND CHANGING WOMEN'S RIGHTS AMONG THE EAST INDIANS IN RURAL TRINIDAD. *Int. J. of Women's Studies [Canada] 1981 4(5): 484-496.* Describes the effects of indenture and social change on the position of East Indian women in Trinidad in the 19th century and examines deculturation in the wedding ceremony, one of the most authentic of retained customs among East Indians.

516. Niño Dios, María Antonia del. EL CONVENTO DE SANTA CLARA DE TUNJA [The convent of St. Clare in Tunja]. *Repertorio Boyacense [Colombia] 1973 (274-275): 3666-3673.* A history of this convent, founded by Juana Macías de Salguero, wife of Captain Francisco Salguero, in 1573.

M. C. F. (IHE 90366)

517. Nobile, Annunziata. ASPETTI DELL'IMMIGRAZIONE ITALIANA IN ARGENTINA NEGLI ANNI DEL GRANDE ESODO: ALCUNI CONTRIBUTI AMERICANI [Aspects of Italian immigration in Argentina during the years of the great exodus: some American contributions]. *Storia Contemporanea [Italy] 1982 13(1): 123-128.* Reviews recent publications on the problems of the immigration and assimilation of Italians in Argentina, especially the problems of literacy and education, the formation of Italian communities, and marriage patterns as a means to test the melting pot theory. 8 notes.

J. V. Coutinho

518. Olwig, Karen Fog. WOMEN, "MATRIFOCALITY" AND SYSTEMS OF EXCHANGE: AN ETHNOHISTORICAL STUDY OF THE AFRO-AMERICAN FAMILY ON ST. JOHN, DANISH WEST INDIES. *Ethnohistory 1981 28(1): 59-78.* This ethnohistorical case study of the American,

formerly Danish, West Indian island of St. John examines the position of Afro-American women during a 260-year period from European colonization of the island to the present. It focuses on the system of social reproduction as it has evolved since slavery and the role of women as agents of production and reproduction, as seen against the background of the socioeconomic units and exchange networks within which women have functioned. The conclusions drawn question the usefulness and validity of the concept of "matrifocality."

J

519. Patterson,   Orlando. PERSISTENCE,   CONTINUITY,   AND CHANGE IN THE JAMAICAN WORKING-CLASS FAMILY. *J. of Family Hist. 1982 7(2): 135-161.* Despite superficial similarities between slave and current working-class families, there is no causal connection. The unstable matrifocal families of the current lower class are not a continuation of the slave family, but a social phenomenon that developed from contemporary conditions. 7 tables, fig., 5 notes, biblio.   T. W. Smith

520. Peña, Devón Gerardo. LAS MAQUILADORAS: MEXICAN WOMEN AND CLASS STRUGGLE IN THE BORDER INDUSTRIES. *Aztlán 1980 11(2): 159-229.* Describes the efforts of Mexican women to achieve better wages and working conditions in the *maquiladoras,* factories primarily in the electronics and garment industries, involved in the Border Industrialization Program in cities along the US-Mexican border. The *maquiladoras* have been seen as transnational capitalism exploiting Mexican workers, but this interpretation ignores the actions of the workers themselves in bypassing the existing labor-capital organizational forms in favor of their own mass actions, especially in the city of Nuevo Laredo. Community networks of self-help efforts are being formed to resist the internationalization of capital. Tables, charts, 132 notes, ref.   A. Hoffman

521. Percas de Ponseti, Helena. REFLEXIONES SOBRE LA POESIA FEMENINA HISPANOAMERICANA [Reflections on female poetry in Latin America]. *Revista/Rev. Interamericana [Puerto Rico] 1982 12(1): 49-55.* Among the great women poets of the 20th century in Latin America are Delmira Agustini, Gabriela Mistral, and Alfonsina Storni; none considered herself a feminist.   J. A. Lewis

522. Perez, Louis A., Jr. WOMEN IN THE REVOLUTIONARY WAR, 1953-1958: A BIBLIOGRAPHY. *Sci. & Soc. 1975 39(1): 104-108.* Compiles as completely as possible, a collection of sources available in the United States dealing with the role of women in the Cuban revolutionary movement. It mainly covers materials printed during 1959-73 as available in the Center for Cuban Studies, the Library of Congress, the Hoover Institution and the University of Florida Library.   N. Lederer

523. Perez-Venero, Mirna M. THE EDUCATION OF WOMEN ON THE ISTHMUS OF PANAMA. *J. of the West 1973 12(2): 325-334.* Though education for girls in Panama began in 1835-36, no secondary school of high caliber for either sex existed even in the city of Panama by 1877. In the interior, primary schools were very scarce. There seems to have been no

antifeminine attitude among the ruling classes. Instead the attitude was: "woman, mother of the future citizen." 29 notes.   E. P. Stickney

524. Persin, Margaret H. GLORIA FUERTES AND (HER) FEMINIST READER. *Revista/Rev. Interamericana [Puerto Rico] 1982 12(1): 125-132.* Gloria Fuertes became a prominent poet during the 1950's and 1960's. Her work illustrates that the female voice in poetry is now equal to its male counterpart. 5 notes.   J. A. Lewis

525. Pescatello, Ann M. THE FEMALE IN IBERO-AMERICA: AN ESSAY ON RESEARCH BIBLIOGRAPHY AND RESEARCH DIRECTIONS. *Latin Am. Res. Rev. 1972 7(2): 125-142.* Examines the role of women in Latin American countries and discusses recent literature, 1960's-70's, on this topic.

526. Pescatello, Ann M. LATINA LIBERATION: TRADITION, IDEOLOGY, AND SOCIAL CHANGE IN IBERIAN AND LATIN AMERICAN CULTURES. Carroll, Berenice A., ed. *Liberating Women's Hist.* (Chicago: U. of Illinois Pr., 1976): 161-178. Woman in the Iberian culture was defined paradoxically as the repository of virtue and, legally, as the *imbecilitas sexus,* in a class with children and delinquents. The protected status and isolation of the upper class woman were derived from the influence of Moorish civilization as well as the turbulent conditions of medieval Spain. Unchallenged by the Amerindian culture in which women were treated similarly, this legacy took root in Latin America. Only in areas with heavy African settlement were women granted substantial prerogatives. This social system remained intact until the advent of modernization and urbanization in Spain and the wars of independence in Latin America. Today the extent of social change for women depends on the degree of modernization in a particular place. Paradoxically, the middle and upper class woman has bypassed the Victorian antifeminine tradition of the Anglo-American world and finds herself in greater positions of influence than women in the United States because an extensive kin network has freed her for devotion to her profession. Secondary sources; 37 notes.
                                                    S. Tomlinson-Brown

527. Pescatello, Ann M. PREFACE: THE SPECIAL ISSUE IN PERSPECTIVE: THE HISPANIC CARIBBEAN WOMAN AND THE LITERARY MEDIA. *Rev. Interamericana [Puerto Rico] 1974 4(2): 131-136.* Introduction to an issue on roles and perceptions of Caribbean women in literature in Brazil, Cuba, Mexico, Colombia, and Puerto Rico. 3 notes.   J. A. Lewis

528. Pichardo, Hortensia. UNA MUJER EN LA CONQUISTA DE CUBA: DOÑA GUIOMAR DE GUZMÁN [A woman in the conquest of Cuba: Doña Guiomar de Guzmán]. *Santiago [Cuba] 1977 (26-27): 35-58.* Traces the life of Guzmán, wife of accountant Pedro de Paz, and subsequently of the young governor Juanes de Avila. Following the death of Paz in Seville, Guiomar de Guzmán remarried and returned to Cuba to look after her financial interests whereupon she became involved in the island's political intrigues. She disputed the accounts of the former guardian of her interests, the powerful bishop of Cuba, Diego Sarmiento, and gained the support of the new

governor Juanes de Avila, whom she soon married. After initial popularity he was accused of malpractice and injustice, and his conduct was investigated by his successor Antonio de Chávez who was immune from Guzmán's extensive influence. Having accompanied her husband to Seville after his recapture and imprisonment she paid his fine and used her resources to have his other penalties reduced and his banishment from the West Indies quashed. They returned to Cuba and anonymity to continue their business in 1563. 93 notes.

R. O. Khan

529.   Porro, Nelly R. CONFLICTOS SOCIALES Y TENSIONES FAMIL-IARES EN LA SOCIEDAD VIRREINAL RIOPLATENSE A TRAVES DE LOS JUICIOS DE DISENSO [Social conflicts and family tensions in the society of the Río de la Plata viceroyalty as seen through judicial proceedings for family discord]. *Bol. del Inst. de Hist. Argentina y Americana [Argentina] 1980 16(26): 361-392.* Discusses court documents relating to family disputes caused by marriages or intended marriages after the promulgation of new royal regulations in 1776. The regulations often caused deep rifts beween parents and children on matters relating to ethical standards, or the status, class, or race of the intended partner. Based on primary material in the Argentine National Archive; 213 notes.

J. V. Coutinho

530.   Prado, César O. LAS MUJERES DEL PUEBLO EN NUESTRA LUCHA POR LA INDEPENDENCIA [Women of the people in our struggle for independence]. *Anuario del Mus. Hist. Regional [Peru] 1971 (21): 3-7.* Provides brief notes on several women who led or participated in various uprisings favoring Spanish-American independence, 1742-1822.

M. C. F. (IHE 87901)

531.   Rachum Ilan. FEMINISM, WOMEN SUFFRAGE, AND NATION-AL POLITICS IN BRAZIL: 1922-1937. *Luso-Brazilian Rev. 1977 14(1): 118-134.* Discusses feminism in Brazil during the 1880's, after World War I, and in the 1960's. Growth of protest movements and radical political parties aided the rise of feminist interest, and liberal governments assisted by approval or acquiescence, but these governments were replaced by authoritarian and conservative ones hostile to feminist movements. In the post-World War I period, Bertha Lutz was the most prominent and active feminist. She organized the Brazilian Federation for the Advancement of Women (FBPF) and was instrumental in achieving the franchise for women in 1932. Secondary sources; 49 notes.

J. M. Walsh

532.   Ramos, Ana. LA MUJER Y LA REVOLUCIÓN EN CUBA [Woman and revolution in Cuba]. *Casa de las Américas [Cuba] 1971 11(65-66): 56-72.* Discusses the historical and social elements which led to the liberation of women within the Cuban revolution of 1959, showing a development from the late 19th century through today and including tables of higher education for various Latin American countries (1963-65) to demonstrate that women are now being educated more equally.

533.   Ramos, Donald. CITY AND COUNTRY: THE FAMILY IN MINAS GERAIS, 1804-1838. *J. of Family Hist. 1978 3(4): 361-375.* Examines signifi-

cant differences in marriage patterns in rural and urban communities in an area northeast of Rio de Janeiro. In the cities families were smaller because there were fewer slaves and fewer children. There were also more female heads of households and more single adults. Urban-rural differences associated with modernization existed early. 11 tables, 14 notes, biblio.   T. W. Smith

534. Ramos, Donald. MARRIAGE AND THE FAMILY IN COLONIAL VILA RICA. *Hispanic Am. His. Rev. 1975 55(2): 200-225.* A study of the 1804 census of Vila Rica, Brazil, shows that few people were married. Contrary to common belief, few of the families were patriarchal extended families. Of the family units, 45 percent were matrifocal; of these, 83.1 percent were headed by women who had never been married. Generalized hypotheses about family life and the role of women in colonial Brazil are not always valid. 13 tables, 73 notes.   B. D. Johnson

535. Randall, Margaret. LA MUJER CUBANA EN 1974 [The Cuban woman in 1974]. *Casa de las Américas [Cuba] 1975 15(88): 63-72.* Studies the impact of the Cuban revolution on the status of women from 1971 to 1974. First the revolution had to resolve military and economic priorities and then address cultural problems, such as *machismo.* Progress in the liberation of women has been achieved both through public awareness and legal changes, such as elimination of job classifications based on sex and application of vagrancy laws equally to men and women. To assure greater opportunities for women in the labor force, women and men must share household duties equally, a spirit evident in the revision of the Family Code. Despite shortcomings, the revolution is effecting a true democratization for both men and women.   H. J. Miller

536. Randall, Margaret. LA PENETRACIÓN IMPERIALISTA Y SUS CONSECUENCIAS PARA LA MUJER LATINOAMERICANA [Imperialism and its effects on the Latin American woman]. *Santiago [Cuba] 1974 (15): 227-247.* The influence of US ideology in Latin America has particularly affected women through the mass media. The latter has been used to promote antifeminism and the values of consumer society. Birth control programs are instruments of capitalistic power in developing nations designed to maintain the economic and social status quo.   P. J. Taylorson/S

537. Randall, Margaret. UNA BRASILEÑA EN LA LUCHA: ADAMARIS OLIVEIRA LUCENA [A Brazilian woman in the struggle: Adamaris Oliveira Lucena]. *Casa de las Américas [Cuba] 1971 11(65-66): 75-82.* Gives the text of an interview between the author and Adamaris Oliveira Lucena, discussing Lucena's work as a member of the revolutionary Brazilian Vanguardia Popular Revolucionaria and her current exile.

538. Randall, Margaret. VENCEREMOS: WOMEN IN THE NEW CUBA. *Can. Dimension 1975 10(8): 49-55.*

539. Recchini de Lattes, Zulma. FAMILY AND FEMALE PARTICIPATION IN THE LABOR MARKET IN LATIN AMERICA. *Latin Am. Res. Rev. 1982 17(1): 101-104.* Summarizes papers presented at the December 1979

meeting of the subgroup on female participation in the labor market of the CLASCO Employment-Unemployment Group.   J. K. Pfabe

540.   Recchini de Lattes, Zulma. LAS MUJERES EN LA ACTIVIDAD ECONÓMICA EN ARGENTINA, BOLIVIA Y PARAGUAY [Women's economic participation in Argentina, Bolivia, and Paraguay]. *Demografía y Econ. [Mexico] 1979 13(1): 19-48.*

541.   Reedy, Daniel R. ASPECTS OF THE FEMINIST MOVEMENT IN PERUVIAN LETTERS AND POLITICS. *Secolas Ann. 1975 (6): 53-64.* The struggle for female equality and rights in Peru during the 20th century owes a great deal to Magda Portal (1901-). Portal's interest in the role of the Peruvian women coincided with her political activity in the Aprista Party and her literary efforts as Peru's foremost poetess. Although deeply disappointed in her life's labor, she remains committed to her earlier goals. Based on primary and secondary sources; 20 notes.   J. Lewis

542.   Riddell, Adaljiza Sosa. FEMALE POLITICAL ELITES IN MEXICO: 1974. Iglitzin, Lynne B. and Ross, Ruth, ed. *Women in the World* (Santa Barbara, Calif.: Clio Books, 1976): 257-267. The small female political elite in Mexico represents neither women in general nor anyone of the lower social strata. From 1910, the feminist movement in Mexico aimed toward suffrage rights, which were granted in 1953. The movement then died out before raising other issues. *Machismo*, an attitude of male dominance, permeates society, affecting women particularly in the lower classes. Very few women are politically active at any level. In 1974 only 20 women were serving as deputies or senators in national government. These women constitute an elite, highly educated and influenced by US styles and standards. European in descent, they adhere to the male-dominated status quo, perpetuating an attitude of colonial condescension over the Mexican population. Secondary sources; 12 notes.
    N. Barron

543.   Rivero, Eliana. HACIA UNA DEFINCION DE LA LIRICA FEME-NINA EN HISPANOAMERICA [Toward a definition of feminine lyricism in Latin America]. *Revista/Rev. Interamericana [Puerto Rico] 1982 12(1): 11-26.* Recent feminist poetry in Latin America has tended to attack traditional customs and values. 16 notes.   J. A. Lewis

544.   Rosenberg, Terry Jean. FEMALE INDUSTRIAL EMPLOYMENT AND PROTECTIVE LABOR LEGISLATION IN BOGOTA, COLOMBIA. *J. of Interamerican Studies and World Affairs 1982 24(1): 59-80.* Evidence does not suggest that Colombian protective labor legislation has hindered employment of female industrial workers. The Colombian legislature should not spend undue energy on revising protective legislation but should seek supportive programs such as day care services and expanded technical training for women. Based on interviews with businessmen, union leaders, and female workers, and on printed materials; 3 notes, 7 tables, ref.   T. D. Schoonover

545.   Russell-Wood, A. J. R. THE BLACK FAMILY IN THE AMERI-CAS. *Jahrbuch für Geschichte von Staat, Wirtschaft und Gesellschaft Latein-*

amerikas [West Germany] 1979 16: 267-309. Recently there has been a great deal of interest in the slave family, much of a general nature. These studies have revealed blacks who ran away to form separate black settlements and who selected surnames reflecting their past or present culture. Significantly, despite the quantity of new work, no definitive history has been written for any region or republic in Spanish or Portuguese America. Secondary sources; 50 notes.

546. Russell-Wood, A. J. R. FEMALE AND FAMILY IN THE ECONOMY AND SOCIETY OF COLONIAL BRAZIL. Lavrin, Asunción, ed. *Latin American Women* (London: Greenwood Pr., 1978): 60-100. Although the role of the urban, white woman was restricted by tradition, law, and religious belief, she had an important impact on Brazilian colonial society, 1500-1822. Concerned with the social problems created by a shortage of white women, the crown issued policies to ensure their migration and settlement and stressed marriage as a panacea. Expected to prepare for marriage or the convent, white women were given high regard as a stabilizing factor. Though physically secluded, they acted as heads of household and were responsible for the education of their children. Although the culture was strongly antifeminine, subordinating women according to canon and civil law, women were entitled to due process, could hold land, execute wills, conduct trade, and bring legal charges. As widows, they could participate fully in economic affairs. Based on wills, inventories, licensing ledgers, fiscal registers; 80 notes.

S. Tomlinson-Brown

547. Russell-Wood, A. J. R. WOMEN AND SOCIETY IN COLONIAL BRAZIL. *J. of Latin Am. Studies [Great Britain] 1977 9(1): 1-34.* As heads of households, and managers of gold mines, cattle ranches, and sugar plantations, white women were active creators of mainstream colonial society. As a stabilizer, a preserver of Lusitanian culture, and as a means of social status, the white woman was held in high regard by the crown, which also protected her through tradition, law, and religion. Unlike her Spanish and English counterparts, who were proportionately more numerous, the Portuguese woman had a more difficult time perpetuating her European culture; but she did organize her resources in convents and retirement homes, as well as in auxiliaries to the lay brotherhoods. Based on wills, inventories, municipal licensing ledgers, brotherhood and conventual records and fiscal registers in private and public archives in Rio de Janeiro, São Paulo, Salvador, and Minas Gerais, and some secondary works; 2 fig., 69 notes.

K. M. Bailor

548. Safa, Helen Icken. THE CHANGING CLASS COMPOSITION OF THE FEMALE LABOR FORCE IN LATIN AMERICA. *Latin Am. Perspectives 1977 4(4): 126-136.* Increasing numbers of middle-class women entering the labor force in Latin America have kept lower-class women either unemployed or in marginal employment and have continued to provide the industrial capitalistic system with a large, cheap labor pool, 1970's.

549. Santos, Fredricka Pickford. THE ROLE OF WOMEN IN THE DEVELOPMENT PROCESS: MARKET INTEGRATION OR FAMILY DISINTEGRATION? *J. of Int. Affairs 1976-77 30(2): 173-181.* The case of Brazil demonstrates that the growth-induced integration of women into the market-

place heralds the eventual demise of the family structure as it was conceived in less advanced stages of development. 9 tables, 7 notes.   V. Samaraweera

550.   Santos, Maria; Engle, Barbara Alpern, interviewer. WOMEN IN THE NICARAGUAN REVOLUTION. *Frontiers: A J. of Women Studies 1983 7(2): 42-46.* Prints an interview with Maria Santos, a member of the Boulder chapter of the Committee in Solidarity with the People of El Salvador. She spent two weeks in Nicaragua interviewing women. The Sandinistas went out specifically to get women involved.

551.   Schmidt, Steffen W. POLITICAL PARTICIPATION AND DEVEL-OPMENT: THE ROLE OF WOMEN IN LATIN AMERICA. *J. of Int. Affairs 1976-77 30(2): 243-260.* To what extent the ideal type of women as wives and mothers has prevailed in Latin America is difficult to ascertain, though there is evidence that in the past some groups of women deviated from the ideal and participated in national development as part of the economically active population and in the political process, the crucial factor involved in the deviation being class. Graph, 3 tables, 56 notes.   V. Samaraweera

552.   Schmidt, Steffen W. WOMEN, POLITICS AND DEVELOPMENT. *Latin Am. Res. Rev. 1983 18(1): 210-227.* Reviews 10 recent (1976-80) books on women in Latin American history. The content of the books ranges from study of prominent women to peasant women. Each makes an important addition to our understanding of women in Latin America. There are some qualifications, however: 1)most are not systematically comparative; 2)there is methodological unevenness; 3)larger objectives dealing with changes in wom-en's roles are often not explained; and 4)this material rarely will reach beyond the Latin American scholarly community.   J. K. Pfabe

553.   Schmidt, Steffen W. WOMEN'S CHANGING ROLES IN COLOM-BIA. Iglitzin, Lynne B. and Ross, Ruth, ed. *Women in the World* (Santa Barbara, Calif.: Clio Books, 1976): 243-255. Conventional indicators—voting rights, party membership, education, careers, and percent of work force—all place women on the outskirts of Colombian society and politics. Their significant role has been in parapolitical activity, such as prison work and campaign activity. Few women have a secondary education; most work "marginally" in domestic and agricultural labor. Representation in party leadership and government is minor; and despite variance in ideology, political parties remain sexist. Although they have had the right to vote since 1957, turnout is lower among women. But competitive politics has only been reinstituted since 1974 and Colombia can expect change in the near future. Primary and secondary sources; 11 notes.   N. Barron

554.   Schmink, Marianne. DEPENDENT DEVELOPMENT AND THE DI-VISION OF LABOR BY SEX: VENEZUELA. *Latin Am. Perspectives 1977 4(1-2): 153-179.* Surveys the impact of imperialism on Venezuela, changes in the structure of the labor force, and its divisions by sex, 1950-70. Imperialism intensifies divisions and the greater oppression of women not only through their use as a reserve army, but by maintaining backward modes of production, by arresting capitalism, and by employing women in the most backward sectors

of the economy. A consequence of this is that women's role in the labor movement is minimal. J. L. Dietz

555. Schmink, Marianne. WOMEN IN BRAZILIAN *ABERTURA* POLITICS. *Signs 1981 7(1): 115-134.* During the 1930's a moderate women's movement successfully achieved women's suffrage in Brazil. This upper- and middle-class reformist movement was not interested in revolutionary models in other countries. When a new movement began in 1975, conservative working women were recruited for the general struggle for political democracy. In neighborhood and working-class organizations, conflicts within the women's movement emerged and the meetings literally dissolved into fistfights. Coalitions were achieved, but elasticity was crucial and the historical context of the movement cannot be ignored. Secondary and primary sources; 44 notes. S. P. Conner

556. Setúbal, Paulo. A IMPERATRIZ LEOPOLDINA [The Empress Leopoldina]. *Rev. do Inst. Hist. e Geográfico Brasileiro [Brazil] 1978 (321): 250-263.* An encomium, based on press sources, of the Empress Leopoldina, consort of Pedro I, first Emperor of Brazil. The Empress, much beloved, was believed to have played a significant role in events leading up to Brazilian independence in 1825 and, dying in 1826, she did not share in the later misfortunes of her husband who abdicated in 1831. J. P. H. Myers

557. Seymour, Arthur James. CULTURE IN ITS BROADEST SENSE: AN INSEPARABLE PART OF DAILY LIFE. *Cultures [France] 1978 5(3): 77-89.* Examines the traditions, social values, and linguistic backgrounds which constitute national cultures in the West Indies from prehistoric times through the 20th century and the threats which urbanization, technology, mass media, cultural diversity, national integration, and foreign cultures now pose to them.

558. Sharkey, Eugene G. THE DIARY OF FLORENCE ATKINSON, 1883-1886. *J. of the Rutgers U. Lib. 1970 34(1): 23-27.* In the 1880's Domingo Sarmiento of Argentina invited North Americans to teach in his country, to reform the Argentine educational system along the lines of that in the United States. In July 1883, Florence Atkinson, and 16 other young women accepted the invitation. Miss Atkinson kept a diary which begins on the ship from New York and continues until her return in 1886, and which includes material on education, politics, religion, and economics, as well as descriptions and interpretations of her life in San Juan and her travels. Based on documents in Special Collections Department of the Rutgers University Library. M. J. Kroeger

559. Silverblatt, Irene. PRINCIPIOS DE ORGANIZACIÓN FEMENINA EN EL TAHUANTINSUYU [Principles of feminine organization in Tahuantinsuyu]. *Rev. del Mus. Nac. [Peru] 1976 42: 299-340.* Examines the concept of parallel hierarchy and hierarchy of conquest as they applied to women in Inca Peru. Gives particular attention to the parallel organization of men and women in areas such as social and religious groups and inheritance. It reflected a cosmological dualism that divided gods by sex and placed "feminine"

characteristics such as creation, fertility, and agriculture on one side as opposed to "masculine" characteristics such as conquest. Balance was maintained through the feminine characteristics. 29 notes.   M. A. Burkholder

560.   Singelmann, Joachim and Tienda, Marta. CHANGES IN INDUSTRY STRUCTURE AND FEMALE EMPLOYMENT IN LATIN AMERICA: 1950-1970. *Sociol. and Social Res. 1979 63(4): 745-769.* Examines changes in female employment in seven Latin American nations, 1950-70, and relates them to the sectoral transformation of the labor force. In all cases, the sectoral transformation favored the employment of women, though often counteracted by declining shares of female employment within sectors. There was a shift in this period to activities favoring the employment of women.   J/S

561.   Smith, Raymond T. THE FAMILY AND THE MODERN WORLD SYSTEM: SOME OBSERVATIONS FROM THE CARIBBEAN. *J. of Family Hist. 1978 3(4): 337-360.* Such social systems as personal interaction, kinship, and family organization, developed very early in the Caribbean societies and have shown strong staying power despite major social, political, and economic changes. The social systems are not holdovers from European, African, or Asian societies but a special system forged in the Caribbean itself. 9 notes, biblio.   T. W. Smith

562.   Socolow, Susan Migden. MARRIAGE, BIRTH, AND INHERITANCE: THE MERCHANTS OF EIGHTEENTH-CENTURY BUENOS AIRES. *Hispanic Am. Hist. Rev. 1980 60(3): 387-406.* Studies 96 merchant families in Buenos Aires, Argentina. The early marriage of women, high fertility, and relatively high survival rate led to a large number of legal heirs. As Spanish law required equal division of the estate between husband and wife, and equal division of each half among all legitimate children, each merchant's estate was greatly divided. This prevented the development of a local oligarchy as each generation had to amass wealth anew, and mobility was often downward. Based on parish records of two Buenos Aires churches and census records of the city; 10 tables, 3 charts, 12 notes.   B. D. Johnson

563.   Socolow, Susan Migden. WOMEN AND CRIME: BUENOS AIRES, 1757-97. *J. of Latin Am. Studies [Great Britain] 1980 12(1): 39-54.* Women were involved increasingly as plaintiffs or defendants in criminal cases after 1777. They were particularly evident in interpersonal crimes and frequently as the victim of domestic disturbances and sexual offenses. Punishment of their abusers was often lenient, with rapists of married women treated most severely. Unreported crime was frequent as many persons lacked access to the judiciary. Based on sources in the national archives of Argentina, the provincial archives of Buenos Aires, and secondary works; 52 notes.   M. A. Burkholder

564.   Soeiro, Susan A. THE FEMININE ORDERS IN COLONIAL BAHIA, BRAZIL: ECONOMIC, SOCIAL, AND DEMOGRAPHIC IMPLICATIONS, 1677-1800. Lavrin, Asunción, ed. *Latin American Women* (London: Greenwood Pr., 1978): 173-197. Although they were temples of worship, the four convents in Bahia served as institutions buttressing an elitist society and system of values by isolating women unassimilable in Bahian society. In order

to maintain their power monopoly, the social elite had to restrict the marriages of their daughters to other members of the elite. Daughters who found no adequate match, widows without guardians, and women of unhappy marriages were disruptive to the hierarchy, but could be accommodated in religious orders. Desterro Convent included women of the highest caliber, who gave substantial dowries and paid high yearly subsidies to maintain their costly life styles. At the same time, illegitimate, unmarriageable, disgraced, or nonwhite women, all misfits in the patriarchal order, were housed in the convents in the secular category. 2 tables, 105 notes.   S. Tomlinson-Brown

565. Soeiro, Susan A. RECENT WORK ON LATIN AMERICAN WOM-EN. *J. of Inter-Am. Studies and World Affairs 1975 17(4): 497-516.* For 400 years, studies on Latin America ignored women or placed them in stereotyped roles. When written about, male-defined images of women reflecting male prejudices are the norm. Some biographies have been written but this has not done much to dispel stereotypical attitudes, since so few women have engaged in public activity to warrant biographical attention. In recent years more objective works have appeared, but much more has to be done. 10 notes, biblio.
                                                                J. R. Thomas

566. Soeiro, Susan A. THE SOCIAL AND ECONOMIC ROLE OF THE CONVENT: WOMEN AND NUNS IN COLONIAL BAHIA, 1677-1800. *Hispanic Am. Hist. R. 1974 54(2): 209-232.* Presents the history of the Convent of Santa Clara do Dêsterro, founded in 1677 in Salvador, Bahia, Brazil, and its relationship to the city's social and economic structure. Women in colonial society were usually secluded, and wealthy and elite women were either married or entered a convent. Most nuns were from planter, landowning, or rich merchant families and were often placed in a convent due to a lack of a suitable partner or a sufficient dowry. Connections with a convent allowed families to obtain credit in times of economic insecurity. Many nuns led active lives within the convent, often with greater freedom than in the secular world. They had access to education and skills often superior to their male peers. Wealthy nuns often engaged in private financial dealings with the secular world. Based on documents from the municipal Archives of Bahia, the Archives of the Convent of Santa Clara do Dêsterro and others, primary and secondary sources; table, 2 figs., 74 notes.   N. J. Street

567. Strout, Lilia Dapaz. HACIA EL HOMBRE NUEVO. UNA ANTO-LOGIA DEL FOLKLORE ANTIFEMINISTRA: MITO Y "MITOS" SO-BRE "EL CONTINENTE NEGRO" [Toward the new man: an anthology of antifeminist folklore: myth and "myths" about "the dark continent"]. *Cuadernos Hispanoamericanos [Spain] 1983 (391-393): 653-661.* Analyzes the role of female characters and the attitudes and behavior of male characters toward them in Ernesto Sábato's *Sobre Héroes y Tumbas* (1961). The novel constitutes an ideal case for the study of instability of personality in partriarchal societies. 5 notes.   C. Pasadas-Ureña

568. Stycos, J. Mayone. RECENT TRENDS IN LATIN AMERICAN FERTILITY. *Population Studies [Great Britain] 1978 31(3): 407-426.* Decline in fertility in Caribbean and Latin American countries (notably Barbados,

Chile, Colombia, Costa Rica, and Trinidad) correlates with primary school graduation, areas of high literacy and declining agriculture, and organized national family planning programs.

569. Stycos, Maria Nowadowska. TWENTIETH-CENTURY HISPANIC WOMEN POETS. *Revista/Rev. Interamericana [Puerto Rico] 1982 12(1): 5-10.* Introduces and summarizes papers read at a symposium at Ithaca College on female writers in Latin America. 10 notes.   J. A. Lewis

570. Suárez-Torres, J. David. CLORINDA MATTO DE TURNER. *Américas (Organization of Am. States) 1979 31(8): 28-32.* Biography of Clorinda Matto de Turner (1852-1909), Peruvian feminist, author, and social reformer, 1880's-1909.

571. Terán, Francisco. THE CONQUISTADORS' LADIES. *Américas (Organization of Am. States) 1976 28(2): 12-18.* Discusses the role of Indian women in the Spanish conquest of Mexico, 1500-1635, as mistress, slave, interpreter, and even soldier.

572. Toledo Sande, Luis. JOSÉ MARTÍ HACIA LA EMANCIPACIÓN DE LA MUJER [José Martí on the emancipation of women]. *Casa de las Américas [Cuba] 1975 15(90): 25-41.* Discusses the writings of José Martí (1853-95) during 1881-90's that reflect his position approaching, but not explicitly advocating emancipation of women.

573. Towner, Margaret. MONOPOLY CAPITALISM AND WOMEN'S WORK DURING THE PORFIRIATO. *Latin Am. Perspectives 1977 4(1-2): 90-105.* Concentrates on Mexican industrialization between 1880 and 1900 and the profound changes in the relationship of women to productive work brought about by that process. Women were brought into the system of productive labor as they were needed by emergent capitalism in Mexico and this had an impact on women's consciousness and political activity. The author analyzes the crisis of 1907 on the employment of women, forcing them out of the active labor force to form a reserve army of unemployed to be drawn upon only when needed.   J. L. Dietz

574. Tron de Bouchony, Claire. WOMEN IN THE WORK OF ROSARIO CASTELLANOS: A STRUGGLE FOR IDENTITY. *Cultures [France] 1982 8(3): 66-82.* An analysis of women's struggle for identity through a review of the work of Mexican writer Rosario Castellanos (1925-74).

575. Tutino, John. POWER, CLASS, AND FAMILY: MEN AND WOMEN IN THE MEXICAN ELITE, 1750-1810. *Americas (Acad. of Am. Franciscan Hist.) 1983 39(3): 359-381.* Colonial Mexican society was dominated by a wealthy elite whose members held large amounts of land even though their fortunes may have originated in other pursuits. In the initial process of amassing wealth, men were wholly dominant. In the conduct of commercial agriculture with a view to perpetuating elite status once it was achieved, patriarchy was again the rule, but with an occasional woman exercising economic power. Normally, such power was shielded from view by use of male

intermediaries. At lower levels of society, power was less concentrated, and opportunities for women increased. Based on family papers of the Condes de Regla in Washington State University and documents in other Mexican and US repositories; 47 notes.   D. Bushnell

576. Valdés, Nelson P. A BIBLIOGRAPHY OF CUBAN PERIODICALS RELATED TO WOMEN. *Cuban Studies 1982 12(2): 73-80.* Lists 56 Cuban magazines published since 1883 dealing with women. Based on work done with the Biblioteca Nacional José Martí in Havana.   J. A. Lewis

577. Valdés, Nelson P. A BIBLIOGRAPHY OF CUBAN WOMEN IN THE 20TH CENTURY. *Cuban Studies 1974 4(2): 1-31.* A selective, partially annotated bibliography of books, articles, pamphlets, dissertations, manuscript collections, and audio-visual sources on women in Cuba during the 20th century. The article is divided into two historical periods: pre-revolutionary Cuba (1900-58) and revolutionary Cuba (1959-73).   J. A. Lewis

578. VanderMark, E. Abraham. MARRIAGE AND THE FAMILY IN A WHITE CARIBBEAN ELITE: THE IMPACT OF DESCENT FOR THE ETHNIC PERSISTENCE OF THE SEPHARDIC JEWS IN CURAÇAO. *Anthropologica [Canada] 1980 22(1): 119-134.* Because the purpose of marriage of Curaçao's Sephardic Jews since the 17th century was to keep money in the family, inbreeding and extramarital families were common.

579. Vásquez, Josefina Zoraida. WOMEN'S LIBERATION IN LATIN AMERICA; TOWARDS A HISTORY OF THE PRESENT. *Cultures [France] 1982 8(4): 83-102.* Traces the changing status of the women of Latin America in education, employment, politics, and the family from the Spanish colonizers of the 16th century and the Enlightenment of the 18th century to the Latin feminist movements of the 19th and 20th centuries.

580. Vatuk, Ved Prakash. CRAVING FOR A CHILD IN THE FOLK-SONGS OF EAST INDIANS IN BRITISH GUIANA. *J. of the Folklore Inst. 1965 2(1): 55-77.* A study of 900 tape-recorded folk songs collected in British Guiana in 1962 reveals that British Guianese of Indian descent (half of the total population) have preserved the folksongs brought from India. Generally, they deal with trials of the indenture period, 1838-1917. Folk tradition reveals the old Indian theme of childbearing and the male.
                                                                        J. C. Crowe

581. Vaughan, Mary K. WOMEN, CLASS, AND EDUCATION IN MEXICO, 1880-1928. *Latin Am. Perspectives 1977 4(1-2): 135-152.* Mexico modernized within the framework of capitalism, and the state gradually absorbed functions of the family for the purpose of increasing the productive capacity of society and ensuring the continuation of the existing social order. A particular ideology of the family prevails through the school system and other state bureaucracies in which the subordinate and primarily domestic role of women is reaffirmed. Both the public school system and the particular ideology of the family which the state elaborates are important tools in dampening working-class consciousness and organization.

582.   VonWerlhof, Claudia. PRODUCTION RELATIONS WITHOUT WAGE LABOR AND LABOR DIVISION BY SEX. *Rev. (Fernand Braudel Center) 1983 7(2): 315-359.* The different forms of commodity production which are developing without wage labor in Venezuela are organized along the principles of extended-family households. The modern nuclear family is typically capitalist and patriarchal; these Venezuelan cooperatives are capitalistic and patriarchal. Male workers are no better off than they would have been as unqualified industrial workers; the condition of women is worse. 40 ref.

L. V. Eid

583.   Wagenheim, Olga Jiménez. THE PUERTO RICAN WOMAN IN THE 19TH CENTURY: AN AGENDA FOR RESEARCH. *Revista/Review Interamericana [Puerto Rico] 1981 11(2): 196-203.* Puerto Rican women were involved in many nontraditional activities during the 19th century. Secondary sources; 32 notes.

J. A. Lewis

584.   Wainerman, Catalina H. FAMILY RELATIONS IN ARGENTINA: DIACHRONY AND SYNCHRONY. *J. of Family Hist. 1978 3(4): 410-421.* Examines family relationships in Buenos Aires and Catamarca by studying the use of the formal and familiar pronouns. Usage is moving toward the egalitarian-reciprocal; Buenos Aires leads Catamarca in this movement. 4 tables, 4 notes, biblio.

T. W. Smith

585.   Wainerman, Catalina H.; Sautu, Ruth; and Recchini de Lattes, Zulma. THE PARTICIPATION OF WOMEN IN ECONOMIC ACTIVITY IN ARGENTINA, BOLIVIA, AND PARAGUAY. *Latin Am. Res. Rev. 1980 15(2): 143-151.* Large differences exist between Bolivia on the one hand and Argentina and Paraguay on the other. In agriculture, poverty and female labor go together. In manufacturing, women are more likely to be employed in smaller firms which use simpler technology. Women in the service sector possess little or no educational qualifications. In Argentina and Paraguay, education is a more significant factor than family situation in determining employment. Based on censuses since 1947; biblio.

J. K. Pfabe

586.   Walker, Annette. GRENADA'S WOMEN MOVE FORWARD WITH THE REVOLUTION. *Freedomways 1983 23(1): 23-28.* The 1979 revolution has resulted in many benefits for women in Grenada, including reduced unemployment, educational opportunities, representation in the upper echelons of government, and the formation of the National Women's Organization to represent women's interests.

587.   Ward, Marilynn I. THE FEMINIST CRISIS OF SOR JUANA INES DE LA CRUZ. *Int. J. of Women's Studies [Canada] 1978 1(5): 475-481.* Chronicles the life of Sor Juana Ines de la Cruz, a woman who sought intellectual and creative outlets but who, because of the restrictive societal pressures, sexual role stereotypes, and religious and political upheaval in Mexico, was forced to recant, 1669-95.

588.   Watson-Franke, Maria-Barbara. THE ROLE OF EDUCATION IN THE LIFE OF GUAJIRO WOMEN: TRADITION AND CHANGE. *Int. J.*

of Women's Studies [Canada] 1980 3(4): 338-344. Briefly describes the prein-dustrial society of the Guajiro Indians of Venezuela and Colombia, focusing on the functions and goals of the education of women in the matrilineal and matrilocal cattle-herding Guajiro society in light of urbanization and the increasing influence of the male-oriented national Creole culture.

589. Weaver, Jerry L. THE POLITICS OF LATIN AMERICAN FAMI-LY-PLANNING POLICY. *J. of Developing Areas 1978 12(4): 415-437.* Delegates at the World Population Conference (1974) defined population rates as central in the struggle to redefine distribution of resources and power between industrial and Third World nations. They analyzed the influence of government, political parties, labor unions, mass media, Catholic Church, lower classes, and the UN on national population. The role of social norms including racism, and regime ideology such as nationalism were examined. Large families sometimes represented a conscious economic choice. Govern-ment intervention generally was opposed by the military, the Catholic hierar-chy, leftists, students, Marxists, and Indian communities. Secondary sources; table, 104 notes. O. W. Eads, Jr.

590. Wilkie, James W. and Menell-Kinberg, Monica. *EVITA: FROM EL-ITELORE TO FOLKLORE. J. of Latin Am. Lore 1981 7(1): 99-140.* Eva Perón created an elitelore concerning her special role in Argentine history which was eventually adopted by the Argentine masses, foreign journalists, and finally the creators of the popular musical *Evita.*

591. Wolf, Donna M. WOMEN IN MODERN MEXICO. *Studies in Hist. and Society 1976 1(1): 28-53.* Discusses the woman suffrage movement in Mexico, 1916-53, and related political events. Reviews 19th-century laws on women's relationship to the family, and the important changes made after the revolution of 1910, principally the Civil Code of 1928. The Mexican Revolu-tionary Party resisted full suffrage in the 1920's-30's because of the strong influence of the Church, and hence the Right, on women. *Machismo,* as shown by the increasing divorce rate, has been on the decline, while women's role in the work force has expanded along with their educational achievements. Despite modernization the socially ingrained role of subservience in women has continued to be the norm. 15 tables, 84 notes, appendixes.

592. Wrong, Dennis H. TRENDS IN CLASS FERTILITY IN WESTERN NATIONS. *Can. J. of Econ. and Pol. Sci. [Canada] 1958 24(2): 216-229.* Studies fertility in all social classes in Europe, Latin America, the United States and Canada, 1870's-1950's.

593. Yeager, Gertrude M. WOMEN'S ROLES IN NINETEENTH-CEN-TURY CHILE: PUBLIC EDUCATION RECORDS, 1843-1883. *Latin Am. Res. Rev. 1983 18(3): 149-156.* The history of education in Chile—and elsewhere—can provide detailed information on women's roles in society. One category of useful documents focuses upon formulation and implementation of educational policy—information from the Ministry of Education, theses from the University of Chile, the Boletín de Instrucción Pública: Decretos Y Leyes, minutes of the Consejo de la Universidad de Chile, and annual reports of the

Minister of Education. A second category of information includes data gathered by educators to measure the effectiveness of educational efforts. 18 notes.

J. K. Pfabe

594. Youssef, Nadia H. CULTURAL IDEALS, FEMININE BEHAVIOR AND FAMILY CONTROL. *Comparative Studies in Soc. and Hist. [Great Britain]* 1973 15(3): 326-347. Examines the interdependence between cultural values and actual conditions of family behavior in Latin America by pointing out significant inconsistencies and contradictions between the cultural definition of the female role and social actuality, and by identifying some of the circumstances that are responsible for this divergence. Introduces comparative statistics from several Middle Eastern societies which show the close association between asserted ideals and actual feminine behavior, but in Latin America there is a contradition between the "ideal" and the "real" in feminine behavior. Based on primary and secondary sources; 5 tables, 34 notes.

M. M. McCarthy

595. Zoraida Vásquez, Josefina. WOMEN'S LIBERATION IN LATIN AMERICA; TOWARDS A HISTORY OF THE PRESENT. *Cultures [France]* 1982 8(4): 83-102. Traces the changing status of the women of Latin America in education, employment, politics, and the family from the Spanish colonizers of the 16th century and the Enlightenment of the 18th century to the Latin feminist movements of the 19th and 20th centuries.

596. —. AUTORIZACION PARA CONTRAER MATRIMONIO [A marriage license]. *Bol. de la Acad. Nac. de la Hist. [Venezuela]* 1983 66(262): 483-486. The reforms introduced by Charles III caused a number of disputes between parents and children relating to their right to marry the person of their choice. Reproduced here is the facsimile text of a royal authorization granted in Mexico to Fernando García de Quevedo to marry Mariana de Peredo against the wishes of her father. Text of document in the Venezuelan National Archives.

J. V. Coutinho

597. —. CONDICIONES LABORALES Y DE VIDA DE LAS MUJERES TRABAJADORAS, 1914-1933 [Labor conditions and the life of working women, 1914-33]. *Bol. del Archivo General de la Nación [Mexico]* 1979 3(3): 14-22. Reprints eight documents concerning regulations and working conditions of women. Documents from the National Archives; 5 photos.

J. A. Lewis

598. —. DESEMPLEO Y TRABAJO FEMENINO, 1915-1936 [Unemployment and female labor, 1915-36]. *Bol. del Archivo General de la Nación [Mexico]* 1979 3(3): 23-29. Reprints six documents concerning the problems of unemployed Mexican women. Documents from the National Archive; 7 illus.

J. A. Lewis

599. —. LA MUJER Y LA MORAL SOCIAL [Women and social morality]. *Bol. del Archivo General de la Nación [Mexico]* 1979 3(3): 4-12. Reprints three documents showing changes in social morality concerning women in

Mexico. Based on documents in the National Archive of Mexico; 13 illus.

J. A. Lewis

600. —. LAS ORGANIZACIONES DE MUJERES, 1913-1936 [Women's organizations, 1913-36]. *Bol. del Archivo General de la Nación [Mexico] 1979 3(3): 30-37.* Reprints eight petitions and broadsides issued by various Mexican feminist groups. Documents from the National Archive; 4 photos.

J. A. Lewis

601. —. LLAMADO A LAS MUJERES A LUCHAR POR LA INDE-PENDENCIA, 1812 [Call to women to fight for independence, 1812]. *Bol. del Archivo General de la Nación [Mexico] 1979 3(3): 13.* Reprint of a poem from the National Archive of Mexico (Section: Ramo Operaciones de Guerra) calling upon women to fight against the Spaniards. Illus. J. A. Lewis

All titles in this series use ABC-CLIO's unique Subject Profile Index (ABC-SPIndex) and an author index. The following abstract is found in this volume:

Abstract

5.   Copley, Anthony. THE DEBATE ON WIDOW REMARRIAGE AND POLYGAMY: ASPECTS OF MORAL CHANGE IN NINTEENTH-CEN-TURY BENGAL AND YORUBALAND. *J. of Imperial and Commonwealth Hist. [Great Britain] 1979 7(2): 128-148.* The attempt by the Victorians to impose their moral codes through the empire in the quest for political power caused existing codes to be questioned and changed. Different effects were felt by the various social classes and cosmopolitan areas. Here widow remarriage in Hindu India is contrasted with polygamy in West Africa. Based on materials at the India Office Library and Church Missionary Society records, London, and secondary sources; 92 notes.   M. C. Rosenfield

In this Subject Index, each index entry is a complete profile of the abstract and consists of one or more subject, geographic, and biographic descriptors, followed by the dates covered in the article. These descriptors are rotated so that the complete subject profile is cited under each of the terms in alphabetical order. Thus, indexing for the abstract shown above is located in five different places in the index:

Subject Index

Great Britain India (Bengal). Marriage. Morality.
   Niger (Yorubaland). Polygamy. Widows. 19c. *5*
India (Bengal). Great Britain Marriage. Morality.
   Niger (Yorubaland). Polygamy. Widows. 19c. *5*
Marriage. Great Britain. India (Bengal). Morality.
   Niger (Yorubaland). Polygamy. Widows. 19c. *5*
Morality. Great Britain. India (Bengal). Marriage.
   Niger (Yorubaland). Polygamy. Widows. 19c. *5*
Niger (Yorubaland). Great Britain. India (Bengal).
   Marriage. Morality. Polygamy. Widows. 19c. *5*

A dash replaces second and subsequent identical leading terms. Cross-references in the form of *See* and *See-also* references are provided. Refer also to the notes at the head of the Subject Index.

Oceania. *See* Pacific Area.
Persia. *See also* Iran.

The separate Author Index lists the name of the author and abstract number.

Author Index

Cole, Juan Ricardo 184
Contu, Giuseppe 185
Copley, Anthony 5
Costa, Iraci del Nero da 382
Couturier, Edith 383 469

SUBJECT INDEX

Subject Profile Index (SPIndex) carries both generic and specific index terms. Begin a search at the general term but also look under more specific or related terms. This index includes selective cross-references.

Each string of index descriptors is intended to present a profile of a given article; however, no particular relationship between any two terms in the profile is implied. Terms within the profile are listed alphabetically after the leading term. The variety of punctuation and capitalization reflects production methods and has no intrinsic meaning; e.g., there is no difference in meaning between "History, study of" and "History (study of)."

Cities, towns, and other small geographical subdivisions are normally listed in parentheses following their respective countries, e.g., "Brazil (Minas Gerais)." However, certain regions of divided, disputed, changed, or indeterminate sovereignty do appear as leading terms listed alphabetically in the index, e.g., "Alsace-Lorraine."

Terms beginning with an arabic numeral are listed after the letter Z. Chronology of a particular article appears at the end of the string of index descriptors. In the chronological descriptor, "c" stands for century, e.g., "19c" means "19th century."

The last number in the index string, in italics, refers to the bibliographic entry number.

A

Aba riots. Igbo. Nigeria (Calabar, Owerri). Political protest. Social Conditions. 1925. *159*
Abeokuta Women's Union. Independence Movements. Lagos Market Women's Association. Nigeria (Southwestern). Women's Party. 1920-50. *93*
Abortion. Attitudes. India. 1971. *283*
Acculturation. Africa, West. Colonial government. Missions and Missionaries. Polygamy. 19c-20c. *70*
Africa. Agriculture. Inheritance. Prehistory-1973. *79*
—. Bantu. Social Organization. 18c-1980. *106*
—. Bay, Edna G. Economic Change (review article). Hafkin, Nancy J. 1700-1975. *175*
—. Bibliographies. Community. Family. 20c. *83*
—. Blacks. Historiography. Racism. 17c-20c. *102*
—. British Empire. Historians. History Teaching. Perham, Margery (obituary). 1922-82. *130*
—. *Chinjira*. Family. Historiography. Malawi. Methodology. Social Organization. 19c-20c. *162*
—. Colonialism. Economic dependence. Modernization. Political parties. 16c-. *160*
—. Demography. Family. Fertility. Great Britain. Industrialization. Marriage. 1700-1930. *98*
—. Dependency. Modernization. 1970-. *161*
—. Economic Development. Social Change. 19c-20c. *121*
—. Europe. Family. Historiography. Methodology. 1730-1870. *140*
—. Family. Historiography. Methodology. 1981. *111*
—. Government. Law. Marriage. 19c-20c. *131*
—. Muslims (review article). 20c. *86*
—. National development. 1960-76. *104*
—. Phallic symbols. Politics. War. ca 1800-1970. *116*
—. Population growth. 1950-77. *129*
—. Research Sources. Women's history. 1500-1980. *153*
—. Social Customs. 1972. *66*
—. Social Status. 1966-79. *148*
Africa, Central. Bantu. Family. Law. ca 1500-1972. *76*
—. Family Structure. ca 1500-1973. *75*
Africa, East. Food. Kikuyu. Land. Politics. Power. 19c. *56*
—. Kikuyu. Social status. Trade. 19c-20c. *55*

—. Spirit mediums. 1800's-50's. *39*
Africa, North. Middle East. Women (review article). 19c-20c. 1973-79. *1*
Africa, southern. Economic Development. 1931-76. *114*
—. First, Ruth. Historians. Radicals and Radicalism. 1925-82. *112*
—. Historiography. Scholarship. 19c-20c. 1930's-83. *78*
—. Matambe. Nzinga, Queen. 1622-63. *120*
Africa, West. Acculturation. Colonial government. Missions and Missionaries. Polygamy. 19c-20c. *70*
—. Commerce. Sierra Leone. Yoruba. 19c. *169*
—. Converts. Missions and Missionaries. Presbyterian Church. Social change. 1850-1915. *51*
—. Cummings-John, Constance Agatha. Independence movements. Politics. Sierra Leone. Women's Movement. 1918-50's. *64*
—. Elites. Lagos. Marriage. Yoruba. 1880-1915. *110*
—. Family. Kinship. Kongo. Slave trade. 16c-19c. *91*
—. Feminism. Hayford, Adelaide Casely. Nationalism. Universal Negro Improvement Association. 1868-1960. *128*
—. Migration, Internal. 20c. *155*
Africanism. Anthropology. Blacks. Haiti. Hurston, Zora Neale (*Tell My Horse*). 1920-40. *505*
Age. Iran. Marriage. Social Customs. 1956-66. *214*
Agricultural Labor. *See also* Migrant Labor.
—. India (Andhra Pradesh; Nellore). 1881-1981. *298*
—. India (Bihar). Working Conditions. 1765-1875. *282*
Agricultural Production. Birth rate. Jamaica. 1880-1938. *452*
—. Islam. Labor force. 1970's. *32*
—. Zimbabwe. 1973-74. *54*
Agricultural Technology and Research. Beti. Cameroon. Economic Structure. 1920-77. *81*
Agriculture. Africa. Inheritance. Prehistory-1973. *79*
—. Baule. Ivory Coast. Labor, division of. 19c-20c. *71*
—. Beti. Cameroon. Cocoa. Labor, division of. Nigeria. Yoruba. 1950-79. *82*
—. Capitalism. Colombia. Economic Development. 20c. *472*

—. Mestizos. Social Change. 1519-1778. *512*
—. Mexico. Social Status. 16c. *350*
Azzabat. Algeria (Mzab; Beni-Isguen). Social control. ca 1970. *73*

B

Ballet. Alonso, Alicia. Cuba. 1922-78. *481*
Bandi. Folklore. Liberia, northwestern. Oral History. 19c-20c. 1973-75. *125*
Bangladesh. Birth rate. Fertility. 1969-71. *231*
—. India. Pakistan. Purdah. Social Customs. ca 1945-70's. *292*
Bantu. Africa. Social Organization. 18c-1980. *106*
—. Africa, Central. Family. Law. ca 1500-1972. *76*
Barbados. Family planning. Rural-Urban Studies. 1960-70. *457*
—. Family services. 1945-70. *405*
—. Interpersonal Relations. 1971. *404*
Bari. Colombia. Indians. Social Organization. 1960-79. *360*
Barrios de Chungara, Domitila. Bolivia. Memoirs. Miners. Political Protest. USA. 1961-70's. *348*
Baule. Agriculture. Ivory Coast. Labor, division of. 19c-20c. *71*
—. Colonization. Ivory Coast. Textile Industry. 1875-1975. *72*
Bay, Edna G. Africa. Economic Change (review article). Hafkin, Nancy J. 1700-1975. *175*
Bedouin. Burton, Richard. Dickson, Harold. Doughty, Charles Montague. Great Britain. Middle East. 19c-20c. *211*
Beer. Economic Conditions. Islam. Sorghum. Upper Volta. 1978-80. *144*
Begums. British East India Company. Exploitation. India (Oudh). Letters. Malika-i-Jahan. 1720-1881. *305*
Belgian Congo. See Zaire.
Belize. Beresford, Marian Edith. Medical Education. Moloney, Alfred. Nurses and Nursing. 1892-99. *440*
—. Religious Orders. St. Catherine Convent. Sisters of Mercy. 1883-1983. *453*
Belize (Gales Point Village). Leadership. Oral history. White, Cleopatra. 1945-53. *441*
Bell, Gertrude. Great Britain. Middle East. 1889-1926. *197*
Beresford, Marian Edith. Belize. Medical Education. Moloney, Alfred. Nurses and Nursing. 1892-99. *440*
Besant, Annie. Independence Movements. Indian National Congress. 1900-17. *285*
Besant Theosophical College. Education. India (Madanapalle). Theosophy. 1915-75. *312*
Beti. Agricultural Technology and Research. Cameroon. Economic Structure. 1920-77. *81*
—. Agriculture. Cameroon. Cocoa. Labor, division of. Nigeria. Yoruba. 1950-79. *82*
Bibliographies. Africa. Community. Family. 20c. *83*
—. Argentina. Ocampo, Victoria. Periodicals. *Sur.* 1920-79. *413*
—. Capitalism. Iran. 1900-77. *216*
—. Cuba. 1900-74. *577*
—. Cuba. Periodicals. 1883-1982. *576*
—. Cuba. Revolutionary movements. USA. 1953-58. *522*
—. Igbo. Nigeria (Aba). Riots. 1929-30. *74*
—. India. Political Participation. 20c. *222*
—. Iran. 1920's-70's. *207*
—. Latin America. -1975. *463*
—. Latin America. Research. 1960's-70's. *525*
Biography. Bolívar, Simón. Bolívar y Ponte, María de. Venezuela. 1786-91. *423*
—. Dictionaries. Economic history. Muslims. Sakhawi, Muhammad Shams al-Din al-. Social History. 1448-90. *16*

Birth Control. Catholic Church. Church and State. Colombia. 1966-72. *359*
—. Egypt. Population. 1966-77. *183*
—. Family Planning. Fertility. 1959-79. *8*
—. Ghana. Nzema. 1973-75. *157*
—. Guatemala. Modernism. 1970's. *380*
—. Ideology. Latin America. USA. 1950's-70's. *536*
—. Income inequality. Morocco. Rural-Urban Studies. Taiwan. Turkey. 1963-67. *2*
—. India. Medical programs. Midwives. 1956-71. *228*
—. Islam. 12c-19c. *20*
—. Thailand. 1970-80. *272*
—. Turkey. 1963-68. *209*
Birth Rate. *See also* Fertility.
—. Agricultural Production. Jamaica. 1880-1938. *452*
—. Argentina (Buenos Aires). Inheritance. Marriage. Merchants. Social Mobility. 1738-1823. *562*
—. Asia. Marriage. Sex. 1950's-83. *301*
—. Bangladesh. Fertility. 1969-71. *231*
Blacks. Africa. Historiography. Racism. 17c-20c. *102*
—. Africanism. Anthropology. Haiti. Hurston, Zora Neale *(Tell My Horse).* 1920-40. *505*
—. Americas (North and South). Family. Slavery. ca 1550-1850. *545*
—. Authors. Cabrera, Lydia. Cuba. 1930's. *446*
—. Creoles. Family. Slavery. Trinidad and Tobago. 1790's-1820's. *442*
—. Cuba (Havana). Midwives. Mulattoes. 1820-45. *396*
—. East Indians. Family. West Indies. ca 1850-1960. *491*
—. Emancipation. Heegaard, Anna. Reform. Scholten, Peter von. Virgin Islands. 1828-48. *431*
—. Family. Virgin Islands (St. John). 1717-1975. *518*
—. Indians. Latin America. Sexual behavior. Spanish. 16c-17c. *400*
Bolívar, María Teresa de. Bolívar, Simón. Death and Dying. Marriage. Venezuela. 1800-03. *397*
—. Bolívar y Ponte, María de. Cáceres de Arismendi, Luisa. Independence Movements. Latin America. 1792-1810. *415*
Bolívar, Simón. Biography. Bolívar y Ponte, María de. Venezuela. 1786-91. *423*
—. Bolívar, María Teresa de. Death and Dying. Marriage. Venezuela. 1800-03. *397*
—. Latin America. 19c. *353*
—. Love affairs. Novels, historical. Sáenz, Manuelita. Venezuela. 19c. *366*
Bolívar y Ponte, María de. Biography. Bolívar, Simón. Venezuela. 1786-91. *423*
—. Bolívar, María Teresa de. Cáceres de Arismendi, Luisa. Independence Movements. Latin America. 1792-1810. *415*
Bolivia. Argentina. Employment. Paraguay. 1945-76. *585*
—. Argentina. Employment. Paraguay. 1950-75. *540*
—. Barrios de Chungara, Domitila. Memoirs. Miners. Political Protest. USA. 1961-70's. *348*
Bombal, María Luisa. Chile. Novelists. 20c. *479*
Bondsmen. Colombia. Family. Slavery. 16c-19c. *374*
Bongo, Albert Bernard. Foreign policy. Gabon. 1972-73. *63*
Bonny, Anne. Pirates. Read, Mary. West Indies. 17c-1720. *409*
Border Industrialization Program. Foreign Investments. Labor Disputes. Mexico (Nuevo Laredo). USA. 1970-80. *520*
Botswana. Family. Modernization. Social change. Tswana. 1930-72. *156*
—. Historiography. Households. Research. Social Change. 20c. *135*

—. Inheritance. Kgatla. Law. 1875-1970. *137*
—. Men. Migrant Labor. Poverty. 1943-78. *45*
Bracken, Josephine Leopoldine. Myths and
Symbols. Philippines. 1890-1977. *294*
Brazil. Argentina. Peru. Research. Venezuela. 1976.
476
—. Attitudes. Leopoldina, Empress. 1825. *556*
—. Colleges and Universities. Educational Reform.
Lobato de Freitas, Rita. Physicians. 1880-1900.
488
—. Colonial society. 16c-19c. *547*
—. Colonial society. Europeans. Family. 1500-1822.
546
—. Economic Development. Family. 20c. *549*
—. Economic development. Labor. 1940-70. *507*
—. Education. Legal status. Press. 1850-99. *428*
—. Employment. Industrialization. 1920-70. *495*
—. Feminism. Lutz, Bertha. Politics. Suffrage.
1864-1964. *531*
—. Feminism. Moura, Maria Lacerda de. Pacifism.
1919-45. *474*
—. Labor. 1970's. *371*
—. Lucena, Adamaris Oliveira (interview).
Revolutionary Movements. Vanguardia Popular
Revolucionaria. 1960's-71. *537*
—. Mayors. Political participation. 1972-76. *351*
—. Midwives. Physicians. 19c. *487*
—. Politics. Social Classes. 1930-81. *555*
—. Suffrage. 1850-1932. *427*
Brazil (Bahia). Elites. Religious orders. 1677-1800.
564
Brazil (Bahia; Salvador). Convent of Santa Clara
do Dêsterro. Nuns. 1677-1800. *566*
Brazil (Minas Gerais). Family. Rural-Urban
Studies. 1804-38. *533*
Brazil (Minas Gerais; Ouro Prêto). Census. Family.
Households. 1804. *382*
Brazil (Minas Gerais; Vila Rica). Marriage.
Statistics. 1727-1826. *391*
Brazil (Northeastern). Family. Kinship. Politics.
1889-1930. *480*
Brazil (Pernambuco). Education. Sex
Discrimination. 1798. *392*
Brazil (São Paulo). Households. Modernization.
1765-1836. *464*
Brazil (Vila Rica). Family. Marriage. 1800-05. *534*
British East India Company. Begums. Exploitation.
India (Oudh). Letters. Malika-i-Jahan.
1720-1881. *305*
—. Family. India. Social Indicators. 1802. *225*
British Empire. Africa. Historians. History
Teaching. Perham, Margery (obituary). 1922-82.
130
British Guiana. Childbearing. Folk songs.
Indenture. Indians, East. 1836-1917. 1962. *580*
British West Indies. Family. Slavery. 1800-34. *444*
—. Family. Slavery. ca 1750-1850. *384*
—. Resistance. Slavery. 17c-18c. *365*
Burkina Faso. *See* Upper Volta.
Burma. Alenanmadaw, Queen. Hla May, Daw.
Independence movements. Kwin Myaing, Daw.
Suffragette activities. Supayalat, Queen.
1878-1947. *287*
Burton, Richard. Bedouin. Dickson, Harold.
Doughty, Charles Montague. Great Britain.
Middle East. 19c-20c. *211*
Business. Kenya (Nairobi). Landholding. ca
1900-50. *47*
—. Philippines (Cebu). 1970's. *223*

C

Cabrera, Lydia. Authors. Blacks. Cuba. 1930's. *446*
Cáceres de Arismendi, Luisa. Bolívar, María Teresa
de. Bolívar y Ponte, María de. Independence
Movements. Latin America. 1792-1810. *415*
Calypso. Trinidad and Tobago. 1969-79. *330*

Cameroon. Agricultural Technology and Research.
Beti. Economic Structure. 1920-77. *81*
—. Agriculture. Beti. Cocoa. Labor, division of.
Nigeria. Yoruba. 1950-79. *82*
—. Ivory Coast. Social change. Social Status.
1955-71. *58*
Cameroon, western. Demography. Duala. Fertility.
Widekum. 1950-64. *59*
Canada. Capitalism. Imperialism. Socialism. ca
1870-1975. *17*
Canon Law. Islam. Marriage (temporary; *mut'a*).
20c. *9*
Capitalism. Agriculture. Colombia. Economic
Development. 20c. *472*
—. Agriculture. Colombia. Labor. 1870-1970. *477*
—. Argentina. Family. Farms. Labor. 1910-73. *336*
—. Bibliographies. Iran. 1900-77. *216*
—. Canada. Imperialism. Socialism. ca 1870-1975.
17
—. Industrialization. Labor. Mexico. 1880-1907.
573
Carrillo Puerto, Felipe. Alvarado, Salvador. Mexico
(Yucatán). Women's liberation movement.
1920-24. *492*
Castellanos, Rosario. Social Status (review article).
1949. *574*
Castes. Inden, Ronald. India (Bengal). Marriage
(review article). 1450-1800. *318*
Catholic Church. Anglican Communion.
Colonialism. Family. Marriage. West Indies.
1685-1838. *498*
—. Birth Control. Church and State. Colombia.
1966-72. *359*
—. Charities. Chile. 1960's-70's. *422*
—. Cruz, Juana Ines de la. Literature. Mexico.
1668-95. *445*
—. Fertility. Latin America. Modernization.
19c-20c. *389*
—. Mexico (Yucatán). Social Status. 1500's. *379*
Cavalry Regiment, 1st. Argentina. Godoy, Catalina.
Rebellions. 1873-77. *407*
Caycedo, María Clemencia. Colombia (Bogotá).
Convents. Girls. Schools. 1765-70. *412*
Census. Brazil (Minas Gerais; Ouro Prêto). Family.
Households. 1804. *382*
—. Family. Korea. 1392-16c. *265*
Ceylon. *See also* Sri Lanka.
—. Family. Muslims. Singhalese. Tamils. 16c-19c.
314
Chaney, Elsa M. Freyre, Gilberto. Jesus, Carolina
Maria de. Latin America. Pescatello, Ann M.
Social Conditions (review article). 16c-20c. *424*
Charities. Catholic Church. Chile. 1960's-70's. *422*
Charles III. Documents. Marriage. Mexico. Social
Reform. 1783. *596*
Chewa. Family. Malawi. Social Organization.
1830-1965. *136*
Child mortality. Fertility. India. Latin America.
Statistics. 1970-77. *26*
Childbearing. British Guiana. Folk songs.
Indenture. Indians, East. 1836-1917. 1962. *580*
Children. Chile. Indians. Law. Legitimacy.
Marriage. 17c-18c. *402*
Chile. Bombal, María Luisa. Novelists. 20c. *479*
—. Catholic Church. Charities. 1960's-70's. *422*
—. Children. Indians. Law. Legitimacy. Marriage.
17c-18c. *402*
—. Class Struggle. Poder Femenino. Upper Classes.
1970-73. *386*
—. Class struggle. Women's liberation Movement.
1971-73. *345*
—. Condell, Carlos. Letters. Navies. Patriotism.
War of the Pacific. 1879-87. *408*
—. Coup d'etat. Middle Classes. 1973. *502*
—. Education. Labarca, Amanda. 1917-75. *417*
—. Education. Social Status. 1843-83. *593*
—. Fertility. Medical Care. 1965-73. *414*
—. Political Attitudes. Popular Unity. 1970-73. *419*

—. Political imprisonment. 1973-77. *331*
—. Popular Unity. Reform. 1970-73. *335*
—. Voting and Voting Behavior. 1970. *465*
Chile (Santiago, Isla Negra). Decorative Arts. Embroidery. ca 1969-82. *466*
China. Communism. Cuba. Economic development. Tanzania. USSR. 1977-78. *6*
—. Cuba. Socialism. Tanzania. USSR. 1917-81. *7*
Chinjira. Africa. Family. Historiography. Malawi. Methodology. Social Organization. 19c-20c. *162*
Christianity. Elites. Lagos. Marriage. Yoruba. 1880-1915. *109*
Church and State. Birth Control. Catholic Church. Colombia. 1966-72. *359*
Church Missionary Society. Clitoridectomy. Kenya. Missions and Missionaries. 1910-72. *122*
City Life. Anyi. Ivory Coast (Abidjan). Migration, Internal. 1955-65. *60*
Civil code. Lê Dynasty. Social Status. Vietnam. 1428-1980. *313*
Civil Rights. Egypt. Islam. 500-1963. *208*
—. Iran. Islam. Revolution. 1967-82. *206*
Civil servants. Attitudes. Family size. Ghana (Accra). 1954-74. *132*
Class Struggle. Chile. Poder Femenino. Upper Classes. 1970-73. *386*
—. Chile. Women's liberation Movement. 1971-73. *345*
—. India. Peasants. 1960's-70's. *291*
Clergy. Divorce. Ethiopia. Laity. Social Status. 1974. *168*
Clitoridectomy. Church Missionary Society. Kenya. Missions and Missionaries. 1910-72. *122*
Clothing. Egypt. Islamic revival. Social Classes. Veils. 1900-83. *188*
Cocoa. Agriculture. Beti. Cameroon. Labor, division of. Nigeria. Yoruba. 1950-79. *82*
Collective bargaining. Family planning. India. Japan. Social Policy. 1952-65. *249*
Colleges and Universities. Brazil. Educational Reform. Lobato de Freitas, Rita. Physicians. 1880-1900. *488*
Colombia. Agriculture. Capitalism. Economic Development. 20c. *472*
—. Agriculture. Capitalism. Labor. 1870-1970. *477*
—. Bari. Indians. Social Organization. 1960-79. *360*
—. Birth Control. Catholic Church. Church and State. 1966-72. *359*
—. Bondsmen. Family. Slavery. 16c-19c. *374*
—. Education. Guajiro. Indians. Social Change. Venezuela. 1970-79. *588*
—. Labor Law. 1970's. *544*
—. Newspapers. Stereotypes. 1970-73. *433*
—. Politics. 1948-70's. *553*
Colombia (Antioquia). Diaries. Martínez de Nisser, María. Revolution. 1840-43. *510*
Colombia (Bogotá). Caycedo, María Clemencia. Convents. Girls. Schools. 1765-70. *412*
—. Family life. Migrant communities. Urbanization. 1950-74. *410*
Colombia (Boyacá, Cundinamarca). Indians. Muiscas. Rites and Ceremonies. 16c. *347*
Colombia (Pasto). Heroines. Independence Movements. 19c. *361*
Colombia (Tunja). Convents. St. Clare Convent. 1573-20c. *516*
Colonial government. Acculturation. Africa, West. Missions and Missionaries. Polygamy. 19c-20c. *70*
—. Algeria. France. Suffrage. 1919-66. *87*
—. Angola. Nzinga, Queen. Portugal. 1582-1663. *67*
—. Authors. Innes, Emily. Interpersonal Relations. Malaya. Memoirs. 1875-1924. *253*
—. Avila, Juanes de. Cuba. Guzmán, Guiomar de. Political intrigues. 1521-63. *528*
—. Family. Judicial Process. Marriage. Río de la Plata. Social Conditions. 1776-99. *529*

—. Igbo. Nigeria. Political Systems. -1970's. *127*
—. Leadership. Sierra Leone. 1896-1910. *35*
Colonial society. Brazil. 16c-19c. *547*
—. Brazil. Europeans. Family. 1500-1822. *546*
—. Indians. Peru. 16c. *363*
Colonialism. Africa. Economic dependence. Modernization. Political parties. 16c-. *160*
—. Algeria. Islam. 1865-. *152*
—. Anglican Communion. Catholic Church. Family. Marriage. West Indies. 1685-1838. *498*
—. Economic Conditions. Education. Social Status. 1960-70. *14*
—. Racism. Sex Discrimination. Social Classes. 1970-79. *15*
Colonization. Andes. Indians. Marriage. South America. 16c. *364*
—. Baule. Ivory Coast. Textile Industry. 1875-1975. *72*
—. Japan. *Kisaeng.* Korea. Prostitution. 1910-77. *322*
—. Kenya. Land tenure. Luo. Social organization. 20c. *126*
—. Kinship. Tonga. 18c-20c. *324*
Commerce. Africa, West. Sierra Leone. Yoruba. 19c. *169*
Communism. China. Cuba. Economic development. Tanzania. USSR. 1977-78. *6*
Communist Party. Government. Vietnam, North. 1930-72. *320*
—. India. National Federation of Indian Women. 1925-80. *261*
Communists. Egypt. Women's liberation movement. 1955-65. *185*
Community. Africa. Bibliographies. Family. 20c. *83*
Condell, Carlos. Chile. Letters. Navies. Patriotism. War of the Pacific. 1879-87. *408*
Conferences. Mozambican Women's Organization. 16c-1976. *170*
—. Social Status. Sudan. 20c. *174*
Conquistadors. Indians. Mexico. 1500-1635. *571*
Constitutions. Independence Movements. India (Bombay). Parliaments (reserved seats). Suffrage. 1931-47. *293*
Convent of Santa Clara do Dêsterro. Brazil (Bahia; Salvador). Nuns. 1677-1800. *566*
Convents. Caycedo, María Clemencia. Colombia (Bogotá). Girls. Schools. 1765-70. *412*
—. Colombia (Tunja). St. Clare Convent. 1573-20c. *516*
—. Economic Growth. Mexico. Social role. 16c-18c. *471*
—. Franciscans. Mexico (Mexico City). 1524. *511*
Converts. Africa, West. Missions and Missionaries. Presbyterian Church. Social change. 1850-1915. *51*
Cooperatives. Economic Conditions. Households. Labor, division of. Sex. Venezuela. 1970's-83. *582*
—. Nigeria. Yoruba. 1972-80. *100*
Copper Mines and Mining. Migrant Labor. Zambia. 1927-53. *53*
Corpus Christi convent. Indians. Mexico (Mexico City). Religious Orders. 1724-1821. *416*
Corridos. Folk Songs. Mexico. 8c-20c. *439*
Cortés, Hernando. Aztecs. Montezuma. 1519. *499*
—. Malinche. Mexico. Spanish. 1501-28. *370*
Costa Rica. Naranjo, Carmen. Novels. 1966-79. *508*
Cotton. Labor. Mozambique. Sena Sugar Estate, Ltd. 1935-60. *158*
—. Malawi (Shire Valley). Youth. 1906-40. *107*
Cotton industry. India (Bombay). Labor. Textile industry. 1919-39. *273*
Coup d'etat. Chile. Middle Classes. 1973. *502*
Courts. *See also* Judicial Process.
—. Divorce. Senegal. 1872-1946. *143*
—. Ottoman Empire (Kayseri). Sharia court. 1600-25. *199*

Creoles. Blacks. Family. Slavery. Trinidad and Tobago. 1790's-1820's. *442*
Crime and Criminals. Argentina (Buenos Aires). 1757-97. *563*
Crisis. Economic Conditions. Ghana. Liberia. Political Change. Social Conditions. 1970's-82. *119*
Cruz, Juana Ines de la. Catholic Church. Literature. Mexico. 1668-95. *445*
—. Mexico. 1669-95. *587*
Cuba. Alonso, Alicia. Ballet. 1922-78. *481*
—. Authors. Blacks. Cabrera, Lydia. 1930's. *446*
—. Avila, Juanes de. Colonial Government. Guzmán, Guiomar de. Political intrigues. 1521-63. *528*
—. Bibliographies. 1900-74. *577*
—. Bibliographies. Periodicals. 1883-1982. *576*
—. Bibliographies. Revolutionary movements. USA. 1953-58. *522*
—. China. Communism. Economic development. Tanzania. USSR. 1977-78. *6*
—. China. Socialism. Tanzania. USSR. 1917-81. *7*
—. Federation of Cuban Women. 1960's-70's. *343*
—. Health Care. Literacy. Sports. 1959-79. *381*
—. Housework. 1959-77. *461*
—. Labor force. Statistics. Unemployment. 1970-80. *358*
—. Latin America. Revolution. 19c-1960's. *532*
—. Martí, José. Women's Liberation Movement. 1881-90's. *572*
—. Novels. Racism. Slavery. Villaverde, Cirilio (*Cecilia Valdés*). 1882. *473*
—. Poetry. 19c-20c. *434*
—. Revolution. 1971-74. *535*
—. Revolution. 19c-1978. *373*
—. Social status. 1950's. *501*
—. Social Status. 1960's-70's. *538*
Cuba (Havana). Blacks. Midwives. Mulattoes. 1820-45. *396*
Cults. María Lionza cult. Political Protest. Venezuela. 20c. *356*
Cultural ideals. Latin America. Social customs. 1960's-70's. *594*
Cultural liberation. Algeria. Male-female relations. 1830's-1970's. *41*
Cummings-John, Constance Agatha. Africa, West. Independence movements. Politics. Sierra Leone. Women's Movement. 1918-50's. *64*

D

Dahomey. Attitudes. Missions and Missionaries. 19c-20c. *142*
—. Slavery. 1700-1900. *124*
Daily life. Argentina. French. Travel accounts. 1850-80. *418*
—. Mexico. Social Status. 18c. *469*
Dance. Jamaica. Theater. 1929-82. *346*
Dayicing-Beyiji. Mongolia. Qatum, Erketü. 1570-1625. *306*
Death and Dying. Alvarado, Beatriz de. Guatemala. 1540-41. *509*
—. Bolívar, María Teresa de. Bolívar, Simón. Marriage. Venezuela. 1800-03. *397*
Decorative Arts. Chile (Santiago, Isla Negra). Embroidery. ca 1969-82. *466*
DelaPeña family. Argentina. Fernandez de la Corte family. Peña, David. 1795-1879. *458*
Democracy. Gandhi, Indira. India. State of Emergency. 1975-80. *270*
Demography. Africa. Family. Fertility. Great Britain. Industrialization. Marriage. 1700-1930. *98*
—. Cameroon, western. Duala. Fertility. Widekum. 1950-64. *59*
—. Fertility. Rural-Urban Studies. Thailand. 1960's-74. *271*

—. India. Social Organization. 20c. *244*
Dependency. Africa. Modernization. 1970-. *161*
Development Policies. Modernization theory. 1970-79. *13*
Diaries. Argentina. Atkinson, Florence. Educational Reform. Teachers. USA. 1883-86. *558*
—. Authority. Family. India. Singh, Amar. Values. 1872-1942. *302*
—. Colombia (Antioquia). Martínez de Nisser, María. Revolution. 1840-43. *510*
Diaries (review article). Gandhi, Indira. India. Nimbkar, Krishnabai. Political opposition. 1970-78. *316*
Dickson, Harold. Bedouin. Burton, Richard. Doughty, Charles Montague. Great Britain. Middle East. 19c-20c. *211*
Dictionaries. Biography. Economic history. Muslims. Sakhawi, Muhammad Shams al-Din al-. Social History. 1448-90. *16*
Discrimination. *See also* Sex Discrimination.
—. International Women's Year. Labor unions. 1970's. *4*
—. Technology (review article). 1970-80. *12*
Divorce. Clergy. Ethiopia. Laity. Social Status. 1974. *168*
—. Courts. Senegal. 1872-1946. *143*
Documents. Albania. Resistance. World War II. 1942-44. *147*
—. Charles III. Marriage. Mexico. Social Reform. 1783. *596*
—. Mexico. Morality. 1550-1850. *599*
—. Mexico. Unemployment. 1915-36. *598*
—. Mexico. Working conditions. 1914-33. *597*
Dominican Republic (Santo Domingo). Economic Conditions. Prostitution. 1960's-70's. *333*
Doughty, Charles Montague. Bedouin. Burton, Richard. Dickson, Harold. Great Britain. Middle East. 19c-20c. *211*
Duala. Cameroon, western. Demography. Fertility. Widekum. 1950-64. *59*

E

East Indians. Blacks. Family. West Indies. ca 1850-1960. *491*
—. Social change. Trinidad and Tobago. 19c-20c. *515*
Economic Change. Ga. Ghana (Accra; Ussher Town). Social Status. 1960's-70's. *139*
—. Kenya. Luo. 1890's-1940's. *85*
Economic Change (review article). Africa. Bay, Edna G. Hafkin, Nancy J. 1700-1975. *175*
Economic Conditions. Beer. Islam. Sorghum. Upper Volta. 1978-80. *144*
—. Colonialism. Education. Social Status. 1960-70. *14*
—. Cooperatives. Households. Labor, division of. Sex. Venezuela. 1970's-83. *582*
—. Crisis. Ghana. Liberia. Political Change. Social Conditions. 1970's-82. *119*
—. Dominican Republic (Santo Domingo). Prostitution. 1960's-70's. *333*
—. Egypt. Fertility. Social Status. -1970's. *202*
—. Family. Ghana (Amedzofe-Avatime). 20c. *46*
—. Ghana. Government. Markets. Persecution. 1970-82. *138*
—. Households. West Indies. 1942-72. *436*
—. International Monetary Fund. Jamaica (Kingston). Working Class. 1978-79. *354*
—. Marriage. Virgin Islands (Rum Bay). 1823-1970. *401*
—. Ottoman Empire (Bursa). Social Conditions. 17c. *193*
—. Social Status. Vietnam, North. Vietnam War. 1946-75. *321*
Economic Conditions (review article). Latin America. 20c. *387*

Economic dependence. Africa. Colonialism. Modernization. Political parties. 16c-. *160*
Economic Development. Africa. Social Change. 19c-20c. *121*
—. Africa, southern. 1931-76. *114*
—. Agriculture. Capitalism. Colombia. 20c. *472*
—. Attitudes. Education. Fertility. Social Change. Turkey. ca 1940-70. *190*
—. Brazil. Family. 20c. *549*
—. Brazil. Labor. 1940-70. *507*
—. China. Communism. Cuba. Tanzania. USSR. 1977-78. *6*
—. Employment. 1950-67. *3*
—. Employment. 1960-73. *34*
—. Korea, South. 1960-80. *232*
Economic Growth. Convents. Mexico. Social role. 16c-18c. *471*
Economic history. Biography. Dictionaries. Muslims. Sakhawi, Muhammad Shams al-Din al-. Social History. 1448-90. *16*
Economic Policy. Employment. Ghana. 1962-70. *151*
Economic Structure. Agricultural Technology and Research. Beti. Cameroon. 1920-77. *81*
—. Social Status. Vietnam. 1428-1788. *260*
Ecuador (Quito). Inca Empire. Indians. Labor. ca 16c-17c. *475*
Education. Arab States. Modernization. 1950-71. *179*
—. Argentina. Feminism. Philanthropy. Sarmiento, Domingo Faustino. 1860-1926. *484*
—. Attitudes. Economic development. Fertility. Social Change. Turkey. ca 1940-70. *190*
—. Besant Theosophical College. India (Madanapalle). Theosophy. 1915-75. *312*
—. Brazil. Legal status. Press. 1850-99. *428*
—. Brazil (Pernambuco). Sex Discrimination. 1798. *392*
—. Chile. Labarca, Amanda. 1917-75. *417*
—. Chile. Social Status. 1843-83. *593*
—. Colombia. Guajiro. Indians. Social Change. Venezuela. 1970-79. *588*
—. Colonialism. Economic Conditions. Social Status. 1960-70. *14*
—. Employment. Malaysia (Trengganu). Social change. 1952-75. *311*
—. Employment. Zaire. 1960's-70's. *80*
—. Family. Mexico. Modernization. 1800-1928. *581*
—. Family Planning Programme. India (Uttar Pradesh). Population control. Social Policy. 1970's. *245*
—. Fertility. India (Greater Bombay). Migration, Internal. 1966. *299*
—. Ghana. 1961-74. *167*
—. India. -1972. *230*
—. India. 1947-75. *262*
—. India. Marriage. Polygamy. Social reform. Vidyasagar, Iswar Chandra. ca 1840-90. *255*
—. Indian National Congress. Naidu, Sarojini. Politics. 1879-1949. *240*
—. Indonesia (Java). Kartini, Raden Adjeng. Women's Liberation Movement. 1879-1904. *237*
—. Industrial relations. Malaysia. Men. Values. Working Conditions. 1960's. *256*
—. Islam. 1950-71. *31*
—. Malawi. 1875-1952. *103*
—. Malaysia. 1817-1975. *277*
—. Panama. 1835-80's. *523*
Educational Reform. Argentina. Atkinson, Florence. Diaries. Teachers. USA. 1883-86. *558*
—. Brazil. Colleges and Universities. Lobato de Freitas, Rita. Physicians. 1880-1900. *488*
—. School enrollment. Tanzania. 1960's-70's. *117*
Egypt. Attitudes. Emancipation. Youth. 1962-66. *186*
—. Birth Control. Population. 1966-77. *183*
—. Civil Rights. Islam. 500-1963. *208*

—. Clothing. Islamic revival. Social Classes. Veils. 1900-83. *188*
—. Communists. Women's liberation movement. 1955-65. *185*
—. Economic Conditions. Fertility. Social Status. 1970's. *202*
—. Feminism. Islam. Social Status. 1900's. *184*
—. Industry. Labor force. 1816-1975. *196*
—. Intellectuals. 1919-39. *189*
—. Public Health. 1832-82. *204*
Egypt (Cairo). Literature. Zaidän, Ğurği. 1891-1914. *213*
—. Taverns. 1850-1900. *219*
El Salvador. Attitudes. 1972-80. *500*
Elections. See also Suffrage; Voting and Voting Behavior.
—. Gandhi, Indira. India. 1980. *315*
—. Gandhi, Indira. India. Marxism. Philosophy of History. Pluralism. State of Emergency. 1975-77. *226*
Elites. Africa, West. Lagos. Marriage. Yoruba. 1880-1915. *110*
—. Brazil (Bahia). Religious orders. 1677-1800. *564*
—. Christianity. Lagos. Marriage. Yoruba. 1880-1915. *109*
—. Gandhi, Indira. India. Political Attitudes. State of emergency. 1947-76. *251*
—. Mexico. Political participation. 1910-74. *542*
—. Mexico. Political participation. 1920-79. *367*
—. Mexico. Sex. Social Organization. 1750-1810. *575*
Emancipation. Atatürk, Kemal. Revolutionary Movements. Social change. Turkey. 10c-1980. *212*
—. Attitudes. Egypt. Youth. 1962-66. *186*
—. Blacks. Heegaard, Anna. Reform. Scholten, Peter von. Virgin Islands. 1828-48. *431*
—. Emigration. Labor. Turkey. 1955-75. *176*
Embroidery. Chile (Santiago, Isla Negra). Decorative Arts. ca 1969-82. *466*
Emigration. See also Immigration; Migration, Internal; Refugees.
—. Emancipation. Labor. Turkey. 1955-75. *176*
Employment. Argentina. Bolivia. Paraguay. 1945-76. *585*
—. Argentina. Bolivia. Paraguay. 1950-75. *540*
—. Argentina. Modernization. 1810-1914. *425*
—. Brazil. Industrialization. 1920-70. *495*
—. Economic development. 1950-67. *3*
—. Economic development. 1960-73. *34*
—. Economic Policy. Ghana. 1962-70. *151*
—. Education. Malaysia (Trengganu). Social change. 1952-75. *311*
—. Education. Zaire. 1960's-70's. *80*
—. Industrial Structure. Latin America. 1950-70. *560*
—. Industrialization. Labor, division of. Textile Industry. 1963-83. *24*
—. Kenya. Professions. 1960-76. *105*
Employment opportunities. Secondary Education. Uganda (Buganda). Youth. 1973. *164*
Equality. Feminism. India. 1900-40's. *250*
—. India. 1947-78. *274*
Ethiopia. Amhara. Family. Nobility. Property. 1750-1860. *61*
—. Clergy. Divorce. Laity. Social Status. -1974. *168*
Ethiopia (Gondar). Land Tenure. 1740-1850. *62*
Ethnic groups. Fertility. Malaysia. 1950-76. *239*
Ethnocentrism. International stratification system. Modernization. Nettl, J. P. Sociology. USA. 1945-70's. *21*
Ethnography. Tonga (review article). Weinrich, Aquina. Zimbabwe. 1850-1975. *115*
Europe. Africa. Family. Historiography. Methodology. 1730-1870. *140*
Europeans. Brazil. Colonial society. Family. 1500-1822. *546*

G

—. Immigration. Intergovernmental Committee for Migration. Refugees. 1956-80. *334*
—. Independence Movements. 1742-1822. *530*
—. Inter-American Commission of Women. 1492-1974. *398*
—. Labor. 1960-75. *388*
—. Labor. 20c. *539*
—. Labor. Migration, Internal. Servants, domestic. 1960's-70's. *456*
—. Labor. Social Classes. 1970's. *548*
—. Literature, historical. 1492-1974. *447*
—. Modernism. Poetry. 1880-1981. *332*
—. Parra, Violeta. Poets. Revolution. 1917-67. *451*
—. Periodicals. 1790-1810. *504*
—. Poetry. Social Customs. 1945-82. *543*
—. Poets. 20c. *569*
—. Political participation. 1960-79. *342*
—. Political participation. Social Classes. 1875-1976. *551*
—. Political participation. Voting and Voting Behavior. 1949-. *454*
—. Power. 1975. *411*
—. Race Relations. Social classes. 16c-19c. *362*
—. Research. 1970-79. *514*
—. Research. Women's studies. 16c-20c. 1960's-70's. *429*
—. Revolutionary Movements. 1940's-70's. *377*
—. Sex Discrimination. Sociology. 1974. *462*
—. Social change. Spain. 15c-20c. *526*
—. Social Status. 16c-20c. *595*
Latin America (review article). 16c-20c. *552*
—. 20c. *565*
Latin American Studies. Family. 19c-20c. *369*
Law. Africa. Government. Marriage. 19c-20c. *131*
—. Africa, Central. Bantu. Family. ca 1500-1972. *76*
—. Botswana. Inheritance. Kgatla. 1875-1970. *137*
—. Children. Chile. Indians. Legitimacy. Marriage. 17c-18c. *402*
—. Islam. Pakistan. 1970's. *229*
—. Jurisdiction. Mexico. Prostitution. 1771-1972. *426*
Lê Dynasty. Civil code. Social Status. Vietnam. 1428-1980. *313*
Leadership. Belize (Gales Point Village). Oral history. White, Cleopatra. 1945-53. *441*
—. Colonial government. Sierra Leone. 1896-1910. *35*
—. Nigeria. Secondary Education. 1977-82. *69*
Legal status. Arab States. Islam. Social Status. 1930-78. *194*
—. Brazil. Education. Press. 1850-99. *428*
—. Ottoman Empire (Kayseri). 1590-1630. *198*
Legislation. Argentina (Buenos Aires). Luisi, Paulina. Prostitution. Reform. Uruguay (Montevideo). ca 1900-50. *485*
Legitimacy. Children. Chile. Indians. Law. Marriage. 17c-18c. *402*
Lelemama dance associations. Kenya (Mombasa). Muslim Women's Cultural Association. Muslim Women's Institute. 1930's-70's. *154*
Leopoldina, Empress. Attitudes. Brazil. 1825. *556*
Letters. Begums. British East India Company. Exploitation. India (Oudh). Malika-i-Jahan. 1720-1881. *305*
—. Chile. Condell, Carlos. Navies. Patriotism. War of the Pacific. 1879-87. *408*
Leva Kanbi Patidars (caste). India (Gujarat). Infanticide. Marriage. Population. 1820-1900. *235*
Liberation. Algeria. 1960-74. *42*
Liberia. Crisis. Economic Conditions. Ghana. Political Change. Social Conditions. 1970's-82. *119*
—. Family Structure. Government Enterprise. Industrial innovation. Markets. 1950-70. *84*
—. Social Status. 1847-1982. *141*

Liberia, northwestern. Bandi. Folklore. Oral History. 19c-20c. 1973-75. *125*
Librarians. Great Britain. Nigeria. Occupations. USA. 20c. *123*
Library education. Morocco. 1912-73. *52*
Lifestyles. Great Britain. India. 19c. *252*
Literacy. Cuba. Health Care. Sports. 1959-79. *381*
Literary Criticism. Argentina. Men. Sábato, Ernesto *(Sobre Héroes y Tumbas)*. Social Conditions. 1930's-82. *567*
—. Feminism. Latin America. 1970's. *483*
Literature. Catholic Church. Cruz, Juana Ines de la. Mexico. 1668-95. *445*
—. Egypt (Cairo). Zaidān, Ğurği. 1891-1914. *213*
—. Gürpinar, Hüseyin Rahmi. Namik Kemal. Ottoman Empire. 19c. *218*
—. India. Urdu. 19c-20c. *259*
—. Middle East. 1840-1980. *195*
—. Puerto Rico. 19c-20c. *450*
—. West Indies. -20c. *527*
Literature, historical. Latin America. 1492-1974. *447*
Lobato de Freitas, Rita. Brazil. Colleges and Universities. Educational Reform. Physicians. 1880-1900. *488*
Local Politics. India (Orissa). Political Participation. 1930's-80. *241*
Love affairs. Bolívar, Simón. Novels, historical. Sáenz, Manuelita. Venezuela. 19c. *366*
Lucena, Adamaris Oliveira (interview). Brazil. Revolutionary Movements. Vanguardia Popular Revolucionaria. 1960's-71. *537*
Luisi, Paulina. Argentina (Buenos Aires). Legislation. Prostitution. Reform. Uruguay (Montevideo). ca 1900-50. *485*
Luisi, Pauline. Feminism. Moral reform. Uruguay. 1875-1950. *486*
Luo. Colonization. Kenya. Land tenure. Social organization. 20c. *126*
—. Economic change. Kenya. 1890's-1940's. *85*
Lutz, Bertha. Brazil. Feminism. Politics. Suffrage. 1864-1964. *531*

M

Maass, Clara Louise. Medical Research. Philippines. Yellow Fever. 1890's-1901. *224*
Mahbuba. Middle East. Pückler-Muskau, Hermann von. Romance. Slavery. 1837-40. *210*
Malawi. Africa. *Chinjira*. Family. Historiography. Methodology. Social Organization. 19c-20c. *162*
—. Chewa. Family. Social Organization. 1830-1965. *136*
—. Education. 1875-1952. *103*
Malawi (Shire Valley). Cotton. Youth. 1906-40. *107*
Malawi (Zomba). Agriculture. Inheritance. Land tenure. Social Change. 1966-81. *92*
Malaya. Authors. Colonial Government. Innes, Emily. Interpersonal Relations. Memoirs. 1875-1924. *253*
Malaysia. Education. 1817-1975. *277*
—. Education. Industrial relations. Men. Values. Working Conditions. 1960's. *256*
—. Ethnic groups. Fertility. 1950-76. *239*
—. Labor force. 1957-70. *258*
—. Political Participation. United Malays National Organization. Women's Association. 1945-72. *278*
Malaysia (Trengganu). Education. Employment. Social change. 1952-75. *311*
Male-female relations. Algeria. Cultural liberation. 1830's-1970's. *41*
Malika-i-Jahan. Begums. British East India Company. Exploitation. India (Oudh). Letters. 1720-1881. *305*
Malinche. Cortés, Hernando. Mexico. Spanish. 1501-28. *370*

—. Zimbabwe. 1970's-81. *166*
Sexual behavior. Blacks. Indians. Latin America.
Spanish. 16c-17c. *400*
Sharia court. Courts. Ottoman Empire (Kayseri).
1600-25. *199*
Shariati, Ali. Iran. Islam. Revolution. 1960's-70's.
192
Shi kingdom. Politics. Zaire (Ngweshe). 18c-1973.
149
Sierra Leone. Africa, West. Commerce. Yoruba.
19c. *169*
—. Africa, West. Cummings-John, Constance
Agatha. Independence movements. Politics.
Women's Movement. 1918-50's. *64*
—. Colonial government. Leadership. 1896-1910. *35*
—. Fertility. Mende. Temne. 1963-73. *65*
Sierra Leone (Freetown). Protestant Churches.
Religious organizations. 1960's-70's. *150*
Signares. Art. France. Racism. Senegal. 1789-1890.
44
Sikkim. Annexation. Gandhi, Indira. India. Nuclear
energy. State of emergency. 1970-75. *236*
Singh, Amar. Authority. Diaries. Family. India.
Values. 1872-1942. *302*
Singhalese. Ceylon. Family. Muslims. Tamils.
16c-19c. *314*
Sisters of Mercy. Belize. Religious Orders. St.
Catherine Convent. 1883-1983. *453*
Sītalā (goddess). India (Bengal). Medicine (practice
of). Myths and Symbols. Smallpox. 12c-20c.
289
Slave mortality. Jamaica. 1780-1840. *385*
Slave plantations. Family structure. Fertility.
Jamaica. 1817-32. *443*
Slave trade. Africa, West. Family. Kinship. Kongo.
16c-19c. *91*
Slavery. Americas (North and South). Blacks.
Family. ca 1550-1850. *545*
—. Blacks. Creoles. Family. Trinidad and Tobago.
1790's-1820's. *442*
—. Bondsmen. Colombia. Family. 16c-19c. *374*
—. British West Indies. Family. 1800-34. *444*
—. British West Indies. Family. ca 1750-1850. *384*
—. British West Indies. Resistance. 17c-18c. *365*
—. Cuba. Novels. Racism. Villaverde, Cirilio
(*Cecilia Valdés*). 1882. *473*
—. Dahomey. 1700-1900. *124*
—. Family. Jamaica. Working Class. 19c-20c. *519*
—. Fertility. Netherlands Antilles. Surinam.
1840-63. *467*
—. French West Indies. Labor. Race Relations.
1635-1848. *421*
—. Mahbuba. Middle East. Pückler-Muskau,
Hermann von. Romance. 1837-40. *210*
—. Nyasa-Tanganyika corridor. 1880-94. *172*
Smallpox. India (Bengal). Medicine (practice of).
Myths and Symbols. Sītalā (goddess). 12c-20c.
289
Social attitudes (British). India. Jhabvala, R.
Prawer. Personal narratives. 1950's. *266*
Social Change. Africa. Economic Development.
19c-20c. *121*
—. Africa, West. Converts. Missions and
Missionaries. Presbyterian Church. 1850-1915.
51
—. Agriculture. Inheritance. Land tenure. Malawi
(Zomba). 1966-81. *92*
—. Agriculture. Marriage. Technology. Tonga.
Zambia. 20c. *171*
—. Atatürk, Kemal. Emancipation. Revolutionary
Movements. Turkey. 10c-1980. *212*
—. Attitudes. Economic development. Education.
Fertility. Turkey. ca 1940-70. *190*
—. Aztecs. Mestizos. 1519-1778. *512*
—. Botswana. Family. Modernization. Tswana.
1930-72. *156*
—. Botswana. Historiography. Households.
Research. 20c. *135*

—. Cameroon. Ivory Coast. Social Status. 1955-71.
58
—. Colombia. Education. Guajiro. Indians.
Venezuela. 1970-79. *588*
—. East Indians. Trinidad and Tobago. 19c-20c.
515
—. Education. Employment. Malaysia (Trengganu).
1952-75. *311*
—. Family. Peasants. Peru. 1900-70. *394*
—. Feminism. Latin America. Poets. 1900-81. *390*
—. Feminism. Nicaragua. Political Change.
Revolution. Santos, Maria. 1979-83. *550*
—. Gökalp, Ziya. Turkey. 20c. *187*
—. Human rights. Islam. Pakistan. 20c. *257*
—. India (Bengal). Tradition. 1960's-70's. *281*
—. Latin America. Spain. 15c-20c. *526*
—. Missions and Missionaries. Papua New Guinea.
1874-1914. *327*
—. Mortality. Sri Lanka. 1920-72. *288*
—. Mozambique. Political Change. Women's
Liberation Movement. 1975-83. *99*
—. Mozambique. Political Theory. Women's
liberation movement. 1970's-82. *90*
—. Social Status. Turkey. Urbanization. 1950's-70's.
200
Social Classes. Brazil. Politics. 1930-81. *555*
—. Clothing. Egypt. Islamic revival. Veils. 1900-83.
188
—. Colonialism. Racism. Sex Discrimination.
1970-79. *15*
—. Family. Latin America. Social Organization.
1971. *352*
—. Feminism. India. Political Factions. 1970's. *246*
—. Fertility. Latin America. Western nations.
1870's-1950's. *592*
—. Guatemala. Personal Narratives. 1978. *438*
—. Indonesia (Java). Social Status. 20c. *310*
—. Labor. Latin America. 1970's. *548*
—. Labor. Mexico (Mexico City). 1950's-70's. *339*
—. Latin America. Political participation.
1875-1976. *551*
—. Latin America. Race Relations. 16c-19c. *362*
Social Conditions. Aba riots. Igbo. Nigeria
(Calabar, Owerri). Political protest. 1925. *159*
—. Argentina. Literary Criticism. Men. Sábato,
Ernesto (*Sobre Héroes y Tumbas*). 1930's-82.
567
—. Colonial Government. Family. Judicial Process.
Marriage. Río de la Plata. 1776-99. *529*
—. Crisis. Economic Conditions. Ghana. Liberia.
Political Change. 1970's-82. *119*
—. Economic conditions. Ottoman Empire (Bursa).
17c. *193*
Social Conditions (review article). Chaney, Elsa M.
Freyre, Gilberto. Jesus, Carolina Maria de.
Latin America. Pescatello, Ann M. 16c-20c.
424
Social control. Algeria (Mzab; Beni-Isguen).
Azzabat. ca 1970. *73*
Social Customs. Africa. 1972. *66*
—. Age. Iran. Marriage. 1956-66. *214*
—. Algeria. Assimilation. France. 1830-1970. *88*
—. Argentina. Ocampo, Victoria. Periodicals. *Sur*.
1900-79. *399*
—. Argentina (Buenos Aires; Catamarca). Family.
Language. 1850-1970. *584*
—. Bangladesh. India. Pakistan. Purdah. ca
1945-70's. *292*
—. Cultural ideals. Latin America. 1960's-70's. *594*
—. Ewe, Abutia. Ghana. Marriage. 1900-80. *163*
—. Family Structure. Marriage. West Indies. 1972.
349
—. India. Urbanization. ca 1960-82. *279*
—. Latin America. Poetry. 1945-82. *543*
—. Modernization. Nationalism. West Indies.
Prehistory-20c. *557*

—. Education. Industrial relations. Malaysia. Men. Values. 1960's. *256*
World Population Conference (1974). Family planning. Latin America. Politics. 1950's-70's. *589*
World War II. Albania. Documents. Resistance. 1942-44. *147*

Y

Yellow Fever. Maass, Clara Louise. Medical Research. Philippines. 1890's-1901. *224*
Yoruba. Africa, West. Commerce. Sierra Leone. 19c. *169*
—. Africa, West. Elites. Lagos. Marriage. 1880-1915. *110*
—. Agriculture. Beti. Cameroon. Cocoa. Labor, division of. Nigeria. 1950-79. *82*
—. Christianity. Elites. Lagos. Marriage. 1880-1915. *109*
—. Cooperatives. Nigeria. 1972-80. *100*
—. Labor, division of. Nigeria. 1500-1980. *37*
Youth. Attitudes. Egypt. Emancipation. 1962-66. *186*
—. Cotton. Malawi (Shire Valley). 1906-40. *107*
—. Employment opportunities. Secondary Education. Uganda (Buganda). 1973. *164*
—. India (Andhra Pradesh). Political Participation. 1969-75. *263*

Z

Zaidăn, Ğurği. Egypt (Cairo). Literature. 1891-1914. *213*
Zaire. Education. Employment. 1960's-70's. *80*
—. Social Status. 1960-79. *36*
Zaire (Kinshasa). Attitudes. Family. Girls. Marriage. Schools. 1969-72. *173*
Zaire (Ngweshe). Politics. Shi kingdom. 18c-1973. *149*
Zambia. Agriculture. Marriage. Social Change. Technology. Tonga. 20c. *171*
—. Attitudes. Nurses and nursing. Tradition. 1981. *146*
—. Copper Mines and Mining. Migrant Labor. 1927-53. *53*
—. Migrant Labor. Peasants. Social Organization. 1930's-78. *57*
—. Political participation. 19c-1974. *145*
Zimbabwe. Agricultural production. 1973-74. *54*
—. Ethnography. Tonga (review article). Weinrich, Aquina. 1850-1975. *115*
—. Sex Discrimination. 1970's-81. *166*

AUTHOR INDEX

A

Abadan-Unat, Nermin 176 177
Abraham, Arthur 35
Abrahemian, Ervand 178
Abu-Laban, Baha 179
Abu-Laban, Sharon McIrvin 179
Adams, Lois 36
Afonja, Simi 37
Aghajanian, Akbar 258
Agnew, Vijay 222
Ahmed, S. 231
Aho, William R. 330
Alarcón, Haydée 331
Albin, Mel 302
Alegría, Fernando 332
Alemán, José Luis 333
Alexandraki, C. 334
Alvarez, J. Benjamin C. 223
Alvarez, Patricia M. 223
Andreas, Carol 335
Archetti, Eduardo 336
Arenal, Electa 337
Ariburun, Perihan 180
Arizpe, Lourdes 338 339
Armagnac, Catherine 38
Arrom, Silvia Marina 340 341
Arvy, Lucie 224
Aviel, JoAnn Fagot 342
Az 181
Azicri, Max 343

B

Badran, Margot Farranto 1
Baer, Gabriel 182
Baily, Samuel L. 344
Bambirra, Varia 345
Barnett, Sheila 346
Barradas, José Pérez de 347
Barrios de Chungara, Domitila 348
Bay, Edna G. 39 43 85 121 127 139 150 154 159
Benjamin, N. 225
Berger, Iris 39
Berkin, Carol R. 373
Berleant-Schiller, Riva 349
Bernus, S. 40
Bhattacharyya, Amit K. 2
Blair, Harry W. 226
Blanco, Iris 350
Blay, Eva Alterman 351
Blitz, Rudolph C. 3
Blumberg, Rae Lesser 227
Boals, Kay 41 42
Bogantes Hidalgo, Olivet 352
Bolinaga de Dúo, María Begoña 353
Bolles, A. Lynn 354
Brain, James L. 43
Breslow, Nancy 355
Brey, Kathleen Healy 228
Briceño, Jacqueline C. de 356
Briceño Perozo, Mario 357
Brooks, George E. 44
Brown, Barbara B. 45
Brown, Susan E. 360
Brundenius, Claes 358
Brydon, Lynne 46
Brzezinski, Steven 359
Buckley, Joan 79
Buenaventura-Posso, Flora 360

Buendía N., Jorge 361
Bujra, Janet M. 47
Burkett, Elinor C. 362 363 364
Burton, John W. 48 49
Bush, Barbara 365

C

Caicedo, Bernardo J. 366
Calabrese, Maria C. 183
Callaway, Barbara J. 50
Camp, Roderic Ai 367
Campbell, Penelope 51
Campo del Pozo, Fernando 368
Cancian, Francesca M. 369
Candelaria, Cordelia 370
Cao The Que Houng 319
Capellin, Paola 371
Carlos, Manuel L. 372
Carr, Shirley 4
Carroll, Lucy 229
Casal, Lourdes 373
Cassell, Kay Ann 52
Chandler, David L. 374
Charbit, Y. 478
Chattopadhyaya, Kamaladevi 230
Chauncey, George, Jr. 53
Cheater, Angela 54
Chen, L. C. 231
Cherpak, Evelyn 375
Chinchilla, Norma Stoltz 376 377
Cho, Uhn 232
Ch'oe Chae-sok 233
Ciancanelli, Penelope 55
Ciski, Robert 378
Clair-Louis, Jean 234
Clark, Alice 235
Clark, Carolyn M. 56
Clendinnen, Inga 379
Cliffe, Lionel 57
Clignet, Remi 58 59
Cobas, José A. 380
Cola Alberich, Julio 236
Cole, Johnnetta B. 381
Cole, Juan Ricardo 184
Contu, Giuseppe 185
Copley, Anthony 5
Costa, Iraci del Nero da 382
Couturier, Edith 383 469
Crahan, Margaret E. 442
Crapuchet, Simonne 60
Craton, Michael 384 385
Croll, Elizabeth J. 6 7
Crummett, Maria de los Angeles 386
Crummey, Donald 61 62
Cubitt, Tessa 387 388
Cuca, Roberto 8
Cuisinier, Jeanne 237
Culhane, Claire 238
Cutright, Phillips 389
Cypess, Sandra Messinger 390

D

DaCosta, Iraci del Nero 391
daSilva, Maria Beatriz Nizza 392
Davanzo, Julie 239
Decraene, Philippe 63
Deere, Carmen Diana 393 394 472 477
Deiner, John T. 395

DelCastillo, Adelaida R. 435 496
Denzer, LaRay 64
Deschamps Chapeaux, Pedro 396
De-Sola Ricardo, Irma 397
DeTejeira, Otilia Arosemena 398
Devanesan, Savithri 240
Devi, Annapurna 241
Devis, T. L. F. 65
Dewey, Clive 242
Dey, Susnigdha 399
Diggs, Irene 400
Dirks, Robert 401
Dobert, Margarita 66
Dodd, Peter C. 186
Dogramaci, Emel 187
Dolghin, Florentina 67
Donaldson, P. J. 243
Dougnac Rodríguez, Antonio 402
Dyson, Tim 244

E

Early, John D. 403
Ebanks, G. Edward 404
Edmonds, Juliet 405
Egboh, Edmund O. 68
Ejiogu, Aloy M. 69
Ekechi, Felix K. 70
El Guindi, Fadwa 188
Elder, R. E., Jr. 245
Eliraz, Giora 189
Ende, Werner 9
Engle, Barbara Alpern 550
Escobar, Gabriel 406
Estrada, Marcos 407
Etienne, Mona 71 72 126 324 360 512
Everett, Jana 246

F

Farooq, S. 190
Farrag, Amina 73
Faulkner, Constance 191
Ferdows, Adele K. 192
Fernandez Larrain, Sergio 408
Fernando, Dallas F. S. 247 248
Fieloux, Michele 74
Finnegan, Oliver D., III 249
Fisher, Michael 300
Fleming, C. J. W. 75 76
Fleming, Carrol B. 409
Flinn, William L. 410
Flora, Cornelia B. 411 433
Forbes, Geraldine H. 250
Forero, Manuel José 412
Foster, David William 413
Francis, Michael J. 465
Fuller, Gary 414

G

Gabaldón, José Rafael 415
Gadant, Monique 77
Gailey, Christine Ward 324
Gaitskell, Deborah 77 78
Galbraith, Virginia 175
Gallagher, Ann Miriam 416
Gallo, María Gowland de 417
García de D'Agostino, Olga 418
Garrett-Schesch, Pat 419
Garriga, María M. López 420